D1010501

This Pen for Hire

Other Books by John Leonard
CRYBABY OF THE WESTERN WORLD
WYKE REGIS
THE NAKED MARTINI

THIS PEN FOR HIRE

By John Leonard

Doubleday & Company, Inc.
GARDEN CITY, NEW YORK

ACKNOWLEDGMENT is gratefully made for permission to reprint the following material:

"News, Views, Reviews," Copyright © 1970 by Associated Councils of the Arts. Published in *Cultural Affairs*, Fall 1970.

"Confessions of a Structure Freak" reprinted by permission of *Esquire* magazine, Copyright © 1969 by Esquire, Inc.

"A Short Rap with the Moonmen," "A Late-Night Taker Who Knows How to Listen," "Frozen Instants: TV at Its Best," Copyright © 1970 Time Inc.; "1971," "The Next Ten Years," "The Irony of a 'Succès d'Emmy,'" "Late-Night Hope for the Republic," "Bigotry as a Dirty Joke," "Ode to a Very Active Verb," "Stand Up and Cher," "Dr. Welby's Tonic Won't Harm You," "One of Our Myths Is Missing," "Private Eyes and Heavy Lids," "On the Street Where Kids Live," "'Mice' Deserve a Better Trap," "The Family That Sings Together," "Why Lassie Can't Come Home," "ABC's Wide World of Sports," "The Basketball Is Black," "They Hardly Ever Knock the Product," "Some Public Credit Where It's Due," "Sorry, No Soap for Fyodor," "A Marvelous Nightingale," "There's Bad News Tonight," "Chicago's 'Underground News,'" "It's Put-Put Time In California," "The Show Biz Conservative," Copyright © 1971 Time Inc.; "The Pick of the Litter," "The Barbara Walters Problem," "Morning Is Less Than Electric," "Nausea in the Afternoon," "Charlie Brown in a Rep Tie?," "Whose Justice Do You Trust?," "Twist and Tact," "Dean Martin: A Las Vegas of the Heart," "Wrong Way Down Sesame Street," "'Subsequent Aggressive Behavior,'" "The Littlest Neurotics," "Prisoners of Corn," "Shuffling the Archetypes," "Soft Vonnegut," "Walter Was There Anyway," Copyright © 1972 Time Inc. Reprinted by permission of *Life* magazine.

"George Kennan's *Democracy and the Student Left*" published under the title "Mr. Generation Gap," Copyright © 1968 by *New York* Magazine Co. Reprinted with the permission of *New York* magazine.

"Death Wish in Chicago," "The Democratic Happening," "The Frustrated Election," Copyright © 1968 by *The New Statesman*. Reprinted with the permission of *The New Statesman*.

FOR FRANCIS BROWN
with respect, affection and gratitude

Warning

In four years I have written almost 500,000 words for too many magazines and newspapers. Looking over those words, I find that I am sometimes fond of what I wrote, sometimes embarrassed, sometimes mystified. These pages are what, for all kinds of not very compelling reasons, I've chosen to preserve. I think the selection fairly reflects my obsessions, enthusiasms, good heart and bad manners. Like me, it is neither systematic nor comprehensive. When you write on assignment, books happen to you like accidents, events are muggings. I never had a chance to review many of my favorite writers; Robert Kennedy was murdered before anybody was interested in my political feelings. And so, if the reader is generous, he will think of what follows as a conversation on which he has stumbled and in which he is temporarily trapped.

The tinkering has been minimal. It consists mainly of removing material I used several times for different publications in different years—what I have stolen from myself I have tried to delete; what I have stolen from others remains. Some tinkering has taken the form of explaining what I *must* have meant when I said something that I can no longer figure out. Rarely—there are half-a-dozen instances—I have restored sentences and paragraphs that were cut from my copy by editors insufficiently sensitive to the wonders of my prose and the reticular formations of my thinking.

There are doubtless certain constants to be discovered in these reviews, little moral bleeps and subliminal signals from repressed biases. If I understand what the physicists mean when they talk about "black holes" in the universe, it has to do with dying stars. When stars lose their thermonuclear power, they start squeezing themselves small with their own gravitational pressure. Some billions of years from now our sun will squeeze itself down to a diameter of 10,000 miles and become what is called a white dwarf. But the larger the star, the more gravitational pressure it will exert on itself and the smaller it will be squeezed, down to the nuclei of its atoms and occasionally beyond—so small, so dense, that it will disappear from sight. A black hole, but still matter. The physicists go on to theorize about black holes turning themselves inside out, like gloves, creating "tunnels," reversing space and time. They believe they have picked up X-ray signals from black holes whose atoms are overly excited; they are trying to check it out.

Well, people—even book reviewers—might be said to be midget universes full of stellar flotsam (intuitions, concepts, presumptions, faith) that are always dying but never entirely disappearing, just become small and dense, still sending off X-rays, still mattering. Other stars are in orbit around these black holes, even if they can't be seen. Distortions occur. An energetic reader might be able to deduce the existence of my own black holes from the distortions and the signals in these pages. But, like Cygnus X-1, I'm not going to explain myself. The white dwarves are obvious enough.

Too many people are to blame for this book, and thus a dedication is difficult. I have singled out Francis Brown, who changed my life by deciding to hire me and who gave me my first chance to write for the New York *Times*. But I owe a great deal to Christopher Lehmann-Haupt, who brought me to New York; to Dave Scherman, who kept me alive; to Dan Schwarz, Nora Sayre, Harold Hayes, Lewis Bergman, Jack Nessel, Clifton Daniel, William F. Buckley, Jr., Abe Rosenthal, Paul Johnson and Arthur Gelb. These are the editors who were responsible for my writing 500,000 words; they are not responsible for what I said, and so I hope the reader will be as forgiving of them as I am grateful to them.

Contents

INTRODUCTION   News, Views, Reviews   xvii

FICTION
Nabokov's *Ada*   3
Gore Vidal's *Two Sisters*   5
Joan Didion's *Play It As It Lays*   7
S. J. Perelman's *Baby, It's Cold Inside*   10
John Cheever's *Bullet Park*   12
Jean Genêt's *Funeral Rites*   14
Günter Grass's *Local Anaesthetic*   16
Hermann Hesse's *Rosshalde*   19
Doris Lessing's *The Four-Gated City*   20
Gabriel Garcia Marquez's *One Hundred Years of Solitude*   22
Joyce Carol Oates's *Them*   24
Kōbō Abé's *The Ruined Map*   26
Harvey Swados's *Standing Fast*   28
Janet Frame's *Yellow Flowers in the Antipodean Room*
   and *Intensive Care*   30, 32
Marya Mannes's *They*   35
Rudolph Wurlitzer's *Flats*   36
Joseph McElroy's *Hind's Kidnap*   37
Thomas Merton's *My Argument with the Gestapo*   39
Elizabeth Cullinan's *House of Gold*   42
Tom McHale's *Principato*   43
Nicholas Delbanco's *News*   46
Marge Piercy's *Dance the Eagle to Sleep*   48

CRITICISM
Richard Gilman's *The Confusion of Realms*   53
Irving Howe's *Decline of the New*   56
Philip Rahv's *Literature and the Sixth Sense*   59
Leslie Fielder's *Nude Croquet* and *Being Busted*   61, 63

Flannery O'Connor's *Mystery and Manners*   66
Randall Jarrell's *The Third Book of Criticism*   68
Stanley Burnshaw's *The Seamless Web*   70
Samuel French Morse's *Wallace Stevens*   73
Marshall McLuhan's *Counterblast* and *The Interior Landscape*   75
Two (?) Modern Masters   77
Camus and Fanon   81

POLITICS AND OTHER INADEQUACIES
Politics   87
Death Wish in Chicago   87
The Democratic Happening   91
The Conspiracy   95
The Tales of Hoffman   97
Show Biz and Serious Biz   100
Confessions of a Structure Freak   103
James Simon Kunen's *The Strawberry Statement* and Dotson
     Rader's *I Ain't Marchin' Anymore*   109
Paul Cowan's *The Making of an Un-American*   113
George Kennan's *Democracy and the Student Left*   115
Margaret Mead's *Culture and Commitment*   121
Raymond Aron's *The Elusive Revolution* and *Marxism and the
     Existentialists*   124, 126
Odyssey of a Friend: Letters from Whittaker Chambers to William
     F. Buckley, 1954–61   128
Arthur Koestler's *Arrow in the Blue* and *The Invisible Writing*   131
VARIATIONS ON VIETNAM   134
     Townsend Hoopes's *The Limits of Intervention*   134
     Willard Gaylin's *In the Service of Their Country*   137
     A Nation of Veterans   139
     Telford Taylor's *Nuremberg and Vietnam* and Mark Lane's
          Conversations with Americans   142
John Kenneth Galbraith's *Ambassador's Journal*   145
Running Against the Machine   147
Who Killed John F. Kennedy?: *American Grotesque,* An Account of
     the Clay Shaw–Jim Garrison Affair in the City of New Orleans,
     by James Kirkwood; and *A Heritage of Stone,* by Jim Garri-
     son   150

BAD DREAMS   153

   The Ultimate Folly, War by Pestilence, Asphyxiation and Defoliation, by Congressman Richard D. McCarthy   153

   Let Them Eat Promises, The Politics of Hunger in America, by Nick Kotz   155

   Nader's Raiders, The Ralph Nader Study Group Reports on the Food and Drug Administration, Air Pollution and the Interstate Commerce Commission   157

   The Politics of Ecology, by James Ridgeway   160

   The Real Majority, by Richard M. Scammon and Ben J. Wattenberg   162

COMMISSION REPORTS—A BRIEF SELECTION   165

   The History of Violence in America, A Report to the National Commission on the Causes and Prevention of Violence, edited by Hugh Davis Graham and Ted Robert Gurr   165

   The Politics of Protest, A Task Force Report Submitted to the National Commission on the Cause and Prevention of Violence under the Direction of Jerome H. Skolnick   168

   Soulside, Inquiries into Ghetto Culture and Community, by Ulf Hannerz   170

INTERPRETERS OF BAD DREAMS   174

   Love and Will, by Rollo May   174

   The Freudian Left, Wilhelm Reich, Geza Roheim, Herbert Marcuse, by Paul A. Robinson   180

FIXERS OF BAD DREAMS   184

   Life on Man, by Theodore Rosebury   184

   The Future of the Future, by John McHale   186

NO MORE PRIVACY   189

   The Death of Privacy, by Jerry M. Rosenberg   189

   The Second Genesis, The Coming Control of Life, by Albert Rosenfeld   191

NO MORE ANYBODY?   194

   Anti-Ballistic Missiles: Yes or No? A Special Report from the Center for the Study of Democratic Institutions; and *ABM, An Evaluation of the Decision to Deploy an Antiballistic Missile System*, edited by Abram Chayes and Jerome B. Wiesner   194

SOCIOLOGY (1): UP AGAINST THE WALL, FUNCTIONALISTS   197

   The Coming Crisis of Western Sociology, by Alvin W. Gouldner   197

Policy I, for Freshmen   201
Predestination Without Grace   204

THE TUBE
Television   211
1971   213
The Next Ten Years   215
EMMYS   218
  A Short Rap with the Moonmen   218
  The Irony of a "Succès d' Emmy"   220
  The Pick of the Litter   222
The Barbara Walters Problem   224
Morning Is Less Than Electric   226
Nausea in the Afternoon   227
A Late-Night Talker Who Knows How to Listen   229
Late-Night Hope for the Republic   231
Charlie Brown in a Rep Tie   233
Whose Justice Do You Trust?   235
SITUATIONS VARIOUSLY COMEDIC   237
  Bigotry as a Dirty Joke   237
  Twist and Tact   239
  Ode to a Very Active Verb   241
  Dean Martin: A Las Vegas of the Heart   243
  Stand Up and Cher   244
ADVENTOURISMS   247
  Dr. Welby's Tonic Won't Harm You   247
  One of Our Myths Is Missing   249
  Private Eyes and Heavy Lids   251
SUBSPECIES (1): CHILDREN   254
  On the Street Where Kids Live   254
  Wrong Way Down Sesame Street   256
  "Mice" Deserve a Better Trap   258
  "Subsequent Aggressive Behavior"   260
  The Littlest Neurotics   262
  The Family That Sings Together . . .   264
  Why Lassie Can't Come Home   266
  Prisoners of Corn   268
SUBSPECIES (2): SPORTS   270
  Frozen Instants: TV at Its Best (Football and Television)   270

ABC's Wide World of Sports   272
The Basketball Is Black   274
They Hardly Ever Knock the Product   276
TV AND THE PUBLIC   278
Some Public Credit Where It's Due   278
Sorry, No Soap for Fyodor   280
A Marvelous Nightingale   282
Shuffling the Archetypes   284
Soft Vonnegut   285
TV VS. THE PUBLIC   288
There's Bad News Tonight   288
Chicago's "Underground News"   290
It's Put-Put Time In California   292
Walter Was There, Anyway   294
The Show Biz Conservative   295

FROM THE OTHER SIDE OF THE DESK

News, Views, Reviews

"Insects sting," said Nietzsche, "not in malice, but because they want to live. It is the same with critics: they desire our blood, not our pain."

1. Adjectives and the 800-Word Mind

A book reviewer isn't really a critic. He may want to be one, seizing each tome in his teeth like a beaver and dreaming the dam he could build with a little gnawing here and there. But he hasn't a critic's space, a critic's time or a critic's audience. The editors of his newspaper and the readers of his column aren't interested in his systems-building impulse. They want a combination of plot synopsis and consumer guide, and they want it in 800 entertaining words.

Thus the book reviewer develops an 800-word mind, which comes in handy at literary cocktail parties and symposia on The Sclerosis of Modernism. One quarter of those words are adjectives. Anybody, stinging a book about the ears and ankles, can suck out enough ink to fill up three quarters of a column, but the professional book reviewer lives and dies by his repertoire of adjectives.

Adjectives are crucial because all book reviews look alike. There is no way in, say, the New York *Times* to make one book review look more important than another. Every day the same number of words appears in the same typeface, whether one is reviewing Ezra Pound or Rod McKuen. Adjectives for a reviewer are a kind of emotional neon sign.

Adjectives are also dangerous. In every reviewer's life will come that awful week when, scanning the advertisements to see if he has been quoted—and all reviewers scan the book ads for that reason, knowing of course that their editors do the same—he finds that his entire vocabulary seems to consist of "superb," "compelling," "explosive" and "exquisite." This makes him look like a jerk. George says to Martha: "According to Pather Parturient of *Aphimixis* magazine, *Three Humps for Every Camel* is a terrifying philosophical romance about sodomists in Nasser's war cabinet." Martha says to George:

"Pather Parturient is a jerk. That's the third time this week he's been terrified. Maybe he should cover Ping-Pong instead of books."

Not wanting to appear a jerk, the reviewer starts using adjectives like "solipsistic," "dodecahedral" and "prelapsarian." Unfortunately, out of the some 20,000 new books published each year in the United States,—of which a daily paper can review perhaps 450—only about three will be in any way solipsistic, dodecahedral or prelapsarian. For that matter, only about two will be superb, compelling, explosive or exquisite. The purpose of a symposium is to complain about this state of affairs; the purpose of a literary cocktail party is to start affairs about which one can get into a state.

2. *Questions and Answers*

Reviewers make mistakes. For instance, they will occasionally accept an invitation to appear on a radio talk show, where the host looks like a rabid coyote and sounds like God. Or they will go innocently to dinner at a friend's apartment, for seaweed and petroleum extract, and the fierce young woman who has just exposed the myth of the vaginal orgasm turns on them suddenly to ask . . . the questions are always the same.

Do the editors of the New York *Times* decide which books you review?

No. Editors have better things to do with their time. Of course, if every other periodical in the world has reviewed a particular book, and you have not, the editors may wonder why. Quite properly. But they never insist. They don't even remind you that the New York *Times* owns Quadrangle Books.

How do you make your selections?

Instinct. Prejudice. Fatigue. Dyspepsia. Anger. Inadvertence. You read catalogues, previews of the spring list in *Publishers' Weekly* and Virginia Kirkus, chapters from forthcoming books that appear in magazines, and *I Ching* hexagrams. You listen to friends. You go to French restaurants for lunch on the expense account of editors and publicity directors, and learn who can be trusted and who sells every company product as though it were a miracle toothpaste or an antiballistics missile system. You get letters from authors, which you ignore; and telephone calls, which you never return. You read other reviews, and depending on whether you think your competitor is serious or an enemy of culture, you can be influenced. You cannot do a respectable job without signals; you have only to determine if the signals come from people who care about books or from the Snow Machines in the advertising departments of Garbage Can & Sons.

How many books do you read for each one you review?

About three to one, not counting jacket copy so inane your brain fries, opening paragraphs that seem to have been translated from the Quechua, and other discouraging first impressions.

What do you do when a friend writes a book?

Try to give it a favorable review. If you don't like the way his mind works, why is he your friend?

How do you feel when you alone like a book everybody else dislikes, or loathe a book everybody else huzzahs?

Smug.

Why waste time on Jacqueline Susann and Harold Robbins?

Why waste time on vacuuming the living room or washing the laundry or fixing the septic tank? We all have to live in this culture. There is in every reviewer an occasional temptation to assume the role of a bottle of Johnson's No-Roach with the spray applicator. You could review only those books about which it was possible to say nice things, three times a week for a year: readers would have no way to gauge your reliability, besides being bored to distraction; you personally would begin to feel like 200 pounds of Silly-Putty, on which the world pressed nothing but valentines; and the book column would be about as relevant to the human condition as Jacqueline Susann or Harold Robbins.

Do you review for special audiences?

Sometimes. If you happen to be interested in experimental fiction or logical positivism or cybernetics or the chemistry of the brain or ex-Communists or anthropology or Richard Nixon or psychoanalysis or haiku, either your reviews are going to reflect those interests or, when you look into your shaving mirror, all you will see is the other side of the room. And 800 words aren't enough to explain a whole field to a million readers, 95 per cent of whom couldn't care less. So you make some elitist assumptions about the people who *will* care, and belly flop straight into deep waters.

Do you have too much power?

Not enough. The front page of *The New York Times Book Re-*

view and almost any television talk show have more power over the
fate of books. Of course, every reviewer believes the world would be
a better place if only the befuddled masses listened to *him*. Every
non-reviewer believes the same.

Don't you ever get sick of the job?

Imagine getting paid each day to sit around reading books, and
then having a column all your own to tell everybody what you think
about those books. Even a pessimist would enjoy it, providing he
liked to read and write. It is one of the few pleasures—one thinks of
sex—that can't be taxed, although the Internal Revenue Service has
been making noises recently about all those free books a reviewer
receives. Why do you suppose marijuana is illegal in this country?
Because the government can't tax it; any dolt could grow it in his
window box. It was inevitable that the IRS should envy book reviewers. Perhaps we should pay our taxes in the form of first novels, and
let the Treasury Department sell them to the Strand Book Store.

3. *The Moralistic Philistine Critic* Manqué

However much he enjoys his job, the book reviewer must still live
like ordinary men and women in a world gone mad. "Would that we
could live in a world of the fauves," wrote Whittaker Chambers once,
"where the planes are disjointed only on canvas, instead of a world
where the wild beasts are real and the disjointures threaten to bury
us." His breakfast cereal will contain no more protein than there is
to be found in a shot of Irish rye. His frankfurters will be one-third
chicken fat. If he stays inside, his air conditioner will be busy converting the atmosphere's sulphur dioxide into sulphuric acid that rots
the pipes; if he goes outside, American manufacturing will dump
300 pounds of contaminants on *him*, personally, every year. If he
conceives a child, it may be one of the 50,000 annual infant mortali-
ties in the United States who would have survived in most modern
European countries. If his child survives, and is a boy, he will probably be eliminating Guatemalans with extreme prejudice nineteen
years from now, unless the MIRV Medusas turn us into stone or
cinders in the interim. If his child is black . . . well, enough.

Like everybody else, then, the book reviewer is a citizen and has a
lot to worry about. The biggest worries are always moral. How he
worries about moral problems, and what he does about them, de-

pend on his sources of information. Books, no matter what Marshall McLuhan cries in whatever apocalyptic seizure, are sources of information; even novels, which Richard Gilman would prefer to be "more purely verbal artifact and imaginative increment," are sources of information. Like plays, movies and politics, they have moral resonance. Does this mean that a reviewer has to brood about that resonance as he clickety-clacks his 800 words on tomorrow morning's ballyhooed excrescence? Yes. Literary criticism, said Leslie Fiedler, can be nothing less "than an act of total moral engagement." If the reviewer, a critic *manqué*, hasn't the habit of mind and craft to ask what such-and-such a book implies in a social and moral context, he is about as useful to the species as a no-deposit, no-return bottle of non-caloric soda pop.

Afflicted with an 800-word mind, I have neither the presumption nor the stamina to propose any theory of aesthetics. Artists do what they want to or have to do. Stanley Burnshaw was probably right in *The Seamless Web* when he advanced the idea that art is an involuntary expression of the artist's total organism; that after each of us has constructed his objectifying "I," we experience "otherness" (estrangement from the biological "web") and start looking *at* the environment through symbolic binoculars instead of continuing *with* it as participants in a unity; that artistic "inspiration" is actually a drive of the organism toward integral equipoise or homeostasis, a discharge of the burden of tension that is a consequence of "otherness." Poets don't compose poems, says Mr. Burnshaw, "for the high purpose of producing objects to give other people pleasure or instruction or knowledge or moral guidance"; they just have to compose poems.

Obviously, any society that tries to tell its artists how to go about their business is sick. But it should be equally obvious that any society which doesn't take its artists seriously is also sick. When critics, reviewers, politicians, businessmen and strung-out pubescents conspire at the pretense that art doesn't matter—intellectually or morally—they aren't taking artists seriously. Susan Sontag may complain about our thralldom to the Greek theory of mimesis, but where does the logic of her complaint lead her? It leads her from a celebration of style (*Against Interpretation*) to an apologia for silence (*Styles of Radical Will*); thereafter, the only thing left to do was to go to Vietnam and review it as though it were a Godard film, and then to make

films herself. Richard Gilman in *The Confusion of Realms* may complain about the "exploitation" of art as a weapon, an escape, a recompense or a blueprint—"To force art into being knowledge has
been the master stroke that cut off its roots in ritual and play"—but
where has *his* complaint led him? To the raptures of the Zeitgeist;
to the lust for and embracing of everything that is *New*, every explosion of form, each seasonal Hula-Hoop from anti-novels to happenings. And then along comes Eldridge Cleaver, and Mr. Gilman
admits he can't review him: black writing, rooted in social and moral
contexts, in a "sense of actuality," simply isn't susceptible to his
approach.

"There is something anterior to technique," wrote Philip Rahv
years ago, "and that is sensibility." The sensibilities of a Tolstoy and
a Céline, a Nabokov and a Genet, of a Doris Lessing and a LeRoi
Jones, are evidently different, and just as evidently crucial to the nature of their achievement, and therefore reviewable. But more: regardless of the intentions of these and other artists, their art *is* going
to be used as knowledge. Neither they nor Miss Sontag nor Mr.
Gilman can say to a culture going up in smoke, "Look, all this
is merely a lot of ritual and play and mysterious otherness of presence. Don't try to make anything *relevant* out of it." The wounded
(and perhaps dying) culture is going to use art as it uses science
and religion; it is going to squeeze the "message" dry for drops of
insight and outlook, for moral, psychological and even political sus-
tenance. You would, too, if you were a culture.

Let's say, along with Mr. Burnshaw, that art is inherently opposed
to any culture. Are the critic and the critic *manqué* also opposed? I
think they've got feet in both camps and obligations on both sides.
Men have to live together (which all of us worry about) but man
must die alone (which artists and philosophers worry about). Each
of us exists in a constant state of tension between what he expects
to receive as an individual and the concessions he must make to society. Our best and worst experiences occur inside ourselves, but we
are at the beginning and at the end dependent on others—for protection and education during our prolonged period of dependency
after birth; for the unending flow of sensations and perceptions from
the *outside*, without which there could be no integrity of the personality; for the goods and services, the division of labor into bits
and pieces of skills, the exchange of experiences abstracted into sym-

bols and words, that permit us to adapt to our environment and survive. Transactions between the individual and society are inevitable, even on a commune, and so is conflict, and so thus is tension. Where the needs of the individual and the needs of society coincide is at the question of *What is the right thing to do?*

When last seen, *the right thing to do* was fleeing across the moors, a moral fugitive. Have the critic and the critic *manqué* a responsibility to pursue it, even in novels? I am astonished that we are all prepared to insist on the moral obligations of the nuclear physicist, the cabinet member, the university president, the sociologist on government contract, the director of General Motors, the construction worker and the newspaper editor, and yet we foist upon art an autonomy as automatic as if it had dropped on us from Mars. And as reviewers, we cloak ourselves in that borrowed autonomy. Without going quite so far as Samuel Butler, who suggested that "Books should be tried by a judge and jury as though they were crimes," I'd say that either we relate our profession to the world we live in or we have no more ethics than a can of Spam.

(*Cultural Affairs*, Fall 1970)

Fiction

Nabokov's *Ada*

Here is Vladimir Nabokov's first new novel in seven years, twice as long as any book he has ever written before, and fourteen times as complicated. Naturally, the reviewer approaches it scared to death. Nabokov's prose is always booby-trapped, and if Edmund Wilson can get bombed (the "sapajou" joke in the Pushkin translation), mere mortals want to stay at home with the comic strips. Which is too bad, for there is more pleasure to be derived from a Nabokov novel than from almost anything else available in contemporary literature—or even, for that matter, from any mixed-media group-grope of deracinated starvelings desperate to groove the East Pillage obscene. Why leave the explications to the exegetes? Or the execration to those radical critics who keep trying to put N. down as some sort of recidivistic White Russian ingrate?

He is, as he once wrote about something else, "a goblet of rays of light and pus,/ a mixture of toad and swan." He is, as well, our only living literary genius. Nobody else could have written an anti-deterministic masterpiece, contemptuous of Freud (there is no guilt) and Marx (there are no politics, no economics, not even any history), that is at once a sexual and philosophical romance, a brilliant science fiction, an awesome parody and a gigantic punundrum.

Let me risk some tentative explications. *Ada* is:

(1) The anthropological description of an alternative world. N., by deciding that certain ancient wars, which were lost, should have been won, has rearranged history to suit himself. There are Russians all over North America, and, because all Russians speak French, they go about obsessively coining trilingual puns. N.'s world is called Antiterra. "Our" world, Terra, is apprehended only by madmen, philosophers and science fiction writers. The two worlds are out of technological phase, allowing N. to pump away on his narrative as though it were a slide rule.

(2) A theory of time which makes time a kind of privately owned supermarket of sensations and events, through which the artist strolls to impulse-buy. Time is always present, and the instant be-

comes eternal insofar as it engages and freezes consciousness into metaphor. (Intense love, for instance, is such a frozen slab of consciousness, always available for a quick fry in the imaginative oven.) Unfortunately, it's a theory of time that only works for geniuses, men of unlimited imaginative capital; the rest of us must live in an empirical funk.

(3) A parody of *Anna Karenina* in particular, the Russian novel in general, and the evolution of The Novel in universal. N. opens *Ada* with a reversal of Tolstoy's opening *Anna* paragraph, and then manages in one book to recapitulate all the various fecundations and despoliations that the great Earth Mother of Prose has had to endure from an army of ravishing innovators for centuries.

(4) A love story. *Ada* is, really, the memoir of a philosopher who, at age fourteen, fell in love with his cousin, age twelve. But the cousin, Ada, turns out to be his sister, and they spend the next seven decades solving the togetherness problem. During those decades, Ada sleeps around and the philosopher, Van, writes the treatises—"catching sight of the lining of time . . . the best informal definition of portents and prophecies"—which account for Explications 1 to 3.

It should be pointed out right here that Ada, as a character, is lovable. There are those critics who—resenting the fact that N. enjoyed a happy childhood—complain of his cerebral chill. They have ignored Pnin, Fyodor, Luzhin, Krug and even Humbert Humbert in the earlier novels; but if they ignore Ada, there isn't a lyric spark in their gray clay hearts.

It should also be pointed out, before I give the one and only true explication of *Ada*, that the book is full of incidental games: N. makes fun of existentialism, of his own annotators, of Jorge Luis Borges, of Balzac, Kafka, Proust, Joyce, John Updike (very affectionately), and especially himself: "Her spectacular handling of subordinate clauses, her parenthetic asides, her sensual stressing of adjacent monosyllables . . . all this somehow finished by acting upon Van, as artificial excitements and exotic torture-caresses might have done, in an aphrodisiac sinistral direction that he both resented and perversely enjoyed."

Exactly. And what he's done in *Ada* is to write his own artistic autobiography, a companion piece to *Speak, Memory*, a treatise on his own internal Antiterra. He has constructed an entire shimmering culture out of his exile and wanderings, a language out of his own experience. Combine Van (chess-playing, tone-deaf "old wordman") with Ada (butterfly collector, amateur botanist); superimpose them on a Russian America; add masks, deceit, memory, dreams, conjuring, apostasy, acrobatics, the zoo and the cage; celebrate the crime (which was that of Cincinnatus C.) of being opaque in a transparent world—and you have the elusive N., like "a bifurcated spectre . . . a candle between mirrors sailing off to a sunset."

He has written elsewhere that "the future is but the obsolete in reverse," and that "the only real number is one, the rest are mere repetition." *Ada*, dedicated to his wife, is his jeweled butterfly, singular, timeless, the man himself. If he doesn't win the Nobel prize, it's only because the Nobel prize doesn't deserve him.

(April 1969)

Gore Vidal's *Two Sisters*

Whether *Two Sisters* is "a novel in the form of a memoir," as the jacket declares, or "a memoir in the form of a novel," as the title page insists, it is nonetheless inadequate. "Out of desperation," writes Mr. Vidal, "I have abandoned the usual form in order to deal directly with myself." Nonsense. He has made fun of Mr. Mailer, whose popularity he envies: the novel as history, history as a novel. And he has parodied Mr. Nabokov, whose reviews he covets: incest, a game the whole family can play. But he is neither desperate nor direct. He seems rather to have felt a lack of literary impulse and so gone to his icebox, pulled out all the cold obsessions—ancient history, hedonism, Hollywood, bisexuality, Jacqueline Onassis—mixed them in a bowl, beat too lightly and baked too long. Aspiring to a soufflé, he achieves a pancake, at which the reader saws without much appetite.

Two Sisters begins in Rome, shortly after the publication of Nabokov's *Ada*. V. is playing verbal badminton with Marietta Donegal, an aging vamp apparently modeled on Anaïs Nin, who has written five volumes of memoirs on her famous bedmates. Marietta gives V. the twenty-year-old diary of Eric Van Damm, plus a screenplay Van Damm wrote called *The Two Sisters of Ephesus*. The

screenplay, all about Persians and Greeks and the destruction of the
Temple of Diana in 356 B.C., includes an incestuous affair between
Herostratus and his sister, Helena. (Since Van is the incestuous
brother in *Ada*, V. proves that he has at least read Nabokov's reviews. Infra dig it.)

V. broods gloomily on these materializations of the past, because
once upon a time he lusted for Eric Van Damm. He had, however,
to settle for Eric's twin sister, Erika, whom he believes he accidentally impregnated. V. is not very big on fatherhood, what with the
population explosion and all that, but still it's nice to know the
family line goes on. Imagine, then, V.'s discombobulation on learning that the child he thought was his actually belongs to Eric and
Erika. Oh, there are too many ironies in the fire!

Not only do we get the whole of Eric's diary, but the whole of his
wretched screenplay as well. We also get, in sections conveniently
marked "now," V.'s emendations: chit-chat with Tennessee Williams,
Gide, John Kenneth Galbraith, Jack Kerouac, Arthur Schlesinger,
Jr., and other roustabouts; plus V.'s views on politics and American
provincialism. The screenplay, after sneering at Nabokov and tele-
graphing Eric's punches with his sister, turns into a nasty little
burlesque about "the *ci-devant* tragic empress of the West," Mrs.
Onassis. (V. tells us on page 175 that there *is* an analogy, just in
case we weren't already sniggering.)

There is no reason why a writer as accomplished as Gore Vidal
couldn't have whipped these materials into convincing shape. "I do
not believe in ghosts, astrology, palmistry, graphology, John Cage,
love or God," he says. Love is the key word. Even in his best novels,
there is no love, only the power of one partner over the other—control, manipulation, pleasure cruelly exacted under circumstances of
unequal option, according to a kind of vicious algebra that cancels
out individuality. Everyone becomes X. For V. to find that Eric and
Erika used *him*, manipulated not only his pleasure but also his memory, is surely the stuff of confessional literature. It might have worked;
it might have caused pain.

It doesn't, because he presents himself under so many coats of
lacquer that one knows reality will never soil him; nor are Eric and
Erika real; he made them up, as he made up Marietta, and tells us so.
Two Sisters works neither as a novel (all the news happens off-stage)

nor as a memoir (the "I" is far too coy). Which leaves V.'s views on the macrocosm as its only justification. He has always been a better literary critic than social analyst—buggery will save the world, or what my colleague Hilton Kramer has called "orifice politics"—but here he chooses merely to bite his betters on their kneecaps. To be told that Victor Hugo is high culture and, by implication, that William Faulkner is provincial, is to be told balderdash.

There is one genuinely amusing moment in this book, when V. reports: "I have usually found that whenever I read about an occasion where I was present, the report (except once) never tallies with my own. The once was Jack Kerouac's *The Subterraneans*, in which he describes with . . . astonishing accuracy an evening he spent with William Burroughs and me. Everything is perfectly recalled until the crucial moment when Jack and I went to bed together at the Chelsea Hotel and, as he told me later, disingenuously, 'I forgot.' I said he had not. 'Well, maybe I wanted to.' So much for the tell-it-like-it-is school."

It is not enough. The author of *The City and the Pillar, The Judgment of Paris, A Thirsty Evil* and *Myra Breckinridge*—yes, *Myra Breckinridge*, one of the better novels and worst movies of recent years—comes on like the Billy Graham of the Pleasure Principle, peddling second-hand goods. Maybe Norman Mailer was right more than a decade ago, when he said of Mr. Vidal: "I cannot resist suggesting that he is in need of a wound, which would turn the prides of his detachment into new perception." Mailer being right might be precisely that sort of wound.

(July 1970)

Joan Didion's *Play It As It Lays*

There hasn't been another American writer of Joan Didion's quality since Nathanael West. She writes with a razor, carving her characters out of her perceptions with strokes so smooth and economical that each scene ends almost before the reader is aware of it; and yet the characters go on bleeding afterward. A pool of blood forms in the mind. Meditating on it, you are both frightened and astonished.

When was the wound inflicted? How long have we to live? Miss Didion's new novel combines this surgical prose with a crushing fatalism—the title refers to a crap game—that obliges her people endlessly to circle themselves, reducing their radii of possibilities, seeking an exit from the "I"—and sets it all in the cities of the desert (Los Angeles, Las Vegas). While the result is not exactly pleasant, it seems to me just about perfect according to its own austere terms.

Maria Wyeth is an internal refugee. She was born in Nevada to parents who were always waiting for the next roll of the dice, and always losing. She went to New York, became a model, survived a disastrous affair with one man and disastrously married another (Carter Lang, demon filmmaker). We pick up Maria after she has starred in two of Carter's movies, given birth to a little girl with an "aberrant chemical in her brain," aborted a second child, divorced, and retired in her thirties to Southern California with a terminal fatigue of the body and the spirit. The only game she has the energy to play is for her daughter, whom she wishes to rescue from a mental home.

Inside and outside Maria, there is only desolation. Carter; the homosexual BZ; BZ's bitchy wife, Helene; and all the other characters seem perfect children of the desert, plastic toys with spring mechanisms coiled inside them, wound up and sent out to whir and spin, dangerous in their very motion. The emotional terrain (brain damage, abortion, sexual inversion, suicide, moral exhaustion) is a mirror image of the landscape (rattlesnakes, freeways, gambling casinos, motorcycle gangs, drive-in churches). One feels that, just as the characters consume themselves in circles and games, so the desert will swallow the ersatz on its surface, leaving everything to the lizards and the snakes.

What makes the world of this novel, a world in which the only reply to the question "Why?" is "Why not?", so heartbreaking and inescapable is Miss Didion's selection of details. There is nothing superfluous, not an incident, not a word. Personalities are more than sufficiently evoked in a single phrase—"Felicia always spoke on the telephone as if a spurious urgency could mask her radical lack of interest in talking to anyone"—and whole chapters are condensed into a single page. Such economy testifies to a vision as bleak and as precise as Eliot's in *The Waste Land*. And if Randall Jarrell was right in saying that Eliot would have written *The Waste Land* about the Garden of Eden, I suspect Miss Didion would have written *Play It As It Lays* about Our Town or Woodstock or Monaco. Sylvia Plath with brains.

For it is the condition of a woman's mind that is her subject; it is the "nothingness" after one has been used as an object that she explores; it is the facts beyond "answers" or "explanations" that she plays with: "This morning I threw the coins in the swimming pool, and they gleamed and turned in the water in such a way that I was almost moved to read them. I refrained." Or: "My father advised me that life itself was a crap game: it was one of the two lessons I learned as a child. The other was that overturning a rock was apt to reveal a rattlesnake. As lessons go those two seem to hold up, but not to apply." And earlier Maria has written, "with the magnetized IBM pencil"—"NOTHING APPLIES."

Cheerless, then. And there will undoubtedly be readers who ask: Why doesn't this girl get her head together? Join her local Women's Liberation chapter or the Peace Corps? Go to Esalen? Read Marx? Find God? If we conceive of the novel as a kind of Drano for dissolving the sludge in the clogged plumbing of fictional characters, then certainly Miss Didion isn't going to win the Good Housekeeping Seal of Approval—which is to say, the Pulitzer Prize. But so long as novels are permitted to be about visions, to identify truths beyond redress of grievance, then Miss Didion need not equip Maria with a Roto-Rooter or a dose of ideological uplift. Maybe God doesn't want to be found. The courage to say "Why not?" to nothingness is more than enough. Faulkner and Mauriac were fatalists, too. So was Freud, who had the courage of his pessimism, before the epigones co-opted him for Disneyland.

Because Miss Didion is not the sort of writer who goes in for tricks on the reader, I doubt whether "Wyeth" is an intentional play on names. But one *is* reminded of Andrew Wyeth's painting "Christina's World," with Harold Pinter's thumbprints all over it. Maria looks up at the house on the hill. Only the house is burning. Perhaps she will get up, and run to save her daughter. But it is her soul burning, as well; and it's only a picture; and ultimately the world belongs to the rattlesnakes. Nothing applies. A terrifying book.

(July 1970)

S. J. Perelman's *Baby, It's Cold Inside*

[This review originally appeared in *Migraine, the Quarterly of Cultural Obfuscation.*]

The S. J. Perelman story, like the Godard film, is a mode of proof, an assertion of accuracy in the spirit of maximum vehemence. The Perelman speech is purified and condensed by disparateness, a speech of *need.* The Perelman world is a world of aggression, beautiful as Lautréamont defined beauty: "The fortuitous encounter of a sewing machine and an umbrella on a dissecting table." Why, then, isn't Perelman taken seriously? He knows more about the "instant character" of Camp than Susan Sontag. He was throwing around "the purely verbal artifact" twenty years before Richard Gilman pumped *The New Republic* full of William Gass. Yet he is trivialized as a mere humorist. A mere humorist! The brother-in-law of Nathanael West? The spiritual grandfather of Russell Baker and R. Crumb? The Admirable Byrd of punitive comedy, stylized reticence and radical juxtaposition?

One might explain this shameful disregard by the fact that his stories appear regularly in *The New Yorker.* (Indeed, typically puckish, he hints at such a misconception by dedicating *Baby, It's Cold Inside* to J. D. Salinger.) It won't do. In this collection alone, seven stories speak of "vengeance," four of "concussed," three of "expunged," two of "David Susskind." Almost all evoke the fantasy figure of a female "a shade too voluptuous" or "a shade too sensual" for "true beauty," with whom nothing is ever consummated. The Black Museum of Scotland Yard—almost as difficult to penetrate as "King Faisal's harem, the council chamber of the Politburo and Secretary Rusk's cerebellum"—the Southern towns, Irish castles, English hotels and Pennsylvania Dutch barns; the predatory doctors, bankers and dentists that throng this book suggest a darker aspect to his genius.

That aspect is the Self as Hero and the Hero as Scapegoat, instead of the Self as Victim and the Reader as Scapegoat. Seldom does Perelman exact the vengeance for which he lusts; his cruelty is on-

tological: "To Err Is Human, to Forgive, Supine." Like Sartre, he has
gone beyond the notion of action as a mode of self-conservation, and
glimpsed the autonomy of the aesthetic: "Anna Trivia Pluralized."
Inspired by newspaper clippings, TV commercials, movies he saw as
a Providence, Rhode Island, prepubescent and what Freud called
"the rubbish-heap" of the quotidian, he leaps from hermeneutics to
erotics in a single bound.

Yes, baby, it *is* cold inside. For instance: "At dusk we warped into
Wilhelmina, a decayed hamlet obviously subsidized by Carson Mc-
Cullers to furnish her with literary material. Eight of its stores were
untenanted, the ninth occupied by a waxworks portraying a group
of pellagra victims frozen around a pinball machine." Or: "Minutes
before I was to join a Welsh couple taking me to an eisteddfod in a
Nonconformist chapel in Dorking, I received word that a gas main
beneath the church had exploded and reduced the place to match-
wood." Or: "A matter of four months later I happened to be up on
Martha's Vineyard, and dropped into a stationery store in Edgar-
town, looking for a mechanism of sorts with which to run a staple
into my thumb."

Such a triptych of quotations reveals the Perelman imagination
pondering its obsessive themes: the Gothic nightmare, the decline
of traditional religious values, and the "reification" of modern man,
the essential hostility of *things*. How can a contemporary sensibility escape this perceptual trap? Perelman is tricky. First, he reverses
Brecht's Alienation Effect as though it were a raincoat: "'Kid, I'll
be honest with you,' he said through his knees. (The armchairs in
his office were so deep that we could hardly see each other's face.)"
Having thus achieved a kind of liberating anonymity, *he simply leaves*.

Perelman's leave-takings—"boarding a dhow to Zanzibar," on the
houseboat *Sleepyhead* in "an endless dismal network of canals
bordering a potash plant," "steaming eastward aboard the *S.S.
Leviathan*, which was conveniently steaming in the same direction"
—are as metaphorical as they are infamous. They are voyages to the
psychic interior, in search of the Wintergarten aerialist or the thun-
der under the Kalahari. As such, each is doomed to disappointment,
a wild goose chase, *eine wilde Gänsejagd*. Inside, it is cold.

Does the fact that it is always cold inside mean that Perelman has
painted himself into an epistemological pigeonhole? Perhaps. But
so do we all, those of us at any rate who refuse the Skinnerian

quadrille, the cyanide pellet of conditioning. Eight times he reminds us that for six months he was once a medical student. He has volunteered a philosophical diagnosis of himself and, going into the cold without any mittens, disclosed the opacity of mere detail in the transparent reality of Now. We laugh because we are afraid of his courage.

(September 1970)

John Cheever's *Bullet Park*

Welcome to Cheever country. Eliot and Nellie Nailles, sitting at their breakfast table, "seemed to have less dimension than a comic strip, but why was this? They had erotic depths, origins, memories, dreams and seizures of melancholy and enthusiasm." Eliot says: "I can't see that playing golf and raising flowers is depraved." And Nellie thinks: "I'm a *good* woman . . . I've never once run over a squirrel on the highway. I've always kept seed in the bird-feeding station." And the reader slips comfortably into their lives, as though the prose were an old sport coat.

For the reader knows what to expect. A tale will be told of life under a glass bell in some suburban cul-de-sac. Of decent people feeling guilty about desires and goals we all share, apologizing for themselves before some blind and deaf tribunal—Youth, perhaps, a hanging judge with acne. Of plaintive Sisypheans on a plastic slope, losing their grip when luck, or charm, runs out. There will be dark currents in the swimming pool, skeletons in the liquor closet, that domesticated desperation of which "a pink plush toilet-seat cover" flying from a clothesline is the mocking symbol.

This time, however, the reader slips not into a sport coat but into a straitjacket. Bullet Park's topography may be recognizably Cheeveresque—railroad stations are "war-like ruins"; people burn to death when cans of charcoal igniter explode at barbecue parties—but an alien wind blows over it. Like many Cheever characters, Eliot Nailles exhausts his luck; but this time the exhaustion triggers an attack on "that sense of sanctuary that is the essence of love," and the glass bell shatters in a fantasy of self-redemption.

Nailles is a chemist who hustles mouthwash. He is "incurably" monogamous: "The success of his marriage was not an affair of the heart—it was a matter of life and death." He believes, "like a child on a hill, that purpose and order underlay the roofs, trees, rivers and streets that composed the landscape." He thinks "of pain and suffering as a principality, lying somewhere beyond the legitimate borders of western Europe." His love for his wife and only son is "like some limitless discharge of a clear amber fluid that would surround them, cover them, preserve them and leave them insulated but visible like the contents of an aspic."

Then one day his young son Tony goes to bed because "I just feel terribly sad," and doesn't get up again. Comforters and specialists fail to rouse him. Nailles, frightened by his inability to protect "his beloved world—his kingdom," starts gulping down illegal "tranquilizers," blowing his mind every morning while waiting for the commuter train. "Without his son, he could not live. He was afraid of his own death."

Enter Hammer. (Yes: Bullet Park, Powder Hill, Hammer and Nailles, a real estate agent named Hazzard, a minister called Ransome, etc.) Hammer is the temperamental opposite of Nailles: illegitimate child of "anarchy and change," cosmopolitan vagabond, raised in loveless privilege, longing for "yellow rooms," emerging from "a timeless moral vortex." Halfway through the book, Hammer assumes the narrative voice. He has come to Bullet Park (an exclusive world of yellow rooms) to claim a mad compensation, "to awaken the world." Hammer choses Nailles, "for his excellence." Nailles is called upon to sacrifice his own son.

Now, Hammer is something new in Cheever's fiction. He is the principle of chance elevated to an irrational evil. As a character, he is wholly unbelievable, but I suspect he isn't intended to be believable. He is an aspect or fantasy of Nailles' mind (perhaps a by-product of the "tranquilizers"), an *Other* fashioned from anarchic depths, a creature of repressed libidinal ferocity. Nailles has invented him out of the very materials Bullet Park denies: chance, the energy of evil, the existence of a moral universe, the meaningfulness of guilt, the necessity of ritual. Hammer is a manufactured darkness.

But why manufacture him? Because Nailles, fearful for his son, is without the means of grace. In a community with only four altars "and none of them sacrificial" (the cul-de-sac is secular), he can *demonstrate* neither his love for his son nor the significance of his own life. And so he must dream the defining violence, batterwhip the whirlwind, from which he will rescue Tony and redeem himself.

Bullet Park is John Cheever's deepest, most challenging book. It has the tone of a summing-up and the tension and luminosity of a vision. For the inhabitants of the glass bell, the citizens of Cheever country, are only vulnerable through their children. Whether the children reach them through sadness (like Tony), or are lost to them in the cheap mysteries supplied by pushers (Nailles in the graveyard, buying his "high"), the message is the same: If we have only each other, the proof of love is the risk of self. And if we fail to risk, we are spiritually impotent. Hammer awaits us; and fire, and water, and night.

(April 1969)

Jean Genet's *Funeral Rites*

Perhaps the only thing more irritating than a novel by Jean Genet is a critical text on his fiction. Indeed, it sometimes seems as if he were a figment of the diabolical imaginations of Jean-Paul Sartre and Susan Sontag. "His intention," says Sartre, "is to harm, and his work aims at being an evil action." It is, Miss Sontag adds, "an extended treatise on abjection—conceived as a spiritual method." They agree that some sort of "transubstantiation" is involved, whereby the "onanistic meditator" annihilates the world we know. Whoopee. If then you graft to this palette of apocalyptic posturings a little Black Mass and an overmuch of resurrection myth (the "self-transfigured" foundling/thief/homosexual/artist), and apply a urethane spray of prose that is gorgeously smutty, what aesthete wouldn't swoon? We have apparently reached the terminal stage of a cancer of the culture, where the surgeons unzip flesh-flaps and gasp in admiration at the rioting cells.

Funeral Rites is exemplary in its noxiousness. It purports to mourn the death of Genet's young lover, Jean Decarnin, a Resistance hero slain by a Nazi collaborator in 1944. It is actually (1) an exercise in cannibalism and necrophilia; (2) the proclamation of an aesthetic of fascism; (3) a masturbatory fantasy that should shame

Portnoy all the way to Sweden for an organ transplant; and (4) an outrageous bore.

It is outrageous on a moral level. We have been fed a lot of nonsense recently about the conceptual autonomy and moral neutrality of art. The loftier criticism today by special dispensation exempts literature from moral categories; it is considered sufficient to identify the artist's intention and to report on how much damage he has done to your sensibilities. All the rest is agitprop.

Yet Western art since the Greek tragedians has presupposed a moral dimension to creative utterance, and the utterer is no more "neutral" than Jack the Ripper or St. Augustine. We must live together and we must die alone, and that tension is one of the things that art will always be about—ways and reasons for living and dying. The novel, especially, is a prose transaction which assumes the existence of readers who will absorb or reject or modify or misinterpret the organizing vision of the artist.

Genet has an organizing vision; and if we are to take him at all seriously, we must cope with it. *Funeral Rites* is a calculated series of degradations—first, of society; then of love (or the memory of it); and finally of consciousness itself. The universe is transformed into Jean D.'s corpse. The corpse is then transformed into Genet's penis. Genet then abuses himself while entertaining fantasies of a submissive Hitler. The parody of Holy Communion, the celebration of fascism, is explicit and complete.

His imaginings are themselves a theft. Knowing the heroic Jean D. to have been a secret homosexual, Genet "steals" him from society. The safely dead and therefore cherished love must then be betrayed by his submitting himself to Jean D.'s murderers. At the last, his mockery of himself obliterates even the fantasy. An ultimate solipsism, an ultimate permissiveness, is proposed: a consciousness capable of experiencing others only through manipulation and total control, employing and enjoying brutality, at once death camp commandant and eager victim.

Unless we refuse this vision, we deserve it. To be neutral about it is to flirt with our own personal fascism; it is either a failure of nerve . . . or immoral. It won't do to blather about the "witness" of a "victim"; and then to turn the victim into a hero and the victimization into an aesthetic principle; and thus to presume that the victimization—of homosexuals, blacks, political dissidents—can be experienced aesthetically. You aren't necessarily good just because you have suffered. When you are told that you are, by those who haven't suffered, they are stealing your reality from you and using it as a coaster on which to deposit their mugs of voyeurism. No rings on the complacent coffeetable soul; only ideas that have become book jackets that clash with the Mondrian. As Genet exploits Jean D., so his claque exploits Genet.

Funeral Rites is also a bore, simply because it says the same things Genet said in *Our Lady of the Flowers* and *Thief's Journal*. Once more we are offered a self-portrait of the artist on his back, metamorphosing himself from brutalized child to wicked angel. Once more we are asked to endure a self-swallowing infantile narcissism, a lust for nullity: I am the Universe; the Universe is a Shuck; I am a Shuck, and therefore I am free. To make a career out of narcissism, even victimized narcissism, is to become a bore, no matter how sumptuously expressive that bore may be.

I admire Genet's plays—*The Maids, Deathwatch, The Balcony, The Blacks*—and I think it no accident that they are superior to his fiction. The theater obliged him to get off his back and deal with a social context, to admit the existence of other people into the cell of his self-consuming fantasy, his automated putrefactory. The very dialectic his fiction seeks to abolish is forced upon him by the inconvenient presence of other "I's" in continuing approximations, and so in the plays there are consequences as well as dreams. Art, like life, is a game of untruths and consequences.

(June 1969)

Günter Grass's *Local Anaesthetic*

Günter Grass has lived for years in the bestiary, occasionally liberating his grotesques—Oskar's glass-shattering scream, Mahlke's Adam's apple, Amsel's mechanical scarecrows—to savage the sensibilities of the burgomasters. His fourth novel is a slight departure because he leashes those grotesques and takes them out for a stroll. They are under control, although they sometimes drag the reader into recesses where he really wouldn't want to go. The result is an unlikely combination of *Man's Fate* and *Portnoy's Complaint*. Not that there's a revolution in *Local Anaesthetic*, or even very much sex. But it is, like *Man's Fate*, a splendid novel of ideas, a meditation on history and violence (and pedagogy and student radicalism). And, like *Portnoy's Complaint*, it employs as a literary device a first-person narrator explaining himself, confessing himself, talking around himself to an unforgiving professional ear—in this case, not an analyst but a dentist.

First, the device. Eberhard Starusch, a forty-year-old professor of "German and history," brings his throbbing prognathic jaw to a dentist for repair. The dentist uses a television set to distract his patients. Onto the TV screen, Starusch projects his life, his violent fantasies and not a little twentieth-century German history, in between commercials. Sometimes that autobiographical videotape is the only scheduled program; sometimes the screen writhes in "live" coverage of demonstrations in the dentist's office; sometimes the commercial products (a deep freezer, a hair rinse) represent abstract problems (memory, disguise). Always the conceit permits Mr. Grass to explore the limitations of "cinematic" authority.

Second, the characters. Starusch has what Kurt Vonnegut calls a "karass": Sieglinde, his ex-fiancée, whose murder he innocently imagines; Sieglinde's father, Field Marshal Krings, a war criminal who devotes his dotage to re-fighting in a sandbox all the battles he lost in reality; Schlottau, the electrician who seduces Sieglinde; Scherbaum, Starusch's disillusioned student, who wants to burn his dachshund in public as a gesture against American napalm; and Vero Lewand, Scherbaum's Maoist teenybopper playmate. Even the dentist belongs to the karass, for, unlike Portnoy's Dr. Spielvogel, he never hesitates to interrupt the action.

Third, the ideas. One might play a jejune game of exegesis: Starusch was earlier a cement engineer, involved with centrifugal dust removal (the Jews?); his dentist describes tartar as "calcified hate" (inflammation of the German soul's notorious romantic-beast gland?); local anaesthetic ("No more pain!") might apply to selective conscience and selective memory. There is obviously a scheme: The dentist with his utopian "Sickcare" could symbolize a senile socialism, a talking tranquilizer, a carpetbagfull of reformist nostrums. Starusch, for all his bulldozer visions, belongs with the dentist ("Humanity is terrorized by overproduction and forced consumption"). Scherbaum seeks only an act that can bridge the discrepancy between what is and what should be. Vero quotes Chairman Mao and knows nothing.

Fourth, the complications. Scherbaum the student is our only hope, no matter his compromises. His example, ideologically unafflicted, saves Starusch, who knows perfectly well that there will never be enough anaesthetic or enough distraction to dull the moral ache. Overtly and inadvertently, Starusch and Scherbaum educate each other. Scherbaum learns that action can be promoted by fear, laziness, evasion or stupidity. Starusch learns that being rational "doesn't prevent you from being stupid." Scherbaum's fantasy of sacrificing his dog for Vietnam is as absurd as Starusch's fantasy of a "pedagogical prophylaxis," a preventive "against all evils." Scherbaum blames Starusch, but that is an enmity as old as Abelard.

Now, all that I have left out is everything. The humor, the exacting eye, the demonic imagination, the human sympathy, the dazzling play of language—when they get around to giving Günter Grass his Nobel prize, they should give one as well to Ralph Manheim, his translator—are not nearly so susceptible to the exegetical fraud as is Mr. Grass's intellectual design. I could go on about the subtleties of Seneca-quoting versus Nietzsche-quoting (Stoic versus Zarathustra); or irony as a stylistic glaze over every post-Auschwitz (post-Hiroshima) literary venture; or the novel about the difficulties of writing novels ("The artist as savior," says Starusch: "He helps sin to safety"); or the past as Super-Ego and the instant as bed-wetting. But . . . will it help sell books? No.

What *Local Anaesthetic* does is to explore the relationship between teachers and students with the empathy of Lionel Trilling in "Of This Time, of That Place"; with the wit of Randall Jarrell in *Pictures from an Institution;* and with the passion (Hegel, help us!) of Hermann Hesse in *Narcissus and Goldmund.* And what Günter Grass has done is to demonstrate once again that he belongs—along with Cortazar, Doris Lessing, Mailer, Nabokov, Sartre and Solzhenitsyn—among that handful of contemporary Western writers we must either read or else confess our cultural illiteracy.

(April 1970)

Hermann Hesse's *Rosshalde*

After fifty-five years, Hermann Hesse's *Rosshalde* has at last been made available in English. It is a transitional novel. Hesse stopped meditating on the anguish of adolescence to ponder for a while the alienation of the artist before groping toward his ultimate role: as a tourist among mysteries. Indeed, at the end of *Rosshalde*, the artist-protagonist Veraguth, having "taken leave of the sweet twilight of youth . . . without resignation, full of defiance and venturesome passion," is about to embark on a journey—to the East, of course. The odd agency of Veraguth's deliverance from a loveless marriage and a life that has "stagnated in the swampy lake of indecision" is the death of his young son, Pierre. Since Pierre, before dying of meningitis, moons about the Rosshalde estate talking to the flowers and feeling sorry for himself, Hesse gets to touch all the usual bases.

Veraguth is a famous painter, full of "demands and moods, my passionate yearning and in the end my disappointment." His wife, alas, is "solemn and heavy." His oldest son, Albert, plays the piano and worries about heredity. Pierre is a hostage, for whose affections the parents compete. Rosshalde itself is a cinematic set, at once embodying the trap of a bourgeois marriage and that "ethos of ethereal asexuality" Theodore Roszak has noted in Hesse's fiction.

At Rosshalde, everything is strange. Feelings are "strangely desolate," flowers "strangely glassy," eyes "strangely questioning" when they are not "strangely bright"—or "staring forlornly" or "peering eagerly" or "glowing with pleasure" or "flashing with indignation" or filled with "an injured, questioning look." Sorrows are "secret," confirmations are "bitter," hearts either bleed or rejoice, people "cry out" in either "despair" or "torment," and suffering is invariably "unbearable." Suffering is also potable: "He would soon have to drain the cup of suffering to the lees"; "to sidestep no suffering, to drain the cup to the last drop"; "I shall drink my suffering to the last bitter drop."

None of this is really the translator's fault. Ralph Manheim has previously proved himself excellent, particularly with Günter Grass. Hesse is the villain, addicted to the extravagant adverb as a substitute for precise scene-setting, even as he was addicted to self-pity as an aesthetic principle, to world-weariness as a sort of meningitis of the soul, an inflammation of the spiritual membranes. His fatigue fell somewhere between Swinburne's and Salinger's. That he sought an end to it in mysticism no doubt accounts for his popularity with the Now Generation. If only young Werther had Turned On, that bummer of a suicide trip would have been unnecessary . . . the universe itself is a dilation of one's wounded sensibility.

Hesse was admired by his betters—Rilke, Gide, Thomas Mann, T. S. Eliot—and therefore such caviling may seem impudent. Ah, well, yes. Western materialism is vulgar. And, understandably, the romantic suffering German soul, seeking a cure for its Faust hangover, chose—in Mann's nineteenth-century dichotomy—a "musical bond with night and death" instead of the obsession with progress. And, agreed, no one impugns the aspiration for salvation, even if all the aspiring is done on a tricycle.

But Hesse was in general as "solemn and heavy" as Frau Veraguth. He so stylized the aspiration, so muddied the motivations, that his novels seem a motion picture still of adolescent attitudinizing, frozen *Angst* licked like a lollipop. And Hesse in the particular of *Rosshalde* manipulates emotions, affecting us only as any account of a child's death affects us, never earning (through characterization or technical innovation or distinction of prose and thought) our commitment. He was a kind of anti-Disney; in his controlled environment, everybody was always weeping; and while they wept, Hitler ate the sleeping princess.

(February 1970)

Doris Lessing's *The Four-Gated City*

On finishing this book, you want to go out and get drunk. *The Four-Gated City* is less a work of art than an act of despair, and its cumulative effect is numbing. It depicts a world—from 1950 until 1997—in which technology and fascism have triumphed; a world in which sex and imagination and intelligence have been brutalized; a world of figurative and literal plague; and a world for which the only hope is drastic biological mutation. What makes Doris Lessing's black vision so compelling is that it is not the product of a literary debauch. It is not a satanic self-indulgence. It is not a tract. It is, instead, a painstaking extrapolation of the present, a sort of elephantiasis of the already obvious and the perfectly ordinary. It is the inevitable terminal point toward which the modern mind is monorailing. Those logical lunatics described by Wallace Stevens in *Esthetique du Mal*—men like Konstantinov, who "would not be aware of the clouds,/ Lighting the martyrs of logic with white fire" —have taken over; and our blank uneasiness has turned to terror.

Martha Quest arrives in London in 1950 with an advanced case of blank uneasiness. The intellectual and emotional terrain she has crossed to get there has been exhaustively cartographed by Doris Lessing in the four previous volumes of the *Children of Violence* series. She has gone through a "Zambesian" (Rhodesian) childhood, two husbands, motherhood, racism, the Communist Party and a war. *The Four-Gated City* will not only finish her off, but will finish off the series and England as well.

After some preliminary skirmishing, Martha settles down as a combination nursemaid-housekeeper-editorial researcher in the home of Mark Coldridge, a novelist. At first the Coldridge household seems a domestic mirror image of the world outside: private madness taking refuge from public madness. Outside, there are totalitarianism and genocide; spiritual impotence and scientific evil. Inside, there are hallucinations and despair. And Martha Quest, somehow hanging out the window, videotapes it all.

But we become gradually aware that this time Miss Lessing is up to something different. Mark Coldridge has written a fantasy novel, part prophecy and part racial dream, about an ancient city ruled benignly by a clairvoyant priesthood. This "four-gated" golden city was betrayed—a kind of original sin ushering in our modern, postlapsarian civilization—and the clairvoyants went underground. Somehow their psychic powers were dispersed.

Coldridge's novel takes over from Doris Lessing's novel. Suddenly we are no longer living in the world of Doris Lessing's indefatigable realism, but in a nightmare of evil. The city and its destruction and its meaning can only be apprehended fleetingly in dreams; or perceived at the odd angle of madness. We are made to understand that the psychic powers dispersed at the time of the city's betrayal attach now in bits and pieces only to the dislocated and the outcast, the drugged and shocked and suicidal. Our final, chilling realization is that, after the bombs and the nerve gas and the holocaust, the children of these mad believers will be the new clairvoyants, the mutant hope of a new world.

Miss Lessing, in other words, has given up: on politics, on rationalism, on psychoanalysis (except for a dose of R. D. Laing). This most exemplary of modern women, who has moved like a relentless tank over the abstractions, aggressions and dependencies of the twentieth century, who has noticed and remarked on everything, who has entertained and ultimately refused almost every illusion that tempts the contemporary intelligence, has given up. She seeks now, in prehistoric recesses and unconscious memory, a new sustaining myth, an island of the mind on which to hide.

And what is terrifying about her giving-up is the absoluteness of the documentation. She has never been an elegant writer, and she has usually been a humorless one. But her mind is formidable, her integrity monumental and her operating methods wholly uncompromising. She has not spared herself and she will not spare the reader. So she is not content merely to show us the asylum and the hospital. She grabs us by the lapels and drags us inside. She forces us to touch the slavering idiots and the haunted children, the ideas that fester and the flesh that rots. If hatred is the underbelly of "all this lovely liberalism," then she will take the knife to that belly. And if monsters then climb out of the knife wound, she will introduce them to us. The monsters are our fathers and our children and ourselves, and we can't ask Miss Lessing to dispatch them for us. She has done her job, and what a staggering one it is.

                                                        (May 1969)

Gabriel Garcia Marquez's *One Hundred Years of Solitude*

You emerge from this marvelous novel as if from a dream, the mind on fire. A dark, ageless figure at the hearth, part historian, part haruspex, in a voice by turns angelic and maniacal, first lulls to sleep your grip on a manageable reality, then locks you into legend and myth. *One Hundred Years of Solitude* is not only the story of the Buendia family and the Colombian town of Macondo. It is also a recapitulation of our evolutionary and intellectual experience. Macondo is Latin America in microcosm: local autonomy yielding to state authority; anti-clericalism; party politics; the coming of the United Fruit Company; aborted revolutions; the rape of innocence by history. And the Buendias (inventors, artisans, soldiers, lovers, mystics) seem doomed to ride a biological tragi-cycle from solitude to magic to poetry to science to politics to violence back again to solitude.

Which isn't to say that the book is grimly programmatic. It is often wildly funny, and superbly translated by Gregory Rabassa. Nor does the specific get buried under the symbolic. Macondo with its rains, ghosts, priests, Indians, Arabs and gypsies is splendidly evoked. So richly realized are the Buendias that they invite comparison with Karamazovs and Sartorises. Indeed, specificity overwhelms incredulity, setting up the reader for imagist explosions more persuasive than mere data can ever be: Anything goes, and everything comes back.

Would you believe, for instance, men with machetes in search of the sea, hacking their way through "bloody lilies and golden salamanders" to find in a swamp a Spanish galleon? A plague of insomnia? A stream of blood feeling its path across a city from a dying son to a grieving mother? A mule that eats sheets, rugs, bedspreads, drapes and "the canopy embroidered with gold thread and silk tassels on the episcopal bed"? A Sanskrit manuscript predicting the 100 years of Macondo, down to the very deciphering of the prediction by the last Buendia? A paterfamilias chained to a tree in the garden, muttering in Latin? Or, when that paterfamilias finally dies, this consequence:

"A short time later, when the carpenter was taking measurements for the coffin, through the window they saw a light rain of tiny yellow flowers falling. They fell on the town all through the night in a silent storm, and they covered the roofs and blocked the doors and smothered the animals who slept outside. So many flowers fell from the sky that in the morning the streets were carpeted with a compact cushion and they had to clear them away with shovels and rakes so that the funeral procession could pass by."

I believe—in the last Buendia infant born as prophesied with the tail of a pig, and eaten alive by ants. In the brothel with alligators. In the 3,000 dead strikers against the banana plantation, hauled away by silent train; and Remedios the Beauty, plucked up by the wind and flown to God as she hung up bedsheets to dry; and Melquiades, who introduces Macondo to the miracle of ice. I believe in all the Buendias, from the original José Arcadio and the original Ursula (cousins who marry and by mythic mitosis divide into generations of Arcadios and Aurelianos and Armarantas) down through "the most intricate labyrinths of blood" to the end of the family line in a room full of chamber pots in "the city of mirrors (or mirages)" as the wind comes to sweep away all memory.

Family chronicle, then, and political tour de force, and metaphysical romp, and, intentionally, a cathedral of words, perceptions and details that amounts to the declaration of a state of mind: solitude being one's admission of one's own mortality and one's discovery that that terrible apprehension is itself mortal, dies with you, must be rediscovered and forgotten again, endlessly. With a single bound, Gabriel Garcia Marquez leaps onto the stage with Günter Grass and Vladimir Nabokov, his appetite as enormous as his imagination, his fatalism greater than either. Don't miss this one.

(March 1970)

Joyce Carol Oates's *Them*

Them, as literature, is a reimagining, a reinventing, of the urban American experience of the last thirty years, a complex and powerful novel that begins with James T. Farrell and ends in a gothic dream: of the "fire that burns and does its duty." *Them*, as people, is all of us under the plastic, even those of us whose careers, like slide rules, prove our natural sense of logarithm; those of us who are adepts in the economic exponential, knowing how much it takes to raise the base, forgetting where we (the base) came from, how we survived, which are the dangerous and vulnerable parts of ourselves. *Them* is really about all the private selves, accidents and casualties that add up to a public violence. "Escape," thinks one of the characters: "As

long as he had his own car he was an American and could not die."
An hour later he is shot.

Miss Oates begins her book in 1937, in the working-class district
of a small Middle Western city, with a sixteen-year-old girl admiring
herself in the mirror on a warm Saturday night. Before the night is
over, Loretta's lover will be killed by her brother, Loretta will be
raped by a policeman. And the reader will become a partner, an accomplice, in the excavation of lives that are shaped by accidents, people to whom the world "happens," whose fates are the result of
discontinuous and unrelated "moments."

For over 200 pages—as Loretta marries, moves to Detroit, raises
her two children, Jules and Maureen, finds and loses one man after
another—we seem to be in Farrell country. The kitchen tables of the
poor (the white poor), the terrible drunken arguments, the overcrowding and sexual cruelties and suffocated hopes are all familiar to
us from the realistic novels of the 1930's. Preconditioned, one awaits
the catalytic appearance of the union organizer or the radical storm-
bird.

But Miss Oates isn't interested in trifling with agitprop. No carpet-
baggers of the millennium descend with revolutionary nostrums. Instead, the realistic novel slips almost imperceptibly into gothic
fiction, as though the gothic were—as perhaps it is—a realistic mode
for apprehending the way we live now. Monsters and benefactors,
madness and flight, appear and deploy themselves, exemplify options,
in defiance of any mechanical logic. Coincidence and enigma are
conditions, dimensions. Chance is fate. Miss Oates herself enters the
narrative, as the recipient of letters from Maureen, who flunked her
night school writing course.

"You said," writes Maureen, "'Literature gives form to life.' I remember you saying that very clearly. What is form? Why is it better
than the way life happens, by itself?" Jules at one point thinks, "My
life is a story imagined by a madman!" Both, like their mother,
Loretta, are clumsy strategists at their own survival. Their idea of the
future is crippled by their memory of a hated past. The past must be
cauterized; the self must be reinvented in the present, by fire. That
Loretta, Maureen and Jules survive at all is the wonder of the book.

There are love scenes of numbing tenderness, dreams of surpassing
hope. But the motion of *Them* is from the personal to the universal
by means of violence. Private violence accumulates throughout the

book. A burning airplane, a brutal beating, an employer's slit throat,
a gun in a girl's purse—all prefigure the apocalyptic ending, the Detroit riot of 1967. We are made to see that the isolation of each and
every "them"—black, white, poor, wealthy—in cells of self-destroying
circumstance leads inevitably to an explosion that is almost a communal affirmation: a sign of finding and defining one another in a
shared rage, the duty of the fire.

Miss Oates is an extraordinary writer. At age thirty-one, she has
four novels, two collections of short stories, a play and a book of
poems to her credit. Each novel has been a different intellectual and
stylistic exercise, although each in its way has been a meditation on
violence and an imaginative projection of relentless integrity. (Those
critics who complain about the violence in her fiction appear not to
be living in the same urban world the rest of us live in.) *Them* is
the other side of the social mirror from *Expensive People*. Only a
very fine writer can travel back and forth through that mirror so convincingly.

"I dream," writes Maureen, "of a world where you can go in and out
of bodies, changing your soul, everything changed and not fixed forever, becoming men and women, daughters, children again, even old
people, feeling how it is to be them and then not hating them, out
on the street. I don't want to hate. There are too many strangers."

Maureen's accommodation with the world of the 1960's bears
little resemblance to that dream. But as a description of what Joyce
Carol Oates is capable of in her fiction, it is perfect. We know the
stranger, even the one who stares back at us from our own fiery
mirror.

(October 1969)

Kōbō Abé's *The Ruined Map*

Donald Keene has called *The Ruined Map* "one of the rare Japanese works of avant-garde fiction." It is surprisingly accessible to the
Western reader—more accessible than the more orthodox Yasunari
Kawabata, recently Nobeled—perhaps because we have over the years
become connoisseurs of the obscure and the fantastic; adepts at the
dance of shifting identities; archaeologists reconstructing the shards

of exploded plot; hang-ten surfers on the alienation wave. Moreover, Kōbō Abé employs as the vehicle of his dark ride that most conventional of Western narrative forms, the detective story, complete with private eye, missing person, missing person's luscious wife, blackmail, syndicate gangsters, victims and aggressors. So we sit down to his obfuscations with a knowing sigh, and the symbols are so much spinach on our groaning board.

Imagine, then, the private eye as an Ahab, and the modern city as his whale. Re-imagine the whale as a kind of white meaninglessness, the yawn of anonymity. Identify the labyrinth (borrowed from Borges?) and the nausea (borrowed from Sartre?). Note that the "map" is psychological. Observe that the missing person obviously lost himself. Remark that the hunter, significantly nameless, becomes the quarry. Shuffle images of urban hell. Be sophisticated about the cinematic techniques—for wasn't Abé's earlier novel, *The Woman in the Dunes*, turned into a superior art-house movie by Hiroshi Teshigahara?

Indulge in all this critical hugger-mugger, and you are still left with a disquieting and original work of art. For one thing, Kōbō Abé has created in the person of Nemuro Haru, wife of the missing person, one of the most complex and alluring women in contemporary fiction, thus passing a test that his Occidental competitors flunk regularly. She is the enigmatic door—or, in the novel's scheme, the "lemon-yellow window"—through which hunter and hunted exchange identities; the still point in the middle of all the ambivalence.

Then there is the atmosphere, made claustrophobic by an obsessive cataloguing of objects; made geometrical (and alien) by patterns on tiles, the intersecting of streets and housing developments (like "filing cabinets"); made anti-human by its definition of man (that consciousness to which drivers' licenses, commutation tickets, ration cards and passports adhere); made mysterious by repetitive signs (the telephone number that always keeps turning up, like a formula for some separate reality, or a recipe for the destruction of that reality).

And there are passages that nibble at the mind: "One could scarcely hope to arrive at any place worth mentioning along such a street"; "an hour like distilled water when nothing strange ever happens"; "It would take considerable courage not to protect this woman"; and "Outside the sun was shining more and more intensely, and the dark door had taken on a green color; my shadow slanted almost parallel with the sofa, my shoulder sprawling over the opposite arm. My head was severed and nowhere to be seen."

Finally, there is the horrifying process of identity conversion itself: when Nemuro Haru "crossed in front of the lemon-yellow curtains, her face became black, her hair white, and her lips white too, the irises of her eyes became white and the whites black, her freckles became white spots, white like dust that has gathered on the cheek-bones of a stone image." It is a photographic reversal, a positive into negative, extinguishing the detective and preparing us to realize that the concluding pages of the book are really the beginning pages of the book: loss, then searching.

The Ruined Map is a metaphysical detective story. It creates a world according to an alien algebra, formal in its mysteries, an abstraction which ultimately obliterates the intelligence seeking to give it meaning. It is a world in which we are all of us missing persons. And, as Abé says, "Nothing would be served by being found."

(June 1969)

Harvey Swados's *Standing Fast*

In his new novel, Harvey Swados takes a handful of American radicals from the Molotov-Ribbentrop pact to the assassination of John F. Kennedy. In the beginning, they are all associated with a Trotskyite faction calling itself the New Party, opposed equally to Hitler and Stalin, organizing factory workers for the socialist millennium. At the end, they are refugees from themselves and the twentieth century. In between, are World War II, the labor movement's purge of its own left wing, Henry Wallace, Korea, Eisenhower, Joe McCarthy, Budapest and Montgomery, Ala., not to mention marriage, children, careers, accommodations, small deaths of pride and conscience. The narrative machinery creaks; the prose is flat; the conversation is cliché-ridden; the love scenes are embarrassing; the resolutions arrive with a clumsy sort of inevitability, like a march of the viaducts on Klee feet. And yet—*Standing Fast* breaks the heart.

It breaks the heart not only because such a century will always break such hearts as Mr. Swados has given to his characters, but also because he pays his way into the reader's trust. He doesn't pay with cleverness or stylistic tricks or lyrical afflatus. He pays with honesty. He was there, a witness, and he reports, unflinchingly. *Standing Fast* is written in defiance of the dominant attitude (device, disguise, defense mechanism?) of the last thirty years in American fiction. It is wholly without irony. Either as a way of coping with atrocities or as a cure for our own ennui, we're so accustomed to irony that a novel without it carries an electric shock. Neither for himself nor for the reader does Mr. Swados permit any "distancing" from his characters and events.

So the college instructor deserts the wife who worked his way through graduate school, and becomes a Charles Van Doren on TV. The factory worker blacklisted on the West Coast builds tract houses and decides to write a book. The radical labor organizer ends up an international representative of a conservative union. The political cartoonist receives a bronze medal of honor from a national institute for the arts. One character takes to journalism, another to Israel, a third to drink. One child in the second generation is born with too much conscience, another with no conscience at all; and since a sacrifice is called for, of course the wrong child dies.

Cop-out? Sell-out? Drop-out? One hears the mutterings of Weathermen in an ill wind, the snap-crackle-and-pop of the Marcusian Rice Crispies every young utopia-head eats at every breakfast after every night of bombs. Yet most of the people in *Standing Fast* lasted a long time. They didn't go into a violent snit the morning after the world refused to change. Mr. Swados explores the reasons why they failed, why the world refused to change, without for an instant compromising the dream, the "idea" they sought to fan to life. You know he is angry; you are amazed at his tenderness; you are moved by a generosity, a precise historical sense, a sympathetic dismay that isn't written in neon or other people's blood.

"Work. That's all there is," says Vito near the end of the novel. And Mr. Swados knows about work—the aircraft and automobile factories, the union offices, the picket lines, the symposia on theory, the loft and the law library; he has earned his right to his psychic scars, instead of exploiting his psychic acne. "The trick," says Norm, "is to go on living even after you've found out what kind of world it really is." Which the characters in this book manage to do. "One way or another," says Sy, "we tried to keep an idea alive. There

weren't enough of us, there never are. We were ridiculously wrong
about a lot of things but who wasn't? And what idea did they keep
alive, the others?" None. Absolutely nothing.

Pride, then, and fatigue, and the not inconsiderable feat of raising children who are more than leeches on the social teat; children
who ate their fathers and grew strong on the diet. Murray Kempton
in *Part of Our Time* said of the 1930's radicals: "We were, most of us,
fleeing the reality that man is alone upon this earth. We ran from
a fact of solitude to a myth of community. That myth failed us because the moments of test come most often when we are alone and
far from home and even the illusion of community is not there to
sustain us."

But the community in *Standing Fast* is not an illusion. At least, it
tries to sustain. In his novelistic appetite, Mr. Swados suggests John
Dos Passos. In his period of concern, he reminds one of Clancy
Sigal—whose *Going Away* would seem to complement *Standing Fast*
in both title and resolution. Dos Passos was the superior craftsman,
although his devices in retrospect seem a kind of cover-up for his inability to create a believable character; Sigal worried his soul to the
sometime exclusion of a social context, and one had to read Doris
Lessing's *Golden Notebook* to find out what happened to him after
he Went Away. Mr. Swados's characters are believable. The context
smothers us. We know what happened, alas. And we have in *Standing Fast* a document of such accuracy and integrity and compassion
that we should not only buy it and ponder it, but we should as well,
as a result, feel ashamed of not having lived it.

(May 1970)

Janet Frame's *Yellow Flowers* in the Antipodean Room

You can't approach Janet Frame's extraordinary novel without resorting to metaphor, because it is more like a dream than fiction.
Imagine yourself inside, alone, looking out a window whose pane is
fogged with rain; familiars dissolve into alien patterns; unsought
shapes flex and contract; water whorls behave as worms. You are

bemused and a little edgy. Then someone suddenly taps you on the shoulder to explain: it isn't a window, it's a mirror.

The dream is one of madness. Miss Frame doesn't call it madness. Ostensibly, she has written a book about the resurrection of the dead. Godfrey Rainbird is a disquietingly ordinary clerical worker who emigrates from England to New Zealand; marries; spawns children; watches television. "A man," writes Miss Frame, "made of paper with a tiny dream-pulse fluttering under his eyelid like a breath of wind blowing a petal or paper scrap through the streets on a Sunday morning."

Then one night Godfrey is struck by a car and dies instantly. Only he doesn't; a coma is mistaken for death. He rises again, to return to a family and a community that had accustomed themselves to the fact of his death. Grief was, perhaps, inherently inappropriate for a man like Godfrey, but the manipulation of the symbols of grief is reassuring to the manipulators. To make of that manipulation something fraudulent, an exercise in self-deception, is to rob ritual of meaning. It is, as well, to rob us of our distinction between life and death, to remind us of the deaths we live, the difference between mere respiration (the ordinary coma thrust upon us) and *living* (a creative uniqueness).

Miss Frame then drops us in a bathysphere down to the sediment of the subconscious: the citizens of Dunedin loathe Lazarus. The smell of their own mortality is on him, and he himself is not sufficiently special—heroic, profound—to represent a satisfying psychological alternative to the grief ritual. He loses his job, his children and, ultimately, what was supposed to be his life.

Now, this just doesn't work if we accept death, and Godfrey's flirtation with death, at face value. The psychological resources of the community, any community, are so Byzantine that they can accommodate the crypt-stinking Rainbird; their repertoire of hypocrisies is broad. He might never be invited to the proper cocktail parties, but he wouldn't lose his job and children.

No. Unless we are to take Miss Frame's novel as an allegorical attack on the welfare state (which it isn't), we must transpose some symbols. *Yellow Flowers in the Antipodean Room*, like Miss Frame's earlier novel *Faces in the Water*, is not about death but about madness. She explores the disrelation between inner and outer landscapes, mental and physical colors, cruelty and the withdrawal from

cruelty, the experience of chaos, of inexplicable evils, of broken perceptions and intuitions of dismay and splinters of demonic force. Her
children, Godfrey's children, are the casualties of a terrible innocence, an inability to cope and to absorb that bleak knowledge
inadvertently conferred by happenstance. Godfrey returning from
madness makes sense; death is Miss Frame's metaphor for the loss of
ordinary focus, the glimpse of ordinariness made monstrous.

Thus the poetic idiom of dreams, the Jell-o with cream on top
"like mild white streams set to flow on beds of golden glass." Thus
the reader trapped in a dream of slipping gears, of pistons pumping
mud and blood. Thus the desolating charge that we must, each of us,
make up the world again from fragments, every day, every man. "If
you go there in winter," she writes of Dunedin, "you will have no
help with your dreams, you will have to experience for yourself the
agony of creating within yourself the flowers that you know and feel
will blossom there in summer."

A cold, haunted, brilliant book—a moon in the night's imagination.

(February 1969)

Janet Frame's *Intensive Care*

You can't be a tourist in the novels of Janet Frame. The act of apprehension makes you an accomplice. The landscape is static, a world
of art, frozen images, memories like mirrors gaping at each other,
dreams like cooled lava that once upon a time erupted from a vol-
canic imagination. The only weather in such a world is psychic—
shifts of consciousness, brainstorms, eclipses. Man is the climate.
Color and motion exist only in the mind. Even the rain is "a suc-
cession of avenues of burning fluid mirrors." The snow "swallows, its
big/ white mouth turning over and munching the sugared people/
limbs go down into cool columns of pressure,/ the sky is spinning out
the flakes like webs/ they drift like lantern spiders across the sky/
catching the air/ hammering silver fang-nails into its nothingness."
Nothingness! To perceive is to lose your purchase on the manageable, to give up your citizenship in the nation of the real.

Does that first paragraph seem overly fancy? All right. But I can't think how else to communicate the spell Miss Frame casts on the reader in her extraordinary novels. This one is the best of them; while sometimes a gloss of the poems she inserts in the narrative, it is more often a superb meditation on the dreams which distinguish us from stones. ("Livingstone" is the name of her family in this book.) She is haunted by the idea of the garden (a dream, a cage) and the idea of Bishop Berkeley's tree in the quad (witness makes reality) and the idea of war ("I saw the soldiers standing blind with the blood falling disguised as snow in the persuasion of purity"). And the "I" marooned in history: "It is the company of weather I crave/ in their weatherless room/ the thermometer/ reads me only/ is it safe to be/ inhabited much longer/ by this hot/ inland sea?"

To begin. The first third of *Intensive Care* concerns Tom Livingstone, a New Zealander who goes off to fight in World War I, is wounded, nursed to health by an English girl, Ciss Everest, with whom he falls in love. But he returns to his wife, raises his family, occupies himself for forty-five years as a furnaceman in a cement factory. Only when his wife dies does he return to England in search of "Miss World War I." He finds her, dying of cancer: "This way to see the Ciss Everest Cancer Doll." She does not know him.

All the signals seem clear. The "Recovery Unit" is called Culin Hall. Culin is an old word for "kiln," or furnace. Tom is the master of flame. His dream of the war, forty-five years old, is consumed, even as he is consumed by an unsuspected ulcer. The war is a flame, a dream, a cancer gone out of control, destroying not only cities and men, but areas of the human imagination. A reversal and a distortion are thrust upon us: the intensive care ward becomes a place of wounding; the recovery unit becomes a prison where the wounded rot to death.

Middle section: Tom's children and grandchildren go about ruining their lives from an excess of dreaming. Violence is born in the discrepancy between dreams and reality. As Tom killed Ciss, his grandson Colin murders a whole family. Is the book itself a dream of his daughter, Naomi, supposedly dying of cancer? Perhaps the surgeons aren't taking away parts of her body, but cutting away her dreams, thinking them madness. The garden—with its "pear tree there, in a wilderness, hung with pears as a chandelier is hung with light"—is a dream plot, another reality, requiring witnesses who sacrifice themselves in the act of witnessing. Nightmare: the war internal, self-consuming.

Final third: "All dreams lead back to the nightmare garden." Miss Frame projects us into a new millennium. The descendants of Livingstone in Waipori City, New Zealand, engage in the grandest social experiment of them all. A Third, or Fourth, or Fifth World War has devastated most of the planet. Some nations are growing plastic forests to remind man of nature. Clearly not all people are human; maybe most are animals, and should be—for reasons of deficient I.Q. or social inutility—exterminated. Computers will decide. From the point of view of Molly Galbraith, a supposedly retarded young girl whose father is (yes) a gardener, Miss Frame rewrites the diary of Anne Frank.

For, of course, it is not the future she is dreaming; it is the past, the Nazi in us, the nightmare of us. Tom's brother was made to think on language: "Unvoweled, unconsonanted, unexclaimed, a man must soon die. Even the alphabetical atom may soon be subdued by the hydrogen atom, unless those who work with language, unless people who speak, learn also to split and solve the alphabet." Now the man who administers the division of us into human and animal rhapsodizes: "How I admire the immunity of numbers, their untouchability, their inaccessibility; every moment they shine, newly bathed, concealing, never acknowledging the dark work they do."

And the reader's mind like a police hound must go back over this marvelous novel sniffing out the clues you missed. All the gardeners, all the accountants, all the nurses, all the dreamers, the girl under the pear tree and the reconstructed, cancer-proof Golden Man—you have been taught about dreams and lies. The lies can be as obvious as the welfare state, saying to the sick, "You are well," to the lonely, "You have friends, lovers," to the dying, "You are immortal"; or they can be as enormous as the quantifiability of men, the number like a price tag on a dream.

"The crossword pain./ I have not solved it./ What are the clues?/ Six feet down and three across?" She hasn't solved it, but what a fine book she has written about the process of trying to do so.

(April 1970)

Marya Mannes's *They*

Marya Mannes's first novel in twenty years has suffered a curious reception from reviewers. Many complain that it isn't a novel at all, but more a set of essays and conversations. Since reviewers solemnly accept, as novels, the transcripts of tape recordings, hallucinations of the jugend-lumpen, scatological pastiche, psychiatric case histories, masturbatory fantasies and catalogues of objects so "opaque in their servitude" that one longs for the humanity, the transparency, of a baseball bubblegum card—why pick on *They?* Because *They* is culturally conservative. It rejects the cult of youth. It attacks the yawpers of nihilism. It celebrates tenderness, dignity, grace, craftsmanship . . . discipline, standards, pattern, order, ethics, responsibility . . . *work.* It defends—in the elegiac manner—that whole clutch of humanistic values that are presently reviled by the storm troopers of *me, now* and *why not?*

Miss Mannes's scheme is straightforward enough. The tense is future. The rulers are the young (*They*): having secured control of culture, they seize political power. The civilization is "post-literate": computerized, anti-print, totalitarian. The casualties are all those born before 1925—"the *pons asinorum* between the Puritan and the pornographer"—who are assigned to detention camps, permitted no contact with their children, and doomed to euthanasia at age sixty-five.

Her form is the traditional philosophical romance, like Samuel Johnson's *Rasselas* and Sartre's *Nausea.* Five sexagenarians—a writer, a conductor, a painter, a popular music composer and an artist's model—are exiled to a house on the North Atlantic coast, to amuse themselves as best they might before death's due-date. Their principal amusement is the preparation of "Articles of Revelation," a brief for humanism all the more poignant because it addresses itself to an audience that may no longer exist.

The five, abetted by a young male mute they believe to be "the angel of death," establish a spiritual and sexual commune in the house. Their exploration of one another, their defiant commitment to "meaning," "shape," and risk of self, is the substance of the book.

In the young mute they discover their true vocation (and salvation):
to teach. And so their quarrels and their retrospections build to an
affecting parable—a plea for the relevance of the past, for ethics
and art, for "associations" and the indispensable element of reciprocity in human relationships.

Miss Mannes is a good conservative. She sympathizes with the
folk singers and the flower children. She's against war (*They*, at last
in the driver's seat, immediately launch a pre-emptive strike against
Chinese nuclear installations). She believes in the body, the senses,
animals, nature, love. But she isn't willing to buy righteousness or
intolerance from any source. Nor will she cede to any individual organism, if it calls itself human, a presumptive and exclusive license
to indulge itself at the expense of others—barbarism in the guise of
solving one's identity crisis. Growing up is tough. Hypocrisy is weary-
ing. So what else is new?

I would have liked to find among her five a scientist: anti-
technology is as much a fetish as youthful self-righteousness; her
marriage of science and the young is a little unlikely since the young
hate science for being rational. And a little more humor: she is too
angry to relax. But *They is* a novel, and a neat one. Its virtues are the
very virtues Marya Mannes defends in the text: moral concern, sharp
and relentless intelligence, vision, stylistic felicity. If the "novel,"
that prose python capable of swallowing Alain Robbe-Grillet and
Andy Warhol, is incapable of swallowing *They*, it deserves to die—of
an anti-social disease.

(December 1968)

Rudolph Wurlitzer's *Flats*

When Rudolph Wurlitzer's *Nog* appeared two years ago, the critics
hopped up and down on their pogo sticks so much that all you saw
were scowls and open mouths, not Mr. Wurlitzer. Friendships broke
up; charges were pressed; and *The Village Voice*, ever alert to the
Zeitgeist, parajournalized. Along comes *Flats*, which might just as
well be called *Linoleum* or *Malone Dies with Friends, from an Over-
dose of Epistemology*, and the whole howl is likely to be rerun in
livid color: The old cultural forms are comatose . . . reality is a bad

trip . . . fragments express our existential disrelation, and shards are our shared experience . . . *ad nauseam* and beat vigorously.

Flats is set in a sort of psychic space (forty square feet near a swamp, where the weather is very Wittgenstein), at the end of culture (a smashed statue, a burning log, a constantly throbbing engine, blue technological lights blinking twice overhead almost every paragraph) and populated by refugees who assume the names of cities (Tacoma, Cincinnati, Omaha, Wichita, Flagstaff, Memphis) and appear to be aspects of a single consciousness trying to get his head together ("The third person handles the changes, keeps me from getting popped. I don't want to knock the third person. I like to travel there"). There's a lot of arch conversation—". . . there has been nothing established. There has been no information. Thank God. We are saved an adventure"—steeped in the vapidities of the counter-culture; and for sixty pages it's amusing, the Odyssey according to Sam Beckett and *Head Comix.*

Then, just as you start wondering why not Chicago, New York, Los Angeles (or Husserl, Heidegger, Merleau-Ponty?), Mr. Wurlitzer shifts into a dreary gear of earnestness, almost pomposity; and you must tag along after the spaced-out Chief Head on his leash from the smashed statue, smelling each fire hydrant at every corner of the soul's terrain. Really, unless Mr. Wurlitzer is putting down the drug scene, which is unlikely, this is last year's sports pages. Spatial presence? Language as a pawn shop for hot metaphors? The problematic as a life style? The phenomenologists have already been there, and Godard before Cohn-Bendit bit him in the pineal gland, not to mention recent superior novels by Janet Frame (*Yellow Flowers in the Antipodean Room*) and Joseph McElroy (*Hind's Kidnap*). To quote Louis Zukofsky: "If you want me to understand, you'd better speak in a different anguish."

(September 1970)

Joseph McElroy's *Hind's Kidnap*

Hind is the six-foot seven-inch "long-legged Samaritan," protector, watchman, shepherd of the city. The city is "placental," "some exactly planted emptiness into which he kept falling," a skyscape of helicopters and "plastic values," a soulscape of the abducted to whose brains transistor radios have been strapped, in whose eyes the "neon gumdrops" add up to an informational dyspepsia, "for in the city there are gaps inside you the city fills up, but here [the country, Hind, the novel] the gap outside gets into you, and you think about your every move." The moves are detective, because Hind is obsessed with the kidnapping of a young boy named Hershey Laurel, and to solve that crime he neglects his own wife and child. He is at once the father and the orphan of himself, a refugee from the bombed "lost City of Is"—the past, a "subtle space"—and locked in "the mind's fierce fuss, forever discontinuous."

Threatening? Yes. We are dealing with a novel that will be compared with Thomas Pynchon's V, only because every new novel full of "quests, chronicle, psychic distance and urban idyll" is compared with V to avoid cutting a new stencil for the reviewer's mimeograph machine. We are dealing with an author who is actually more like a young Nabokov than a Pynchon, rewriting Paul Goodman's *The Empire City* instead of V. We are dealing with a Hiroshima of cryptograms, for all is code in *Hind's Kidnap*; and deciphered, it's dazzling.

In the guise of a detective story, Joseph McElroy does violence to traditional conceptions of time (which may be reversible, running backwards from death to birth), perspective (a "triangulation of moments," the third wall of which is the past), grammar (a perceptual trap), art ("abductions of past into present," for ransom, at a sacrifice) and pastoral atavism (a city full of strangers requires abstract relationships; to become "doors" those abstractions must be witnessed, lived). The clue pursued leads back to self, but the pursuit stretches the self's perimeter.

Mr. McElroy plays the sorts of games only the hardiest readers of experimental fiction will endure, but he rewards those readers handsomely. If almost all the paragraphs in the interior monologue of Hind's wife, Sylvia, begin with *v*-words, there's a reason. (We are being asked to cope with vectors.) If the characters wear names like Plane, Plante, Beecher, Wood, Ivy, Ash, Rosenblum, Trellis and Tree, a scheme's at work, not a trick. (The past, the country, is the place of emotions and sensations; the present, the city, is an abstract

mode of thought, a grammar after naming, a death of feeling without witness. The ego, with its rules, is a padded cell imprisoning a
self that once knew trees, flowerings.) When Hind's high-church
grammarian guardian on page 298 talks about "a job that isn't him,"
one knows Mr. McElroy wants us to wonder why. (Art is opposed
to grammar; kidnapping the past, making it present, unlocks the
doors of the city—freedom to see and feel, anterior to language.)

Architecture, education, sports, logic, fatherhood and love—forms
and conventions—come in for a thorough bleach during this launder
of the language. Among the brilliant conceits: inside, the men's
health club; outside, the conspiracy of rollerskaters who investigate
incinerators. Hind's intention—not announced, but ultimately disclosed—is to "dekidnap" all of us; to make each man an end and not
a means; to assert art's credentials and capacity to impose, by its own
creation and access to the pre-grammatical, order on the discontinuous and the fussy.

I have made this novel sound difficult. "Difficult?" said Dr.
Johnson; "Sir, I wish it had been impossible!" But it is also full of
marvels, a "special mode of prethought," an exploration of the roots.
Hind at one point in the narrative "phoned for the time but got a
busy signal, he'd called the wrong number—his own." Mr. McElroy's
switchboard is a blaze of signals, but we listen in on every conversation and learn more than one mere reading will allow us to report
with confidence. This novel, like Hind's city, crash-tests our "brains,
stamina, and looks . . . in soundproof phone duels and at the
bronze base of some fragile office mountain." The only trees in the
city are men, dialing their own numbers and getting busy signals.

(November 1969)

Thomas Merton's *My Argument with the Gestapo*

More than a surprise, this book is an astonishment. Thomas Merton
destroyed three of his unpublished novels when he became a Trap-
pist monk in 1941. He saved the manuscript of this one for more
than a quarter century, finally approving its issue shortly before his
death last year at age fifty-three. Compounded in equal parts of auto-

biography, spiritual passage and incantatory tour de force, it is less a conventional novel than the word-drunk, panic-stricken, sorrowful-hilarious journal of a man hounded by and hounding after the idea of God. *My Argument with the Gestapo* details the activities of a young man (called "Merton") in England and France during World War II. But Merton left Europe for the United States in 1934. And so he writes of London without having lived through the Blitz; of the Gestapo without having tasted it personally.

Imaginary, then. But not wholly so. For he *had* been there: his memory contained the discrete and demonic—faces, houses, words, emotions, played out according to a dark scheme, as though each recollection were a broken colored filter to be plucked up and peered through at the moral landscape. When he says, "No, I would not sneer at anything, even human institutions," he is being charitable. His war was beyond politics; his Gestapo was inside himself, questioning him endlessly about his pride and guilt.

And that part of the book which is wholly imaginary seems in its manipulation of literary devices to have been conceived by an unlikely amalgam of Stephen Crane, Joseph Heller and St. Francis of Assisi. The word play blinds; the laughter convulses; "the gasworks are monuments like the cathedrals, and maybe they will last longer."

Honoring no nationalism, no theory of economics, no pleasure principle, no objectification of identity in passports and thumbprints and university degrees, the young Merton seeks an elusive self in a world of masks ("inside the reticent houses, long, inarticulate insanities"); a world of mythicizing cinema ("1909 movies that flicker like an old gray storm of rain . . . Europe swims and expands in pictures, according to the subtle methods of the propaganda film") in which heroes die singing beer commercials; a world afflicted by machinery—steel, sirens, bombs—and spiritual fatigue.

Thus a German officer explains himself: "If he isn't a German, how can he aspire to perfection? How can he long to live in a house as big and black as a big black beer hall with rings on his fingers and nine-pound heavy iron boots on his feet and gold teeth in his head and medals all over the pocket where he keeps his cigars? How can he long to live in a heaven of expensive body belts and big frowning stone dames and nineteenth-century underwear, and paintings of women and serpents . . ."

Thus an English officer remembers his alma mater: "Your memory, old Cambridge, shines in my precise mind as clear as a triangle, and here in the time of disorder I make up all the new mental pictures from minute to minute, of my life, upon the base of your isosceles peace."

Or Merton will say of British courage that it is "like the careless, quiet, grave wit of Ralph Richardson in the films . . . we believe we are above war by our humor and our instinctive nicety of feeling, and that if we cling to what we know is humorous and sincere, if we make no wrong gestures, we will, in the end, catch the spy, as if by mistake, and it will be over."

And he will say of German heroism, "What do I care for the Germans, dying bravely with their heads full of algebra, potato soup, camera lenses, incomprehensible jokes, rectangles, unexplained hatreds and fears?"

Plus (the "macaronic," a mixture of Latinate tongues with vulgar vernaculars) interior monologues conspired at by Wodehouse and Joyce: "We sitzen in the Sigsfreed Line with our feelings hurt to the point of intense agony, for one whole winter. German feelings smart like sunburn. Oh, wow! . . . The generals scream and beat their heads against the walls of forts, in an attempt to restrain their delicate feelings. O noble rage tudesque! Hundreds of infantry sergeants weep like bulls . . ."

It is a dangerous game, using the war as a private Rorschach, the self as a reel locked into a projection booth, while the bombs come down on the movie house. For beyond the buffoonery is a horror (abstract, impersonal) he couldn't guess at while he wrote. And beyond language (which he used, like Blake, to fill paper with words "for the angels to read") is silence, the silence he sought in his monastic vows, the silence he forsook to write *The Seven Storey Mountain*, the poems, the Vietnam protests.

But it is a game he won with this extraordinary book, hating the plucky posture as much as the blubbering beast, living again "in a world where, for despair, the young men hanged themselves in the showers of colleges. Your pride was not the world's fault, but yours, because you were the one who finally consented to be, also, proud. Look now where the Crucifixion flowered in London like a tree, and the wounds were made in Cambridge, red as oleanders." I hadn't before realized the rage and exuberance of this writer, the gambler in

the cassock, for all things human and the will to write his appetites
on stone and offer the tablets to a void and hope that the void has
eyes that can weep.

(October 1969)

Elizabeth Cullinan's *House of Gold*

There is no sex in *House of Gold*, although there are children.
There is no violence, although there are deaths: by cancer, cardiac
arrest, tropical fever, drowning. There are no politics, although
there is religion: two priests, three nuns, enough extreme unction
to anoint an army. There is no history, except of a family: the
American-Irish Devlins, circa now. There is no scourge by pity or
terror, no new forms, no stylistic flummoxing, no escape. There are,
instead, the details of domestic pain, unflinchingly perceived and
remorselessly recorded: packaged in the sort of sandwich—a slice of
naturalism between two leaves of irony; Spam on wry—we usually
associate with *New Yorker* fiction. (Which association is indiscriminate, for what have John Updike, Jorge Luis Borges, Donald Bar-
thelme and Elizabeth Cullinan in common but publication in the
same magazine?)

Miss Cullinan has, then, committed a crime against the Now Sensibility. Another first novel about another American family lost in
the thickets of self-deception, O'Neilling every night before the altar
of some fabulous image of their ordinary selves. Devlins believe Devlins are special; the reader knows they are not. They haven't power,
money, glamour or wit. They have only their Roman Catholicism,
which they have turned into a substitute for life instead of an enhancement of it, as though by a monstrous clanking of mechanical
forms they can camouflage their blunted awareness.

And yet, the inevitable "and yet": this is a book of flabbergasting
integrity. Beginning with the deathwatch over old Mrs. Devlin, to
which her surviving children are summoned, and ending with her
wake, Miss Cullinan refuses to spare us any ramification of complicity. She resists the temptation to saddle any one character with her
own sensibility; to make the family jokes any funnier than they
would have been; to superimpose an artistic knowingness on the

gropings of each Devlin toward postures of dignity, of possibility. Ironic consciousness passes like a cloud outside the novel.

Thus a door is opened to the Devlin house; the reader walks in; the door is locked behind us. We are trapped in Miss Cullinan's lacerating exactitude. The effect is, intentionally, claustrophobic. Mrs. Devlin expects to die in sacramental style, having but to "spit" at Purgatory on her way to God. The discrepancy between her life as she imagines it (a perfect preparation for her just reward) and as it is demonstrated in her children (frightened, guilty, dutiful, casualties of character) horrifies. By spending her humanity on a graceful death, she mortgages the lives of her children; they are paupers at the shop window of what-might-have-been.

Her love is life-denying. The difference, the "specialness," the Devlins sense in themselves depends on their fidelity to her forms, forms that are suffocating rather than liberating. The mythical specialness of Devlinism is a flight from reality. Her children, raised to seek approval instead of fulfillment, botch her death. Whether their mismanagement will ultimately release them from their myth, their thrall, is left ambiguous.

Thus, after all, *House of Gold* is history as each family is a history. Family is the beginning of culture, the first dependency and the first commitment, the initiation into consequences, the prototype of subsequent complicities, responsibilities, ways of coping, forms of expression. Until the laboratory synthesis of life (there goes Oedipus; who'll take the rap?); until human "cloning" (planting father's somatic cell into mother's egg, thereby exactly replicating father and making incest a much more complicated problem)—novels as honest as this one will continue to remind us of our own beginnings and continue to serve the liberation of novelists from their own pasts. We may even be in for a run of Catholic novels now that the Jewish novel has self-destructed.

(September 1970)

Tom McHale's *Principato*

It all comes rushing back: the Irish father who sang tenor and died young, perceived darkly through a bottle of rye; the mother weeping over her saints' cards, into her beads; the daughter married to

Christ; the young son sold into priesthood as partial payment of the family tithe; the mourners at wakes working their grief like a slot machine . . . Not precisely the house Tom McHale has built in this wonderful novel, but a related wing of it. I know these people, the Principatos of Philadelphia, and their claustrophobic preoccupation with eternity, their inglorious roles in the death racket. How do they escape? Some hatches have been opened in the fiction of James T. Farrell, Edwin O'Connor, J. F. Powers and, most recently, Elizabeth Cullinan (*House of Gold*), but those hatches keep turning into closets in which other shapeless oppressions hang, straitjackets with brass buttons.

Mr. McHale's thirty-four-year-old protagonist, Angelo Principato, does better. He escapes through a crack in his own perception. It's as though that perception were so brittle, as though his whole life were such a fragile bowl, that when it breaks in two and he stands there with the parts in either hand—jagged masks of comedy and tragedy—he simply decides to walk between them and out of the house into a world of possibilities.

Angelo is surrounded by the death racket. His father, who cherishes a thirty-five-year-old "Defiance" of the Roman Catholic Church, owns a funeral service, providing the best of coffins. His uncle digs graves for a living. His brothers-in-law, the unspeakable Corrigans, run a fleet of hearses. Even his five children, spawned upon the unlovely Cynthia, partake of death: ". . . always, they preferred the shade. A choice that grieved their father, who believed fervently in the curative powers of the sun; as babies, if they were put out on the lawn, they would crawl away into a shadow, as if their sallow skins and strange russet-colored hair had marked them out to become some special breed of night people. Groping in the dark for a hallway light switch, he often found them walking easily about, their blue liquid eyes glowing in the darkness. Occasionally, he even thought of them as moles."

Only Angelo is a bringer of life. A social worker, he begets a child with one of his clients, and holds out more hope for that black-white baby than for his official brood of night people. A harassed husband, he leaves a sort of group therapy session one night in the company of a huge woman named Corky, and promptly fathers a child on her, too. A son, he inherits from his father not only the "Defiance" of the Church but an enigma at least as large as Corky. A nice guy, he survives a marriage he agreed to in order to make sure he passed theology in college, as well as physical beatings by his brothers-in-law and spiritual beatings by the most motley crew of priests ever collected in one house—lonely, but laughing.

Laughing. What we have here, in spite of the foregoing grisliness, is a comic novel, something like what Bruce Jay Friedman might have written were he an Irish or Italian Catholic. Hold it. Why Friedman? Or Joseph Heller? What a poverty of references! All black humor doesn't derive from urban Jewish dislocation, as we know from Vonnegut. Or John Updike, the Updike of the Kennedy assassination party in *Couples*. (See the rush of approval for Updike, now that he writes amiably about an urban Jewish dislocated *Commentary* type. Shame on him for writing brilliantly all his life about people and places his critics weren't interested in!) A comic novel in what I hope will become the McHale tradition . . .

Whether Angelo is out trying to find a woman for his paraplegic brother; or fleeing "Superpriest" (to whom he confesses that he punched a Monsignor, to which Superpriest responds: "Just a minute, penitent! I've got to hear more of this story. After years of waiting since the seminary for the big one to walk into the box, I'm not letting you go that easily"); or comforting his neurotic case supervisor over the telephone; or seeking in his father's deathbed scene some dignity, some "balance," some crude justice of give-and-take—Angelo is splendidly his own man. His integrity, his comic quasi-saintliness, redeem him.

At a retreat where Catholic husbands go on weekends to be refreshed and affirm their vows, Angelo is made to play baseball. He regrets that "he had never played baseball when he was a kid. Somehow it seemed an unforgivable omission that contributed to making Principato a person that neither he, nor many others, it seemed, was completely satisfied with. Because of it, he judged, he would always exist many degrees to one side of the reading for mean American excellence."

Not at all. If there is an American excellence, it is perfectly embodied in him, almost as though he has a built-in moral compass whose needle points always to decency in a venal, death-filled wilderness.

(June 1970)

Nicholas Delbanco's *News*

Nicholas Delbanco is not yet thirty years old, and *News* is his fourth novel. The first three—*The Martlet's Tale*, *Grasse 3/23/66* and *Consider Sappho Burning*—delighted and perplexed reviewers, when they were reviewed at all, for they seemed to refer to a world consisting wholly of words; to posit an autonomy of the imagination; to seek in language itself the solution to moral problems conceived of as perceptual problems: the way one sees accounts for the discrepancy between one's motives and one's motions. Very modern novels, to be sure, substituting memory for time, myth for logic, poetry for the long train of qualifying clauses—all those freight cars of fact. Faced, then, with *News*, which the publisher describes as a "novel about black separatism and the white revolutionary," a reviewer must wonder whether Mr. Delbanco has been traumatized out of his autonomy by the headlines, or set upon by Bennington Maoists and forced to sign an oath of relevance.

Apparently not. Comparisons ought to be required by law to come equipped with warning labels ("Caution: This Analogy May Be Hazardous to Your Mental Health"), but I think *News* stands in relation to *Grasse 3/23/66* as *Man's Fate* stands to *The Temptation of the West*. Delbanco, like Malraux, has extended his method to explore a different context; a sensibility of enormous sophistication stretches itself to take in both the private and public domains. The news of *News* is that an excellent writer is among us, and if we neglect him as we have (until recently) neglected Kurt Vonnegut and (still) John Hawkes, we shall have to apologize to posterity.

News purports to tell us how four young white New Leftists cope with American racism. Allan, Gifford, Harrison and Sam (think about those names for a moment) grew up together, children of an atypical affluence; participated as a group in voter registration drives, draft resistance, rent strikes; split up according to their various marriages to pursue their various dreams; and yet seem to require one another more than they require their wives and almost as much as they require the idea of blackness as an energizing principle.

We meet Allan on a farm in Vermont, trying to put together his life after a shattering liaison with a black girl. Gifford is busy in Oakland, Calif., organizing a ghetto insurrection. Harrison in Yucatan fantasizes an irredentist march of the Mexicans through Texas. Sam seeks on Georgia's off-shore islands the spirit of Tunis G. Campbell, an actual historical figure who ruled a Georgia black belt after the Civil War. Thus *News* would appear to be about the points of the compass as much as headlines; and about points of the psychological compass at that.

(Have you thought about the names? How about Matthew, Mark, Luke and John? Tunis G. Campbell as a black Christ? The metaphysics of ideological commitment? Blackness as a necessary mystery for affluent whites of a certain sensibility?)

Allan's letters to Elaine, Sam's letters to Allan, presumably authentic excerpts from Tunis Campbell's autobiographical essay and his manual on hotel management, Gifford's journals and memoranda, and Harrison's interior monologues are the stuff of the novel. Allan is deserted by Elaine; Gifford is betrayed by the Oakland blacks; Harrison's Mexican wife dies needlessly; Sam in Georgia fails to find a black prince, a primeval innocence, a martyred God. Suicide, assassination and madness result. Separatism is not just black, but implies a larger alienation of each white revolutionary from his family, his privilege, his friends and himself.

"Disjunct" is Delbanco's favourite word. Next come "distance" and "dispossession" and "dismiss," "loss" and "obsolete." Harrison "named himself a private person, carried distance like a cross." A "sense of loss" is precious to Allan, "and that of exile, the self held aloof." Gifford's despair derives from "the fact that I am white and therefore obsolete." Sam suffers from "the sense of severance . . . and though he felt philosophy to be a condition of distance, though he wished perspective," there is only blood.

Blackness, then, refers not only to pigmentation, to mystery, but also to the islands of blackness in these four white minds, the sense of discrepancy, an otherness not susceptible to rhetoric or even (more horrifying) to action. Delbanco's vision is bleak indeed: perhaps the Civil War was a national wound that will never heal; perhaps privilege itself is a psychology that can't be changed; perhaps our modern God isn't going to waste any of his children on "distant" crosses—some sins being irredeemable. The language of his novel, as difficult as often as it is surpassingly beautiful, seems rooted

in images of violence, commercials, overheard conversations made
incantatory, the ordinary heightened to the dreamlike and so slipping away from the grasp of consciousness. "Disjunct," after all,
means not only "disjoined, separated" (the four witnesses), but, in
music, "progressing melodically by intervals" (an idea of history?).
And I suspect Mr. Delbanco of such a stylistic progression—from
fragments to Sam's tortured epiphanies.

Intimidating, yes. Profoundly pessimistic, yes. And compelling—
"past fused with present and both of them gerunds, ongoing acts
that were future forever"—also, very much, yes.

(June 1970)

Marge Piercy's *Dance the Eagle to Sleep*

It should be possible to approach Marge Piercy's second novel—the
first was *Going Down Fast* (1969)—from a variety of now-this-is-
culturally-significant angles. For instance, why are Marge Piercy
and Sol Yurick the only serious young American writers producing
"radical" fiction? Which is to say, novels of some craft, reflecting
radical political opinions, instead of autobiographical debauches in
which the omnipresent "I" pretends to be synonymous with authenticity, as though craft were a trick instead of a method of organizing
one's perceptions. (I am thinking of the Mungos, Myersons, Cowans,
who write autobiographies almost before they've begun their lives. I
am excluding Nicholas Delbanco, whose *News* was about radicals,
among other things, but not *with* them.) And why does radical fiction nowadays seem to end inevitably with a disaster? Are the radical novelists mainlining on despair? Is writing a novel about radical
political activity an admission that the activity is futile, or otherwise
the writer would be acting instead of writing? Is the intuition of
futility an aesthetic hype, a species of self-indulgence? Or are young
radicals with writing talent mostly as contemptuous of the novel—
a bourgeois form, after all, and intrinsically moralistic—as the
McLuhanatics keep on insisting?

But *Dance the Eagle to Sleep* is a vision, not an argument. You
can't quarrel with a vision, any more than you can quarrel with a
Scientologist or a Jesus-freak or Eli Siegel's night school Hegelians

or your mother; either you accept its terms or you dismiss it as pathological. I accept Miss Piercy's terms; they are brilliant. She was a published poet before she resorted to the novel, exploiting its didactic capacities, and her prose crackles, depolarizes, sends shivers leaping across the synaptic cleft. The "eagle" is America, bald and all but extinct. The "dance" is performed by the tribal young, the self-designated "Indians," after their council meetings, to celebrate their bodies and their escape from the cannibalizing "system." The eagle isn't danced to sleep; it sends bombers to devastate the communes of the young. And yet the naked dancing, as an idea, survives the violence that is "the pornography of our culture."

Miss Piercy establishes the time of her novel a little bit in the future, but the principal difference between her "then" and our "now" is the eighteen-month period of military service all her characters are obliged to undergo on achieving their nineteenth birthday. Shawn, the rock singer who might have allowed himself to be merchandised but chooses instead to murder a merchandiser; Corey, the part-Indian who dies instead of becoming "plastic"; Billy, who could have gone to Cal Tech but decides instead to manufacture hallucinogens and be a warrior; Joanna, the Army captain's daughter whose head is put permanently un-together by electro-shock and insulin treatments; Ginny, whose agonized liberating of herself from the chauvinisms of family, state and male bedmate is the dramatic spine of the book—these people lead a revolution. It collapses; a few of them survive, to face God knows what . . . and if He did know, He would probably drop acid.

They establish communes. They organize against the idea that they are objects, consumers, fodder, "children of the gray box, children of the print-out, children of the death ray, of the comic book and the Pentagon." They seek also to escape "the cinematic floodlit pools of youthcult: an eternal wave coming in on an antiseptic beach, high midnight on the Strip, strobe-spastic boutiques. The carbonized freeways of the brain. Los Angeles: city that was nothing but a slot machine dispensing plastic toys." They dance; they farm; they fail. Miss Piercy can come up with no better ending to their experiment than John Steinbeck settled for in *The Grapes of Wrath*—the birth of a new child, the image of motherhood and renewal, the precious increment of unsullied consciousness. It is not enough, but it is all there is.

Along the way, we have a war against the young that is little more than an extrapolation of Orangeburg, Jackson, Kent State and the Vice President of the United States. We have speculations on the bankruptcy of *machismo*. We have gestures of surpassing tenderness and betrayals of enormous dimension—the more personal, the more enormous—and the seed drowned in blood and "the Garden of Mammon, full of glass headstones glaring in the sun," and the urban guerrillas, the street people, dying for an idea of the dance, "the cold ring of liquid stars," the instrument of the flesh.

A vision. Not necessarily Corey's, of the buffalo; or Shawn's, of the knife in the belly of the whale; but Billy's: "He would never live to be human. Nobody like him or these people could imagine what it might be like to be human, in a society people ran for the common good instead of the plunder of the few. Dimly, like a blind man imagining the sun, he could call up fancies of a person who was strong, unafraid, social, generous, ready. The brother. He could almost imagine. Tenderness swept his body. Someday there would be people. But that coming would not be gentle." Naïve, of course, but biologically the best in us. We've come a long way from the opium dreams of Malraux, the stormbirds of Odets, the line from Pasternak —"To open a window is like opening a vein." They were skirmishes. The imagination of disaster, the dream of blood, the ritual exorcism, the end of property, the death-sleep of the eagle populate Miss Piercy's teeming vision. She writes it down on bandages, and we are suddenly aware of our wounds. What a book. The novel lives.

(October 1970)

Criticism

Richard Gilman's *The Confusion of Realms*

Of Susan Sontag, Richard Gilman writes: "I think her one of the most interesting and valuable critics we possess, a writer from whom it's continually possible to learn, even when you're most dissatisfied with what she's saying, or perhaps especially at those times." Yes. And equally true of Richard Gilman himself, professor of playwriting and criticism at the Yale Drama School, former literary editor of *Commonweal* and *The New Republic*, former drama editor of *Newsweek*. One might (I do) disagree with at least 65 per cent of of what he says in *The Confusion of Realms*, and yet to grapple with his perspective is to grapple with one's own flaccid preconceptions; to be roused from torpor for a cultural wrestling match and to find oneself a gastropod pitted against a Viking. What's more, the Viking wears hobnailed boots.

The athletic metaphor is employed advisedly, for Mr. Gilman practices a kind of confrontation criticism. He is almost as rough on his friends (Norman Mailer?) as he is on his enemies (John Updike, Barbara Garson, the Living Theater). I can't help thinking that should he chance one night upon some grandchild of Balzac, some hapless recidivist still trying to write "stories about men in society," Mr. Gilman would flog the fellow comatose with a quotation from Kierkegaard.

Because he doesn't like such stories. He considers outdated "the notion that novels are superior reports on social or psychic or moral phenomena." He disapproves of characters (except as "pretexts, arenas for inquiry") and of narrative ("that element of fiction which coerces and degrades it into being a mere alternative to life . . . a way out, a recompense, a blueprint, a lesson"). He thinks "fiction is better off stripped of its burden of 'information,' of portraiture and sense of actuality; denuded in this way, it can begin to be . . . more purely verbal artifact and imaginative increment."

To persist in writing books with stories and characters is to indulge a defunct humanism ("the old Mediterranean values"), to abet "rational control over culture," and to subserve the "confusion" that gives his collection of essays its title. Art is a "reinventing" of worlds that never were, an autonomous imagining of new forms, new realities. To use it as a weapon, an escape, or for moral instruction, is to exploit it. "To force art into being knowledge has been the master stroke that cut off its roots in ritual and play and mysterious otherness of presence."

Thus Updike is suspect since he is "his own chief character, or rather his sensibility is its own chief object." Thus William Gass, whose *Omensetter's Luck* Mr. Gilman calls "the most important work of fiction by an American in this literary generation," compromised himself by resorting to narrative, "which every major novelist since Flaubert has either abandoned or used ironically." Thus, distressingly, "Painters have gone on painting portraits decades after Picasso blew up the genre with those three noses . . . And people still go to the theater to identify with characters, not having been apprised of their death." Thus Mailer ("intellectual action painter, prophet without portfolio and philosopher *maudit*") wrote unacceptable novels because he was confused "about the nature of imaginative writing." He only resolved his literary and ego problems by stumbling on a nonfiction form (*The Armies of the Night*) that put self and history into a creative relationship. This "rather wonderful achievement" was made possible by his very "impurity" as an artist, his unseemly desire to change the world and oblige that world to admit that Mailer was responsible for the change.

There are several ways to respond to such a prescriptive idea of art—autonomous, a-historical, a-psychological, a-social, a-moral. One can quibble: Updike is underrated, and deserves the same long leash to sniff around his own sensibility that Gilman allows Eldridge Cleaver. (Gilman says he can't review Cleaver because he isn't black, and being black is very painful, and therefore black writing is bound to be rooted, for the time being anyway, in that "sense of actuality" that is so tiresome to the swinging white critics of the 1960's. There is condescension in this attitude, but more: an inadvertent confession of failure. All these people keep doing things with fiction that they should not be doing. Why? There must be a political reason. Forgive them; they've got problems. The argument is circular. Everybody has problems. One of the biggest problems is society in general and our society in particular. Critics telling novelists what they should or shouldn't be writing about tend to look a little silly, even though their criticism is in its way a creative effort. Beware the commissar lurking inside each cultural newsman.) The "every major novelist since Flaubert" assertion about narrative is absurd. (Dostoyevsky? Proust? Mann? *Dubliners?* Faulkner? Günter Grass? Garcia Marquez? Etcetera, ad absurdum.) Aren't some forms worth repeating? (New life, after all, emerges out of the same old sex act. Maybe, though, human beings—rooted in history, psychology, sociality, morality, genealogy—are insufficiently autonomous to be as splendid as art.) Surely his fine dissection of *MacBird!* (severing "our lifelines—to the past, to our moral bases and the bases of our judgment, to our possibilities of acting") implies an ethical imperative: If Gilman denies an emasculation of *his* self by history, after seeing a wretched little masturbatory dream masquerading as political satire, why can't Mailer do the same thing? Or Updike? Or even Irving Wallace? The world keeps on intruding on Gilman's reinvention of it.

But finally one resists two prongs of his argument:

(1) Gilman presumes a kind of built-in obsolescence to all art forms. The presumption leads to a toy manufacturer's psychology. New models every season. More chrome, longer fins. Less chrome, no fins at all. The anxiety to be with it, the fear of the death of a notion. Inevitably, there is in these pages a lust for, and cult of, the New. So what if Salinger and Updike "remain a number of years behind the truest current feeling"? Art isn't the same as the sports pages, and critics aren't sports columnists trying to write the Odyssey every morning about last night's baseball game. So anxious is Gilman on this score that he must in his preface apologize for using the words "broadjump" and "happening" in the course of his collection. Why? Because different words have replaced them in the interim. Usage. But usage is irredeemably utilitarian; there is nothing about it that partakes of "mysterious otherness of presence." Exponents of traditional aesthetic forms don't suffer from this anxiety to be on the street wherever an accident has happened. (They suffer from other anxieties, including a fear of the unknown and that which cannot immediately be translated into their grammar, a grammar not of usage but of faith. Nevertheless, they ask useful questions about each innovation as it pops out of the print factory or the developing fluid: Is this "new reality" anything more than a spastic

rapture of the Zeitgeist, a Hula-Hooping sort of culture cough, a media hiccup?)

(2) Gilman's disapproval of art "exploited" into knowledge is about as meaningful as my disapproval of the truck that runs me down at an intersection. The culture is in trouble, and the culture is going to look for help wherever it can find it, regardless of the intentions of artists and critics. Gilman once recklessly defines "the conditions of existence" as "finiteness, sacrifice, hierarchy, reciprocity, debt, time"—an excellent definition. Mustn't an artist, who is also a citizen, be allowed to try to cope with these conditions every once in a while? And mustn't a culture, to survive, try to absorb the artist's manner of coping—insights, outlooks, partakings, leave-takings, angles of moral, psychological, structural vision—as it tries to absorb the researches of science and religion? Gilman also describes artistic consequence as "imaginative increment." One dictionary definition of "increment" is "profit; gain." Can he then complain that the rest of us seek some intellectual dividend from art? Anyway, we do; and, to wrench from context a quote by A. J. Ayer, it is perverse to see tragedy in what could not conceivably be otherwise.

(January 1970)

Irving Howe's *Decline of the New*

By the "decline of the new," Irving Howe means the breakdown of "literary modernism," the end of literature as we have known it for 100 years—the years of Baudelaire, Dostoyevsky, Kafka, Proust, Joyce, Eliot, Faulkner and Samuel Beckett. It is a literature of desperation, of extreme subjectivity, in which "the object perceived seems always on the verge of being swallowed up by the perceiving agent, and the act of perception in danger of being exalted to the substance of reality." It posits a "historical impasse . . . an apocalyptic cul-de-sac in which technological ends and secular progress are called into question." It strips man "of his systems of belief and his ideal claims, and then proposes the one uniquely modern style of salvation: a salvation by, of, and for the self." It seeks "to reinvent the terms of reality," to "re-create the very grounds of being, through a permanent revolution of sensibility and style." Above all, it is difficult.

Now, ten new novels arrive each week on a reviewer's desk full of such subjectivity, positing, stripping and seeking. Mr. Howe would dismiss most of them as a "vulgar reincarnation and parodic mimesis" of the masters, and he would be right. Unlike other cultural movements, modernism will not die decently. The media machine keeps transfusing it pints of ink. It must suffer the indignity of cartoons written in its name, of "publicity and sensation," of "savage parody," of being approved of by those slicksters and flacks against whom it sought to construct an alternative reality. It is cannibalized by its children.

Very dangerous children they are, too, as Mr. Howe points out. While most of his book consists of essays on writers he variously admires—and there isn't a page that doesn't shine with intelligence— the motion is from "The Culture of Modernism" to "The New York Intellectuals." It is a motion as much political as literary. Mr. Howe to his credit has never stopped worrying about morality and politics, in literature or in life. The authoritarian opinions of Eliot, Yeats, Pound and Lawrence bothered him years ago; the new sensibility or intellectual style of the children of modernism (mixing "sentiments of anarchism with apologies for authoritarianism; bubbling hopes for 'participatory democracy' with manipulative elitism; unqualified Populist majoritarianism with the reign of the cadres") dismays him now.

His problem is that, as one of the sympathetic interpreters of modernism early on, he helped create a kind of cultural permissiveness, a cult of self-reference, from which the new sensibility derives. A salvation "by, of, and for the self" leads too easily to the "psychology of unobstructed need" he now deplores. (Granted, Mr. Howe spent the mid-1950's editing *Dissent* instead of celebrating, like most of the *Partisan Review* and *Commentary* crowd, the near perfection of America. How ironic, then, that *Dissent* should have published Mailer's "The White Negro," the first significant expression of the new gangster style: if I "dare the unknown" by beating up an old candy-store owner, it's probably good for me. As usual, the writers are ahead of the critics. Lionel Trilling has been teaching modernism most of his life, and only recently began to worry about the consequences.)

Howe copes with his problem (and ours) in several pages of
prose so tough-minded and persuasive that they are alone worth the
price of his book. According to the psychology of unobstructed need,
everybody should satisfy all his organic and psychic needs. The way
to do this is "to discard or destroy all those obstructions, mostly the
result of cultural neurosis," that stand in his way. "Sexuality is the
ground of being, and vital sexuality the assurance of the moral life."
But what if "the needs and impulses of human beings clash . . . if
the transfer of energies from sexuality to sociality" doesn't go
smoothly?

Howe finds the pronouncements of Norman O. Brown on this
subject "a curious analogue to *laissez-faire* economics . . . by means
of which innumerable units in conflict with one another achieve a
resultant of cooperation. Is there, however, much reason to suppose
that this will prove more satisfactory in the economy of moral conduct than it has in the morality of economic relations? . . . Against
me, against my ideas, it is possible to argue, but how, according to
this new dispensation, can anyone argue against my *need?*" Or, for
that matter, against Hitler's?

But the new sensibility is impatient with ideas, with literary struc-
tures of complexity and coherence, with the habit of reflection, the
making of distinctions, the weight of nuance. "It despises liberal
values, liberal cautions, liberal virtues. It is bored with the past: for
the past is a fink. . . . It seeks to charge itself into dazzling sentience
through chemicals and the rhetoric of violence. . . . It *ordains* life's
simplicity. It chooses surfaces as against relationships, the skim of
texture rather than the weaving of pattern."

Howe professes the best sort of liberalism, not as a version of current politics nor as a theory of power, "but liberalism as a cast of
mind, a structure of norms by means of which to humanize public
life. . . . We have paid dearly for the lesson that democracy, even
'bourgeois democracy,' is a precious human achievement, one that
. . . has been wrested through decades of struggle by the labor,
socialist and liberal movements." He is not willing to scrap it for a
herd of mind-blown storm troopers, and he quite properly disdains
intellectuals who play at revolution by publishing on the cover of a
literary magazine instructions on how to make Molotov cocktails.

(March 1970)

Philip Rahv's *Literature and the Sixth Sense*

Confused times test the literary intellectuals. Today, as in the 1930's, they want to make a connection between aesthetics and politics. Vietnam recapitulates the "crisis of capitalism" of the Great Depression. Once more there is a lust for relevance. "Art" and "history" are knotted up in each other's dangling participles. "Public" and "private" seem but symbolic notations on a page of raw unreadable experience. Surely some theoretical construction, some radical ambidexterity, can accommodate the disarray of our literature and our headlines. Thus on one side there are vulgarized forms of Marxism and/or Freudianism; and on the other, a thralldom to the anarchic "I," what Philip Rahv describes as "that orgastic self-glorification that you may find in our hipster writers who make do with the self (the ravenous, raging self of erotic fantasy and adolescent daydreams of power) when talent and moral intelligence fail them."

Mr. Rahv has been here before. His talent and moral intelligence don't fail him. Ever a swimmer against the Zeitgeist, in the 1930's he debunked "proletarian novels" while simultaneously introducing Kafka to America. His *Partisan Review* was a comfort station for intellectuals who escaped the Stalinist wilderness. The sixth sense he deploys in this selection from thirty years of literary criticism is historical "awareness" or "dimension." It serves him and the reader admirably, by steering us past totalitarian schemes without shearing off the social and moral contexts from a fiction.

Here, then, are his fine essays on "paleface and redskin" (energy *vs.* sensibility, opportunism *vs.* discipline in American literature), the "cult of experience," our classic writers (Hawthorne, Melville, Henry James) and Europe's (Tolstoy, Dostoyevsky, Kafka and Mann). Here are long thoughtful looks at the theory and practice of criticism, and the tergiversations of the mystifiers, whether they are politically radical, psychoanalytically rabid, or slumped in the "complacence and spiritual torpor" of the orthodox. Here, too, are examinations of Bellow, Malamud and Mailer, because Mr. Rahv, unlike Edmund Wilson, Allen Tate, Lionel Trilling and other formidable middle-aged critics, chooses to explore the contemporary as well as poke at the past. Finally, here are the consequences implied

by "historical awareness." Rooted in the observable and demonstra-
ble, the novel is "an experiential art . . . Object and symbol, act
and meaning" must be linked or the structure sinks. Style is a gloss:
"There is something anterior to technique and that is sensibility."

One argues with Mr. Rahv, of course. He dislikes Leslie Fiedler
(gross—*Partisan Review* apparently published his Huck Finn essay
thinking it a parody), Harry Levin (opaque), Hugh Kenner (for lik-
ing Ezra Pound). But all three stretch the mind, and sometimes
the understanding; surely consensus criticism serves us even less than
a clash of gibbering symbolists. He also prefers Saul Bellow to Norman Mailer. Ah. Well, Bellow and Mailer are moving in opposite directions, the one toward Europe and the past, the other toward
himself and the future. Like Fiedler only more so, Mailer takes risks.
I think the risks are well worth taking, even though they make for
messy books.

Mr. Rahv is, however, superb in identifying the New Criticism
with religious orthodoxy and traditionalism: those Southern fugitives from the secular: a fall from style is a fall from grace. Superb,
too, in characterizing Auden's later work as "stylized anxiety," and
for finding in Mann's *The Black Swan* a "sensibility seeking to discover in meaningless enormities a cure for ennui." And who will
not share his disapproval of those critics who seek "to interpose between us and Melville a Talmudic elaboration of mythology porten-
tous to the point of stupefaction"?

Like Fiedler, he is the Jewish outsider looking in on Puritan guilt
("the morality of abstention") and grafting to his portrait of it a
little Marx, a little Freud, a lot of moral intelligence. Like Fiedler,
he hasn't been able to connect aesthetics with politics yet, but keeps
trying—for which we must be grateful. Unlike Fiedler, he does not
seek the approval of the counter-culture—the drugs/rock/polymor-
phous perverse libidinal ferocity of a generation that seems to pride
itself on never having achieved a self at all. He is a man of the Left
who still believes in reason, and barks right back at the yawpers
of "me" and "now."

(September 1969)

Leslie Fiedler's *Nude Croquet*

"All masks abandoned," cried Leslie Fiedler in the preface to his *Love and Death in the American Novel*. If literary criticism could be nothing less "than an act of total moral engagement," the literary critic had not only to escape the locked airless room of textual exegesis, had not only to wrestle with the psychological, biographical, historical, sociological, anthropological and generic contexts of a fiction; he had also to risk his own carefully fabricated identity, to strip personal disguises, to resist the encysting of one's self in unexamined cultural presumptions. If the transactions of the artistic "I" with its materials and its audience were to be traced in all their baroque extravagance, then the critical "I" must be similarly probed, tested, doubted, fed like Darwin's insectivorous sundew flower with bits of urine and cork and tissue from the visceral cavity of a toad.

Fed, too, with bits of Freud (the unconscious) and Jung (the archetypes) and Marx ("the class relations of a culture help determine its deepest communal fantasies"). One result of Mr. Fiedler's moral engagement and self-stripping was an omnivorous "I"-eye, a kind of atomic submarine braving the deeps of American experience, exploring the unconscious sediment, sea anemones and anomies, sending up missiles of fiery insight into our inadmissible obsessions: the innocent, doomed dream of black-white male love; the revenge on women for the cult of art; brother-sister incest; necrophilia; Indian-guilt.

Another result was the institutionalization of Leslie Fiedler, a department of cultural affairs existing to publish cross-categorical Fiedler books, as there are Levi-Strauss books and Marshall McLuhan books and (eventually, hopefully) Hugh Kenner books—unclassifiable inquiries which we do not apprehend as scientific demonstration but as brilliant metaphor. In grasping those metaphors, we alter our perceptions.

Surely Mr. Fiedler has, along with Stanley Edgar Hyman, Edmund Wilson and Quentin Anderson, done more to reveal the richness and complexity of the American literary legacy than all the arid scholiasts combined, upon whose very touch imagination is sclerosed. He permits us to get drunk with our great-grandfathers, instead of

simply worshiping or reviling their semicolons and their subliminal
putt-putts. Just as surely Mr. Fiedler's own fiction deserves the same
sort of interpretative risk on the part of a reviewer that Fiedler himself specializes in as a critic.

Fiedler's novels are not structurally pleasing. His control is faulty.
He doesn't know when to shut up. But there is an energy about
novels like *Back to China* and *The Last Jew in America*, an affecting
sprawl and spill of ideas and intuitions, a groveling with characters,
that is persuasive. They tend to begin just where Portnoy's analyst
was "now, perhaps" ready to begin: with the masks of identity, the
connection of the individual to communal fantasies. You may be
able to kill your mother, with a long sword of words; but the Earth
Mother is as omnivorous as Mr. Fiedler's "I"-eye, and demands accommodation. Being ready to begin is being ready to try out adulthood.

The stories in *Nude Croquet*—about Jewishness, about academia,
about the left-wing failure of nerve after the 1930's—are not quite
up to his novels. The characters in this book usually maintain their
masks; or, if one is peeled off, another is discovered at a deeper layer
of deception. There are trick endings, and rather too much exposi-
tion. And, with the single exception of "The Dancing of Reb Hershl
with the Withered Hand," the stories are unremittingly bleak. To
be sure, we are individually and culturally full of violence and madness. But there is a personal as well as an historical dialectic, an
opposition of moods. Mr. Fiedler is, here, all antithesis. And the
antithesis is not, like Flannery O'Connor's, complete—a bone-hinge
of faith and flesh. It is more of a black joke; nasty.

Which is not to say that *Nude Croquet* hasn't the power to startle
and inform. The title story is superb, though even the rain must
"bang stupidly against the leaded window panes." "The Teeth" is
a bitter anti-valentine. "An Expense of Spirit" corrodes, and "The
Stain" is as disquieting an exploration of black self-hatred as "Let
Nothing You Dismay" and "Dirty Ralphy" are of the Jewish self-
hatred we have come to know and love-hate. "Bad Scene at Buffalo
Jump" and "Pull Down Vanity!" go at Jewishness with a scimitar.
"The Fear of Innocence" combines Marxism, sexuality and betrayal
to enormous effect.

What seems to run through all these stories is a sense of paralyzing
guilt: for having deserted the Left, for having denied Jewishness, for

having betrayed old visions of the self, for having sought in the ano-
dynes of money, irony and even self-contempt a permanent mask,
behind which there isn't any face at all. Perhaps it was the energy
of these denials that propelled Mr. Fiedler into his investigations of
the American unconscious, to define not only the relation of our
earlier writers to that seething continental psyche, but his own relation as well. Perhaps, in fact, having learned that even the computer print-outs come to us with fresh bloody thumbprints of the
irrational on their margins; having learned that, as the masks of
identity drop one by one, the face revealed is a hole in history; having learned, after Auschwitz and Hiroshima, that the Enlightenment
was somehow naïve—he had to plunge into myth and learn how to
swim. And, in the process, teach the rest of us how, too.

There is, in his fiction and his criticism, a kind of groping backwards, as though in search of some secularized version of Original
Sin. Of Hawthorne, Herman Melville wrote: "In certain moods, no
man can weigh this world without throwing in something, somehow
like Original Sin, to strike the uneven balance . . . this black conceit pervades him through and through." Mr. Fiedler, too. But we
know that, like the Vietcong, he will strike again.

(August 1969)

Leslie Fiedler's *Being Busted*

On April 28, 1967, Leslie A. Fiedler, his wife, his son and his
daughter-in-law were arrested in their home by Buffalo police and
charged with "maintaining a premise" where marijuana was used.
"I never would have thought it," an old friend told him. "You're
the kind, Leslie, who always gets away . . . Oh *hell*, you'll just write
a book about it and make lots of money." Here is the book. Yet his
arrest seems oddly peripheral to it. We learn of his legal briefs; of
the young girl who spied on his family with an electronic device; of
the "credit" world that judged him guilty before his trial; of the University of Amsterdam, which canceled his invitation to teach a term
abroad. But *Being Busted* is really about all the other times Mr.
Fiedler "got away," times when he was "a tourist at someone else's
war." He looks at his materialism (the longing "for sleek and shiny
comforts") and his politics ("vestigial, nostalgic: little more than a

function of my desire not to grow old"), at his intellectual style (that "ambivalence" prized by the old, despised by the young) and his professional role ("the teacher teaches himself, diffidently at first, shamelessly after a while").

To be sure, the Buffalo bust was material enough for a minor league game of Kafka ball. According to Fiedler: neither he nor his wife is a pot-head. The police were out to get him because he sponsored a campus group that favored legalizing marijuana. The wretched spy, who would later repudiate her charge and then repudiate the repudiation, planted the marijuana on his premises. Once his arrest hit the headlines, he couldn't insure his house, get a loan, rent a car or enjoy a Diners' Club card. Friends of his family were harassed. In rolled the anti-Semitic mail.

Half the book focuses on these events—legal maneuvering (which still proceeds), article writing (for *The New York Review of Books*), marijuana laws (Prohibition puritanism), the brave new world of bugging ("legitimized stealth," the death of privacy), drug cult vs. whiskey cult, student vs. university, freedom vs. property. What he has to say isn't particularly startling, although it comes irony-enriched with the usual Fiedler sophistication about the vicissitudes of self. He knows that his personal predicament isn't as significant as, say, Vietnam or racism; it is, however, symptomatic of the war between the young and the old that rips this nation apart. (If "maintaining a premise" can be used to arrest college professors, why not arrest all the officers in charge of all the Army posts here and abroad? There's as much marijuana smoking on the posts as there is on campus. "Maintaining a premise," indeed.)

But the better-written and more moving part of *Being Busted* is that half in which Fiedler examines his own past—as teacher, writer, ex-Trotskyite, Freudian, Easterner, Jew: Six Avocations in Search of an Ambivalence. As an exercise in autobiography, it omits much the reader wants to know about his parents, his marriage, just when Freud entered his mind, just why he went to Montana in the first place, how the American Indian came to weigh so heavily on his imagination. It is nevertheless a vulnerable and affecting piece of confessional literature.

Consider his reverie on purchasing a place to live in the exclusive Central Park section of Buffalo: "Those great stone houses, as old as the century, staunch as battlements and crenelated like castles, had been constructed to protest the verdure in whose midst they rose and the peace their WASP owners sought against all ethnic interlopers, all who had come too late to our shores or had gotten rich after the proper moment. But they had long since departed, those original builders, along with the immigrant girls who had polished their silver and scrubbed their floors; and the cruel gray of the stones they had set, grim as a prison or a Florentine *palazzo*, had softened toward green under the moss, and the foliage of the great elms lining the streets had lifted and spread till the light that filtered through made the playing children beneath them seem like dim figures at the bottom of a lake."

Isn't this a Gatsby's gaze on the green light at the end of Daisy's dock? I mean, after we peel the ironic onion to its eye, isn't it a cry for that which is denied, no matter whether it ever really existed? "The orgiastic future," wrote Fitzgerald, "that year by year recedes before us . . ." Guilt-inspiring, at least in Leslie Fiedler's case, for it mocks what Newark meant to him. It suggests as a novelist might (as Fiedler as novelist might) that his crime was not in sponsoring an unpopular campus group, but in wanting too much to be "OK" in Central Park, in buying—on an installment plan—elms that never grew on Bergen Street, green lights that never shone in Trotsky's eyes.

No wonder, then, that Naval Intelligence cleared him during the war. No wonder that he gets along better with motorcycle gangs than with the SDS. No wonder that he was never busted until his complicity with youth annoyed the police. No wonder that he never experienced a sense of sin (social, political) until the police defined it for him. He wanted what most of us want. His dream was ours— for elms of whose rot we were unaware until we were told that someone else owned them in perpetuity.

To have paid for those elms with our lives, to have coughed up all that accumulated interest, only to learn that the advertisement was fraudulent, that no one ever had any intention of letting us loll in the filtered light, is . . . well . . . ambivalent-making. Mr. Fiedler, to his enormous credit, admits it: No synagogue in Lame Deer, Montana; no elms in Buffalo, New York; no green lights this side of Timothy Leary. Only "someone who is simply *there*." And a sign in Amsterdam: "Gatsby Go Home."

(January 1970)

Flannery O'Connor's *Mystery and Manners*

You must hack your way through a thicket of pieties to get at Flannery O'Connor's special grace. A recent critical study of her fiction, published by Vanderbilt University Press, went so far as to suggest that she could only be appreciated by readers with "an orthodox understanding of Christocentric religion." Hogwash. But typical of the pronouncements issued *ex cathedra* by those southern writers and critics who milk their psychic trauma as though it were a sacred cow: When they lost the Civil War, they "fell" from innocence and therefore consider themselves experts on redemption, about which they monologize.

Flannery O'Connor fought all her life against the categorizers who would lock her inside a "gothic" or "grotesque" or "degenerate" box. We shouldn't allow her to be expropriated now by autocrats of the orthodox, the people who wear Christ like a campaign button to every symposium on Moral Fatigue—even when she herself conspires at that expropriation, as she sometimes does in this posthumous collection of essays and lectures. Southern Christians no more monopolize "mystery" than urban Jews monopolize *Angst*, or blacks monopolize rage, or Hollywood monopolizes trash.

After chasing the expropriators from the temple, we can see *Mystery and Manners* for the marvelous thing it is: occasional prose —on Christianity and fiction, the creative process, regional story telling, teaching literature, raising peacocks—which should be read by every writer and would-be writer and lover of writing; a painful dialectic between the artist (Flying Dutchwoman on bizarre seas) and her Church (custodian of inflexible verities); and a moving portrait of a unique person we have lost, to our permanent impoverishment.

Roman Catholic (mystery), Southerner (manners) and doomed (knowing it, enduring it, squeezing blood from stony metaphor all the while), she ranks with Mark Twain and Scott Fitzgerald among our finest prose stylists. Her epigrams alone are worth the price of the book: "The Catholic novelist believes that you destroy freedom by sin; the modern reader believes, I think, that you gain it that way." Or: "One old lady who wants her heart lifted up wouldn't be so bad, but you multiply her two hundred and fifty thousand times and what you get is a book club." Or: "Everywhere I go I'm asked if I think the universities stifle writers. My opinion is that they don't stifle enough of them. There's many a best-seller that could have been prevented by a good teacher."

As a meditator on the function of faith in the shaping of fiction, she got herself into some odd and untenable positions. She defends, for instance, the proscribing of books: "The business of protecting souls from dangerous literature belongs properly to the Church. All fiction, even when it satisfies the requirements of art, will not turn out to be suitable for everyone's consumption." She declares that "in the absence of faith . . . we govern by tenderness," which tenderness, because it is "cut off from the person of Christ . . . ends in forced-labor camps and in the fumes of the gas chamber." (What tenderness are we talking about? Stalin's? Hitler's? A monstrous simplification.) She celebrates the "cultural unity" of the South without ever mentioning the race question, rationalizing the unmentionable by stating that "evil is not simply a problem to be solved, but a mystery to be endured." (By whom? By the objects on which it inflicts itself?)

But her reflections on writing are superb. She knows that "the limitations any writer imposes on his work will grow out of the necessities that lie in the material itself . . . more rigorous than any religion could impose." That fiction "operates through the senses" and stories must begin with concrete, believable details. That "unless the novelist has gone out of his mind, his aim is still communication." And that "in the greatest fiction, the writer's moral sense coincides with his dramatic sense, and I see no way for it to do this unless his moral judgment is part of the very act of seeing."

Flannery O'Connor's mission was to "observe our fierce and fading manners in the light of an ultimate concern." There was no sweetness in her, no forgiveness. Her ultimate concern was a sword with which she struck down her characters in the light of their being seen and judged, art as assassination. She died at age thirty-nine, leaving two novels and two short-story collections in which a visionary prose successfully aspired to a convergence of poetry and prophecy. The violence she employed, finding it "strangely capable of returning my characters to reality and preparing them to accept

their moment of grace," engulfs us. Many of our mysteries seem now
explicitly evil, and one would have liked to talk to her about them.
It is bitter that we can't.

(May 1969)

Randall Jarrell's *The Third Book of Criticism*

Randall Jarrell died before he should have, without finishing this
book. He was a complicated man, and it will be a while before we can
see him in focus. His poetry is neglected by anthologists because
anthologists need the space to inflict on us their own perishable produce and therefore haven't room for, say, *The Death of the Ball Tur-
ret Gunner*, one of the best war poems ever written. His criticism
is considered by some to be suspect because it was both witty and
engaged, which are crimes against the Higher Seriousness. Yet no
anthology could contain such a many-sided man: poet, critic, teacher,
eulogist, advocate, conscience of his colleagues. And as for the Highly
Serious, to whom the Muse appears "with a ruler, a pair of compasses
and a metronome"—Jarrell makes you want to read the book; they
make you want to give up reading altogether.

On the evidence of *The Third Book of Criticism*, I expect many
a living writer only wishes Jarrell had read him and subjected his
work to the same fierce scrutiny here accorded W. H. Auden, Wallace Stevens and Robert Graves. Every aspect of their art—rhetoric,
attitude, aesthetic and philosophical resolution, even the sponsoring
culture—gets comprehensive treatment. It is, to borrow from basketball, a game of one-on-one, for Jarrell belonged to no school of critics
or poets, and respected none.

Criticism, then, as an act of total engagement. Scarcely a page of
it doesn't yield dividends. On Stevens: "We feel like saying that the
process of creating the poem is the poem. Surprisingly often the motion of qualification, of concession, of logical conclusion—a dialectical motion in the older sense of *dialectical*—is the movement that
organizes the poem; and in Stevens the unlikely tenderness of this
movement . . . is like the tenderness of the sculptor or draftsman,
whose hand makes but looks as if it caressed."

On Marianne Moore: "In the world of her poems there are many thoughts, things, animals, sentiments, moral insights; but money and passion and power, the brute fact that *works*, whether or not correctly, whether or not precisely—the whole Medusa face of the world: these are gone."

On T. S. Eliot as the future will probably view him: "Surely you must have seen that he was one of the most subjective and daemonic poets who ever lived, the victim and helpless beneficiary of his own inexorable compulsions, obsessions . . . [Take] *The Waste Land*, which Eliot would have written about the Garden of Eden, but which your age thought its own realistic photograph."

On the Beats: their "iron spontaneity" makes it impossible for them to "write a good poem except by accident, since it eliminates the selection, exclusion, and concentration that are an essential part of writing a poem."

It is an engagement, however, not wholly grim-faced. The fact that "few of the ideas of Auden's last stage have the slightest novelty to a reader acquainted with Luther, Calvin, and Barth" is actually "a Godsend for everybody concerned, since the theological ideas which Auden does not adopt but invents are all too often on the level of those brown paper parcels, brought secretly to the War Department in times of national emergency, which turn out to be full of plans to destroy enemy submarines by tracking them down with seals."

The "erotic procedures of Chinese poetry" are called "those silks that swathe a homely heart." The novel is defined as "a prose work of some length that has something wrong with it." The attitude of poets toward their readers in the 1920's is summed up: "Modern poetry is necessarily obscure; if the reader can't get it, let him eat Browning." A motto is invented for William Carlos Williams: "In the suburbs, there one feels free."

Inevitably, the essays vary in their holding power. If you haven't read Christina Stead's *The Man Who Loved Children*, his essay will inspire you to do so; but if you have read the novel, the essay seems interminable. No one should try to account for fifty years of American poetry in thirty-nine pages, complete with thumbnail appreciations of the principal practitioners. And a forty-page analysis of one poem by Robert Frost seems an exercise in exegetical overkill, while at the same time depressing those of us who are trapped into our daily reviewer's can of 800 calories.

Still, those are the hazards of advocacy criticism, and when the advocate is Jarrell, the hazards are worth it. Yes, he brooded long on what Wallace Stevens called "things dark on the horizons of perception." And yes, M. L. Rosenthal was right in saying that he sought "to evoke an acute feeling of violated sensibility." But stylized anxiety was not his racket. Beyond the anxiety were moral imperatives, and a sense that our possibilities are almost equal to our vulnerabilities, and a profound sympathy for the writers who tried to balance the equation. That he drank himself to death is maddening.

(1969)

Stanley Burnshaw's *The Seamless Web*

Reviewers notoriously bring to books their own conceptual carpetbag, as handymen and plumbers bring tools: yardsticks and saws to measure and reduce, drills to bore, pliers to wrench from context, as though the "word-pack" were either raw material to be fashioned into something agreeable, or a problem, like a clogged drain, needing to be fixed. Perhaps, then, the best way I can signify my enthusiasm for Stanley Burnshaw's extraordinary treatise is to say that it changed my mind. Mr. Burnshaw is a poet. When poets start talking about "the wisdom of the body," one reaches automatically for the chisel and tongs. Yet Mr. Burnshaw disarms at least this chiseler, proposing an idea of poetry as the involuntary expression of a poet's total organism; of the poem as a physical assault on the reader's body; of art—in words, paint, stone or sound—profoundly opposed to any culture.

His "seamless web" refers to a biological "at-oneness" with the world, "all that one senses and knows," a participatory Eden, an envelope of instincts in harmony with nature. Such paradise was lost by man—not because of our weapon making, language, "societality," symbolic thinking, altruism or technology, but because of our experience of "otherness." Otherness (strangeness, alienation) is a consequence of the "I," which each of us forms as our brain is taught "to regard its owner as an other-than-itself," and so objectifies the universe: "I," "it," "them."

With the formation of an "I," says Mr. Burnshaw, "continuity with" the environment ends; "looking at" the environment begins. Which means divisiveness, a human reality wholly symbolic, our experiences translated into symbols, those symbolic representations of experience processed and acted upon, our responses already twice removed from stimuli that issued from another dimension, a non-symbolic reality. We are talking to ourselves, and our only "world" is linguistic.

It smacks slightly, doesn't it, of Norman O. Brown, or even Marshall McLuhan? The polymorphous perverse or haptic harmony, sacrificed on the altar of Reason or the alphabet. But Mr. Burnshaw makes poignantly clear, in some of the best popular science writing I've seen in years, that this "otherness" derives inevitably from the training of the human brain itself. In J. Z. Young's words, "We have to learn to see the world as we do." The reality a child perceives consists of adults operating according to a culture of "otherness," of manipulation. Sprung from the womb, out of our Eden of at-oneness, we know no way to make sense of stimuli. (Ernst Gombrich: "The innocent eye sees nothing.") We must be taught to see; and the teaching makes us see in certain ways, makes us organize our brains linguistically, in categories and dichotomies, symbols and manipulable approximations.

What has any of this to do with poetry? By examining the witness of great artists and scientists through the ages, Mr. Burnshaw demonstrates that the creative process is something done *to* instead of done *by* the human medium. Inspiration isn't a faucet one turns on to pour a poem or a formula; it is a drive of the organism toward unity, an aspiration for the lost Eden, a discharge of the burden of tension the creator experiences, an eruption seeking the integral equipoise, homeostasis, "seamless web." (Our web has seams: the synaptic cleft is 200 angstroms wide. Hydras, experiencing two-way excitation all along the nerve-net, may not have our problem. Mr. Burnshaw doesn't mention this, but it supports his argument, and as an amateur neuroanatomist I want to help.)

Art, then—and it's scandalous to try to condense this book into my 800-word box—is necessarily opposed to culture, because culture is predicated on fragmentation, "distancing," manipulation, causality, all the "I's" seeking an abstract relationship with one another. Poets don't busy themselves "for the high purpose of producing objects to give other people pleasure or instruction or knowledge or moral guidance"; they are, instead, afflicted with a strangeness wanting familiarity, an alienation wanting community, a tension wanting quiescence.

Mr. Burnshaw manages also to look at similes and metaphors, the role of the critic, the preoccupations of linguists, the scientific problem of explaining memory, the difference between poetry and religion (the latter must have some of the former, the former need have none of the latter), the way we read, and why translations are usually garbage. Accustomed as we are to such ambition being packaged in apocalyptic plastic—toilet training is to blame! or genital organization! or capitalism, Gutenberg, aggression, the nuclear family! Repent!—Mr. Burnshaw's patient matter-of-factness, his gentle urging, pleases almost as much as his graceful prose. The man has written an important, challenging, exciting book, without ever asking us to admire him or become his disciples. He is all the more admirable for his reticence.

I would wonder, along with him, on just two puzzles that spin off from his speculation. The first has to do with the poet himself: If the biological economy is an anti-Keynesian as Mr. Burnshaw describes it, does the poet who allows poems to be dictated through him sacrifice a capacity for feeling in other areas that might amount to self-emasculation? (Was it Baudelaire who said that each poem means one less erection?) The second has to do with our experience of strangeness: What if the organism's longing for a "seamless web" is doomed to disappointment? What if otherness is irreversible? What if all our complexity is an evolutionary inadvertence, our question-asking a tragic noise, a static in a void whose (non)existence the question asker would find insupportable? Then we would be left, wouldn't we, in a world full of tense strangers; and be obliged, as we are, to establish relationships with those strangers by signing various sorts of social contracts, enunciating abstract principles of reciprocity, trying to create—through law, science, religion and even art—if not a web to bind us, at least an umbrella under which the community can stand as the fact of death rains down on us from the upstairs nothingness. That seems to be the situation.

(February 1970)

Samuel French Morse's *Wallace Stevens*

About the time Grace Kelly was married to Prince Rainier, someone in Hollywood was asked for anecdotes about her and replied: "Grace is the sort of person who doesn't allow anecdotes to happen to her." Wallace Stevens seems to have been the sort of person who not only didn't allow anecdotes to happen to him, but who also almost didn't allow life to happen to him—at least the kind of life we romantically associate with fine poets. No illegitimacy, drugs, drunkenness, wenching, war, inversion, disease, tragedy or even travel. He was born in Reading, Pennsylvania, in 1879; went to Harvard in the fall of 1897; left for New York in 1900; failed at journalism and at law; joined an insurance company; moved with it to Hartford; eventually became its vice-president, and was eulogized by its house organ on his death fifteen years ago as "an outstanding attorney in the bond claim field." His wife didn't like his poetry.

Can a life that Samuel French Morse accurately describes as "devoid of outward drama and excitement or interest" inspire a satisfying biography? No doubt some mole is already boring his way through file cards toward a monumental footnote, but Mr. Morse—poet, Northeastern University professor of English, editor of *Opus Posthumous*—attempts no such wheezy doorstopper. He neither rhapsodizes nor does he catalogue. Instead, he introduces the poems, sketches the poet, traces the intellectual development of the man, and sifts the ideas through a very fine sieve to remark their essence, all with uncommon grace.

We can conceive of Stevens along the lines of "poetry as life" or "imagination as reality" or "a violence from within that protects us from a violence without." We can accept him as "the poet of the earth" he wanted to be or "the poet of things" Mr. Morse decides him to be. We can meditate on his "evasions" (a favorite Stevens word) or on his politics (". . . apostrophes are forbidden on the funicular./ Marx has ruined Nature,/ For the moment"). We can brood about his acquisitive impulse ("I don't for a moment like the idea of poverty") or his silences (". . . after writing a poem, it is a good thing to walk around the block; after too much midnight, it is pleasant to hear the milkman . . .").

But what Mr. Morse makes clear is that Stevens saw and felt
"things"—landscapes, objects, ideas—more intensely than most of us.
The paintings his agent purchased for him in Paris, the cans of tea,
the books, the languages, the borrowings from Santayana and Berg-
son were all perceived through the peculiar light of his extraterrestrial
imagination ("the yellow moon of words about the nightingale")
and assumed astonishing shapes and meanings. He lived on an internal moon, a Mars of irony and color; there were craters and stars
inside him no astronaut has yet afflicted with a platitude.

Who cares, then, about his tristich? This man made Florida seem
incredibly exotic. What does it matter whether he confused himself
at times with Crispin, or ever winced at Peter Quince belaboring a
clavier? "The poem lashes more fiercely than the wind," and Stevens
the poet never "looked at plainly" anything: ". . . as a wave is a force
and not the water of which it is composed, so nobility is a force and
not the manifestations of which it is composed, which are never the
same." Material comfort? Social Security at the Canoe Club? "The
more than rational distortion,/ The fiction that results from feeling"
testifies to an experience those of us who shape our fantasies in cave-
like movie theaters are incapable even of suspecting.

Movies. Hashish. Ideology. Accustomed as we are to the custom-
ized fantasies of crude imaginations crudely laid on us, a Stevens
distresses. Why didn't his wife like his poetry? What did his colleagues at the Hartford insurance company think of him? Is he resented by political critics because he successfully separated the
making of money and the making of art, and succeeded at both? Is he
resented by sentimentalists because he never suffered in public, and
yet wrote poems only certified sufferers should be permitted to impose on us? How could a conservative, heterosexual, stay-at-home
vice-president of an insurance company write some of the best poems
of this century?

Mr. Morse doesn't answer these questions. Probably, they can't
be answered, like "Is my thought a memory, not alive?" or "Is the
spot on the floor, there, wine or blood/ And whichever it may be, is it
mine?" But his book does belong on that short, distinguished shelf
including the collected poems, Holly Stevens' Letters of Wallace
Stevens and Helen Vendler's On Extended Wings: Wallace Stevens'
Longer Poems. And, who knows, maybe "They will get it straight

one day at the Sorbonne./ We shall return at twilight from the lecture/ Pleased that the irrational is rational . . ." And Wallace Stevens "will have stopped revolving except in crystal." I hope not.

(July 1970)

Marshall McLuhan's *Counterblast* and *The Interior Landscape*

Not that any post-literate needs reminding, but let us, loud enough to fill all the available acoustic space, blabbercast the First, Second and Third Precepts of Mobius the Looped: (1) Western man's fall *from* grace was a fall *into* Syntax, out of the haptic harmony and into the alphabet soupçon. (2) With the invention of movable type, *we sold our Gestalt for a mess of dualities*; eye-cendancy in the sensorium disequilibrates. (3) We shall escape our consequent dynamic of violence through subliminal tribalization (trivialization?) via the LP record, the TV set and the computer. "Circuitry is the end of the neolithic age," boasts *Counterblast.* "Computer speed and inclusiveness is LSD for Business . . . Electricity creates musical politics . . . The prayer mat will succeed the Cadillac." Hanging tense as we surf the electromagnetic wave . . .

Once upon a time, as *The Interior Landscape* demonstrates, Marshall McLuhan was a good literary critic. He wrote harmless essays for the usual quarterlies on the usual subjects: Poe and Pope, Joyce and Pound, technique vs. sensibility, analogical mirrors. Yes, there was an agenbit of Innis-wit, but the stuff was solid. Then on the banks of the *Sewanee Review* he lay down with the Mechanical Bride and they performed all sorts of unnatural acts.

Now, as demonstrated by the typographical acid-trip called *Counterblast,* his thing is manufacturing gloss for the gross. "Bless Madison Avenue for Restoring the Magical Art of the Cavemen to

Suburbia." The bookman (who used to identify technological components in artistic innovation) has become the ad man, *manqué* to
be sure, but nevertheless absolving Madison Avenue and Hollywood
of any guilt for what they're doing to us. He stopped laughing at his
own jokes, the butts of those jokes, and himself. A terrible, messianic
seriousness sidewhelmed him.

Since there is obviously a McLuhan implosion—hail the apologist,
bearing aperçus—it is recumbent upon the reviewer (who takes everything lying down) to wonder whether Mr. McLuhan's typographical
conspiracy with Mr. Parker is anything more than a silly trick.
Wouldn't any other type arrangement have disserved the reader just
as much? Can you have your book and beat it, too? Isn't it odd that
most of his puns are visual (unlike the Joyce he's always squeezing,
and who of course was going blind)? But he has delivered himself
into the claws of packagers, and neither he nor the packagers care
about content.

Equally irrelevant (as content, as criticism) are a reviewer's
qualms about McLuhan's contempt for a "moral," "ethical" or
"cathartic" view of art. He proposes a cognitive recapitulation: the
form of an artwork should imitate the confusions of our perceptual
apparatus. Or help create those confusions. Probe, don't point. Instead of values, we have "strategies for survival." The guilt-edged
insecurities of the wretched dehumanist are so much slag of sloughed-
off awareness; the unconscious itselflessness is a compost of discarded
sense-impressions.

Never mind, then, that the man seems basically to confuse
information-receiving (for which, after all, the eye is the superior
tool) with information-processing (which aspires to an organizing
vision, an abstraction, a communicable "truth"). Never mind that
his celebration of a "field theory" is compromised by his lust for
a Prime Cause, a Causal Crime (Aristotle's Trojan Zebra, foisting
the unconscious dualisms of Greek grammar on the unsuspecting
cosmos). Never mind that "participatory" TV is inconvenienced by

the impossibility of dialogue with an electronic image, the absence of feedback. Never mind that all those medieval readers of illuminated manuscripts were hung up on *every word*, while modern readers at least grasp the syntactic whole of a *sentence*. Never mind the lack of "how" in this injunction to roll with the media punch. We freeze in the programmed Arctic of what George P. Elliott has called "an electronic Chiliasm."

Still: The man who once worried not only about *how* a writer said something, but also *what* the writer meant to say, now proposes an acquiescence in technological manipulation; a "value-free" Herman Kahnoclasm; a rape of the lotus by the robot. The garbage fed us, and the garbagemen who shove it down our throats, are blameless. The way it's shoved down our throats alters our garbage-ratio perception. If we nonetheless choke, we are, demonstrably, unwithit. Zeitgeistless. The Mechanical Bride emasculates.

Enough. The dialogue between self (wherein we experience most of our pain and most of our joy) and society (to which we sacrifice some personal license in exchange for services, upon which we are dependent, with which we must transact) will go on in its messy way. We must live together and must die alone, and no tribe dedicated to the eating of electricity will solve that paradox, even in an age where the electric chair seems our most characteristic medium. The message is part of the message.

(November 1969)

Two (?) Modern Masters

Marshall McLuhan and George Orwell slipped into town last week, off a Viking submarine from England, wearing book jackets that identified them as "Modern Masters" in the Frank Kermode essay series—along with Camus, Marcuse, Levi-Strauss, Lukacs, Wittgenstein, etc. Frankly, the heart sinks. If McLuhan is, according to Mr. Kermode's editorial scheme, a modern master, one of "the men who

have changed and are changing the life and thought of our age," what
does that make Orwell? In orders of magnitude, we are talking about
a light bulb and Sirius the Dog Star. McLuhan exists mostly as an
excuse, the means by which admen and television executives forgive
themselves for their many crimes against intelligence and decency.
Whereas Orwell . . . well, as writers and as people, most of us aren't
fit to carry Orwell's aspidistra.

McLuhan is carved up for Mr. Kermode by Jonathan Miller, the
British doctor best known to Americans for his role in the Broadway comedy sketch *Beyond the Fringe*. Dr. Miller's critical method
consists of ablation and curettage; no vagary of culture or logic escapes his knife. McLuhan's head-heart dualism, his "abdication of
political intelligence," his misapprehension of physiology and linguistics are all scraped out of the corpus and deposited in bottlelike
paragraphs for examination. They can't stand the light of day.

But the real value of Dr. Miller's essay lies elsewhere. Such
McLuhanisms as the tyranny of the eye, the wholeness of village life,
the superiority of the ideogram and the icon over the alphabet and
the ego, the contempt for rationalism and the celebration of some
de-Chardinian noosphere of electronic grooviness, are represented
by the Master "not as [his] privately owned opinions, but as orphan
data sent back to earth, as it were, from an unmanned space probe.
. . . He likes to see himself, not as an author, but as a publicly subsidized payload of sensitive instruments that records information
irrespective of personal values." A one-man Rand Corporation or
Hudson Institute: just the bad news please.

No. Just as Alvin Gouldner in *The Coming Crisis of Western
Sociology* demonstrated the subjective value-bias of sociologists on
government contract, Dr. Miller demonstrates "a hidden bias" in
McLuhan. That bias is at least tripartite: First, his conversion to
Catholicism—a minority culture alienated from the Canadian
majority's "single point of view." (See McLuhan's early articles on
Hopkins and Chesterton.) Second, his upbringing in the western
provinces of Canada—agrarian "distributist" ideas, a cultural and social identity crisis. Third, his postgraduate education at Cambridge
University—the positivism of I. A. Richards (literature conceived "as
a special example of the neural manipulation of artificial signs")
grafted onto the "moral vision" of F. R. Leavis (with his nostalgia
for the rural, "the simplicities of village life"). Add a tour of academic

duty in the American South, trafficking with the Fugitives, and you have a mind that's predisposed to believe the West went wrong at the dawn of the Renaissance.

In other words, McLuhan isn't an accident that happened to an electric typewriter during sunspots. "His investigations of the new media," argues Dr. Miller, "are prompted in a very large measure by his eagerness to find a new form of iconic symbolism through which the redemptive mysteries of God can be experienced." Are Ted Bates, General Sarnoff and Andy Warhol aware that the hammer, the peacock and the soup can are our icons, and that God is merchandising? Probably. What they refuse to believe is that, as Dr. Miller says, "The fate of ideas and inventions is determined by the character of social institutions that choose to exploit them, and not by some hypothetical spiritual flaw ingrained in the imagination . . ." It is of institutions that McLuhan is ignorant. In our time and place, it is an insupportable ignorance.

Dr. Miller is hostile to his subject. Raymond Williams is confused about his. When Mr. Williams's essay on Orwell appeared in England, critics interpreted it in wholly contradictory ways. For example, John Wain (*The Observer*) professed to find in it "the mind of the Left establishment" at work, with "that mind's old hostility to Orwell . . . the bitter lessons Orwell learnt in Barcelona are still no more palatable now than they were then." On the other hand, Cyril Connolly (*Sunday Times*) understood the essay to be arguing that "Orwell was a pioneer of the New Left . . . In one sense this book is a refutation of Mary McCarthy's suggestion that Orwell, had he lived, might have come out on the American side in the Vietnam war."

Mr. Williams, the author of much better books (*Culture and Society, Modern Tragedy*) is at fault. A critical method that consists of the relentless propounding of paradoxes, with never a resolution to be glimpsed, leaves almost everything to be desired. At one point Mr. Williams seems to say that, although disillusioned, Orwell never became a reactionary. At another point, he appears to blame Orwell for helping to "tie the knot" of Western political thinking into the Cold War bind. One can only feel sorry for a critic who finds in Orwell's fiction little more than "defeat, self-hatred." And one can only despair of an author who says "most historians" dismiss the anarcho-syndicalist/POUM revolution in Spain as "an irrelevant distraction from a desperate war."

The image of Orwell that emerges from these pages, after all the psychologizing and sociologizing, is that of the Victim. We learn that young Eric Blair manufactured the "Orwell" persona; that his idea of England as "a family with the wrong members in control" significantly omits all mention of a "father"; that Orwell, like Huxley, Auden, Greene and Isherwood, was afflicted with the double vision of his class; and that the renunciation of an imperial identity troubles the mind. Thus, a victim. Too many subjective biases tart the apple.

Can one welcome Dr. Miller's exploration of McLuhan's "hidden bias" and deplore Mr. Williams's attempt to do the same thing to Orwell? I think so, because McLuhan in his books comes on like a Dennis the Menace, without any motives, any social context, any individual spark of pain or pleasure, so value-free one can properly wonder what if anything makes him tick; Mr. Miller tells us things about him we didn't know and couldn't possibly know from the books. Whereas Orwell was always there in his books, an individual, writing out of his viscera on a specific time, place and personal experience. Mr. Williams promiscuously couples history and suspicion, Freud and dialectics, to come up with his Victim—as we are all presumably victims, the sum of our contradictions, compost heaps of genes, nanny, prep school, war news and economic system—and the portrait just doesn't check out compared with the Orwell books. Orwell was more than a mucky determinism; McLuhan, it now seems, at least partakes like the rest of us in a few human conditions.

Mr. Williams warns against the "body-snatching" of Orwell by ideologues who want a slogan instead of the man. And, to be sure, the ideologues and end-of-ideologists have snatched a lot of bodies, as they always will when an honest man dies and they need his name for a letterhead or a blacklist. But Orwell's body is missing entirely from Mr. Williams's pages. One wishes he were alive, not merely to disappoint Mary McCarthy, but also to write a "Modern Masters" essay on the new Big Brothers our futurists bomb us with so indiscriminately. What, for example, would he have made of an electric iconography, a transistorized God with the Professor as Super-Star handling His static? Inconveniently, Orwell died. The English language and our moral perceptions still suffer from that inconvenience. Which is why Marshall McLuhan is considered a Modern Master.

(June 1971)

Camus and Fanon

The Modern Masters series, edited by Frank Kermode, consists of long essays by distinguished critics on "men who have changed and are changing the life and thought of our age." By choosing to review only two of the first three, I intend no disrespect for Alasdair MacIntyre's *Herbert Marcuse*. Mr. MacIntyre contends that "almost all of Marcuse's key positions are false," and proves it. But Marcuse, like the Hula-Hoop, seems to have had his day; even the young no longer wear his slogans as a sort of sandwich board advertising the revolution.

Whereas Albert Camus and Frantz Fanon go on speaking urgently to the contemporary sensibility. Moreover, they complement each other, having both died young without adequate replacements, having shared a language (French), a preoccupation (Algeria), a philosophical father figure (Jean-Paul Sartre) and a cultural schizophrenia (Europe versus Africa). That the white novelist and the black doctor should have arrived at such different solutions to the same moral problem (colonialism) is a tragedy more keenly felt because it appears likely to repeat itself.

Of Camus, Conor Cruise O'Brien writes: "No other writer, not even Conrad, is more representative of the Western consciousness and conscience in relation to the non-Western world. The inner drama of his work is the development of this relation, under increasing pressure and in increasing anguish . . . Imaginatively, Camus both flinched from the realities of his position as a Frenchman of Algeria, and also explored with increasing subtlety and honesty the nature and consequences of his flinching."

Thus in *The Stranger* Europeans have names, Arabs do not, not even the Arab Meursault shoots. The shooting itself is considered irrelevant. But, according to Mr. O'Brien, the killing of a man is never irrelevant. Did Camus conceive of the nameless Arab as somehow less than a man? Would a European court in Algiers sentence a European to death for killing an Arab who had drawn a knife on him? Mr. O'Brien suggests that Camus in the second half of the novel simply denies colonial reality. Like his play *Caligula, The Stranger* concerns the "truth of feeling—the artist's truth." But

Caligula carried that truth to a hideous extreme. Is it, asks Mr.
O'Brien, that *Caligula*, "fascinating but odious on the historic European stage, becomes humdrum, acceptable, and finally endearing
under the African sun"?

Mr. O'Brien's sort of socio-political criticism is likely to make assistant professors of the French novel grind their teeth. But it seems
more useful to me than the quasi-Freudian interpretation of *The
Stranger* that made the campus rounds a while ago, explaining that
the Arab was really Meursault's mother. And Mr. O'Brien makes it
work the whole of Camus's career. In *The Plague*, a journalist comes
to Oran to investigate medical conditions in the Arab quarter; once
people—all of them Europeans—start dying, we hear no more about
Arabs. There followed the break with Sartre on Algerian policy, the
anti-Communist period, the anguished stories in *Exile and the Kingdom* and, finally, *The Fall*.

O'Brien can play fast and loose, and should be watched carefully.
If he so breezily dismisses Camus's explanation of his intentions in
The Stranger, what right has he to accept at face value Simone de
Beauvoir's disingenuous assertion that *The Mandarins* was not a
roman à clef? Of course it was. And I didn't think anybody still believed that Camus won the argument with Sartre. Sartre wins most
of his arguments, which doesn't prevent him from being morally and
philosophically preposterous half the time. But O'Brien's thesis holds
some heavy water. Having chosen his mother (his roots) over justice
(independence for Algeria), Camus went on to explore the consequences brilliantly in *The Fall*. Irony became the pre-eminent Western intellectual posture toward experience.

Frantz Fanon hadn't the consolations either of irony or of the
absurd. The white intellectual could play his joke on the absurdity
of life by refusing to abide by the logic of suicide. The black intellectual, simply to survive, needed something more. Fanon found it in
"the existential necessity of collective violence for the colonized people." Violence alone, he said, "violence committed by the people
. . . organized and educated by its leaders, makes it possible for the
masses to understand social truths . . ." It is "a cleansing force," free-
ing "the native from his inferiority complex and from his despair and
inaction."

David Caute follows Fanon from his birth in the Antilles to his education in Lyons, psychiatric practice, flirtation with the "Negritude"

of Aimé Césaire and Leopold Senghor (both of whom would betray his trust when they assumed power), disappointment with the Paris intellectuals like Sartre who sponsored him, co-operation with the Algerian terrorists, diplomatic career and death from leukemia at age thirty-six. The conceptual motion is from *Black Skin, White Masks* ("rationalist-abstract methodology") to *The Wretched of the Earth* ("romantic and chiliastic" visions of a redeeming apocalypse).

If he owed his schemata to Sartre; and if the sources of his psychological theory were suspiciously eclectic; and if his acceptance of African "national" boundaries arbitrarily defined by European powers seems perverse; and if his hope for the African peasantry as a revolutionary vanguard seems vain—what does it matter? The doctor who abhorred violence became the poet-prophet of its therapeutic utility, not because of some personal aberration, but because of history. We might argue about the inevitability of that violence, but we certainly can't say we don't deserve it.

(July 1970)

Politics and Other Inadequacies

Politics

In 1968, I wanted very much to go to the Democratic Convention in Chicago. I proposed an article on the California delegation, many of whose members I knew personally, to the *Times* Sunday magazine. The Sunday magazine, alas, had classified me as a specialist in pop culture; I wrote articles on television, on Andy Warhol, on the making of a miserable movie about Che Guevara. They said no. Fortunately for me, and unfortunately for the rest of the world, the Russians chose that moment to invade Czechoslovakia. Andy Kopkind, the Washington correspondent for *The New Statesman*, rushed off to Czechoslovakia. He was to have covered the convention proceedings, inside the hall, for *The New Statesman*, while Nora Sayre, their New York correspondent, was to cover the street action. Nora had been my editor on two novels. When she was asked by *The New Statesman* to suggest a replacement for Kopkind, she suggested me. They decided to give it a try. Off I went. The articles I wrote for *The New Statesman* inspired Harold Hayes to suggest a remarkable scheme. Dwight Macdonald was then writing the "Politics" column for *Esquire*. If, by the first of each month, he hadn't turned in his copy, would I be willing to write the column by the fifteenth of the month? I was willing. As I recall, the arrangement lasted six months, during which time Macdonald generously neglected to turn in any copy at all. It was absorbing work, but frustrating, because *Esquire's* lead-time is two months. My first column was for the January issue of 1969, to appear on the newsstands in mid-December. My copy was due October 15. I was inconvenienced by the fact that nobody was certain who would be the President of the United States.

Death Wish in Chicago

The bold bumper stickers on many cars declare: "Welcome to Prague —Richard J. Daley, Mayor." And it's almost true: Richard Daley is

indeed the Tsar of all the little Prussias which Democratic Party delegates must endure this week in Chicago. The ultimate irony in the
fire is that Mayor Daley has created the perfect setting for the high-
camp exercise in suicide to which his city is the host.

This is not a political convention—it is a death rite. This evening
(Wednesday) the masked players will emerge from a dozen down-
town hotels, wearing plasticized polyurethane badges around their
necks on elastic strings. They will climb into chartered buses and
follow squad-car escorts through streets patrolled by 12,000 police
and 6,000 National Guardsmen. (Another 7,000 riot-ready federal
troops have been airlifted to Chicago on alert.) They will pass
through at least six checkpoints before penetrating the barbed-wire
ring surrounding the International Amphitheatre. They will submit
their color-coded badges to "go/no go" electronic boxes for computerized credentials-approval. They will surrender purses, bags and
envelopes to security agents for inspection against guns and bombs.
They will proceed to assigned seats and stay in those seats until the
session is adjourned. And, when the balloting begins, at least 1,312
of them will nominate Hubert Horatio Humphrey as the Democratic
Party's candidate for President.

Humphrey will lose the election to Nixon in November. The delegates know this, and have been saying it aloud since Saturday. But
the smell of the slaughterhouse which oppresses the amphitheater
area is apparently contagious. The Democratic Party, having realized
most of the domestic reforms proposed by the New Deal in the
1930's, and being unable to resolve the Southeast Asian freak-out to
which its present president has committed the country, is empty of
ideological and moral content, expects defeat and, on some guilt-
ridden substratum of the conglomerate psyche, cherishes that apocalyptic prospect. Afterward, everything will be changed . . . utterly.

Delegates will stay in their seats because there is no place for them
to go if they decide to leave early. Some 80 per cent of Chicago's
taxicabs are on strike: the drivers want bulletproof sheets to protect
themselves from passengers. Half the city's buses are inoperative. A
wildcat strike has immobilized the South Side (predominantly
black) while business as usual continues on the North Side (predominantly white).

They will nominate Humphrey—who loses two to one to Nixon

in the latest national polls—because they are no longer fit to govern. Perhaps disarray (institutional and psychological) seeks a sort of mythic disaster in the same way that consciousness (in representations of objective reality) seeks a mythic "I." Vietnam is an historical trauma from which Americans are trying to awake; disorder in the cities is an agonizing "now." Nixon is the desperate throw of the last dice available to us as we are presently defined.

The only real news from Chicago is the attempt to draft Edward Kennedy for president or vice-president: so, in myth, we lust for a prince to redeem us; failing that, we wait for a revolution. Power brokers as politically and morally opposed as Jesse Unruh (leader of the 174-man California delegation originally pledged to Robert Kennedy) and Mayor Daley, with 118 delegates (pledged to please Mayor Daley), are trying to sell the prince to his party and the party to its prince. The party hasn't collateral of nerve to buy, and the prince has an understandable disinclination to be bought. We are a nation of 200 million persons: two out of our three princes have been murdered. So let the rough beast slouch in 1968 even if his name is Nixon.

What about the alternatives to Humphrey? The South Dakota Senator, George McGovern, from a small agricultural state, is as anonymous as he is virtuous. Governor Lester Maddox . . . not even the Democratic Party of the state of Georgia likes Lester Maddox. Eugene McCarthy: his is a compound of intelligence, diffidence, arrogance, wit (immodest, always at the expense of others), epigrams, compunctions and Catholicism. He is known to loathe the Kennedys because they are "bad Catholics." He is also the kind of poet-patrician who turns off delegates because they feel he holds them in contempt. While their contemptibility may be a fact, they do not wish to certify or mythologize it.

Besides which, McCarthy is anti-government; like Eisenhower, he expresses a midwestern distrust of bureaucrats, a revulsion against "systems," a "throw-the-rascals-out" mentality. He suggests dismantling the power machine. (The youth of America have responded as much to this as to his Vietnam critique.) American youth believes itself dismissed as so many interchangeable labor units. McCarthy— throwing away his *mots* the way he has thrown away his candidacy— represents to youth a rejection of utility as the ultimate criterion of

social worth. In promising to fire General Hershey and J. Edgar
Hoover, he promises to revenge youth on the merchandisers of its
flesh. So youth volunteers itself as chauffeur, babysitter, doorbell
ringer at this convention, and convention delegates avail themselves
of the service, "value-free," impressed with the volunteers but determined to ignore the candidate. McCarthy, in Chicago, preaches
privacy to people who define themselves by public spectacle.

Without McCarthy, though, death in Chicago would be wholly
meaningless. McCarthy is the first pure product of a "new politics"
which John Kennedy suggested in 1960: beat the professionals.
There are constituencies beyond the province of the power brokers;
white youth refusing to be technological managers; black youth refusing to be a service pool; blue collar and white collar alike rejecting corporate depersonalization; an entire country full of individuals
deciding that they don't want to be sub-humanized. The Kennedys,
John and Robert, scared the power brokers: McCarthy ignores them.
Assassins in book depositories and hotel kitchens have made sure
the brokers win this round, but this round may very well be the last
whimper. When Humphrey loses the election, a manipulative system
will have lost its thumbs: it will be able to scratch itself, but nothing
more.

Meanwhile, the forms, the rituals remain. They are being played
out this week in Chicago with the rejection of challenges to lily-white
delegations from the South and the endorsement of Lyndon Johnson's foreign policies. They will continue to be played out in September and October, with Nixon submitting his own color-coded ("law
and order") card to the electric box of public opinion. Like the devices at the International Amphitheatre, that November box will be
incapable of subtle distinction-making, of moral and/or aesthetic
judgments. After it registers its "go," civil strife, counter-insurgency
and the polarization of races and regions will be licensed. There will
be a binge of death so extravagant that even Mayor Daley may experience unease. And after the binge my country will embark upon a
renewal program in which there are no Chicagos. Since every other
industrialized country in the world will have to face the same problem, I can only hope the ritual is worth this week's awful risk.

(*New Statesman*, August 30, 1968)

The Democratic Happening

A critic like Susan Sontag should have been assigned to review it: *The Persecution and Assassination of the Democratic Party as performed by the Inmates of the Asylum in Chicago under the Direction of Mayor Richard J. Daley*, with Hubert Humphrey as the Noël Coward of the Theatre of Cruelty. Miss Sontag has called madness "an authentic metaphor for passion" and happenings "an art of radical juxtapositions." Seldom in the history of American party conventions have the juxtapositions been more radical, and the metaphors more maddening, than last week. Outside: nightsticks, tear gas, jeeps, Mace, baby-blue riot helmets, fixed bayonets, barbed wire and blood. Inside: security guards bullying delegates; security guards passing out stacks of Humphrey posters before the nominating roll call; security guards illegally admitting Daley's hired claque through back doors, to expropriate the press galleries.

"There is something comic in the modern experience as such," writes Miss Sontag, "a demonic, not a divine comedy, precisely to the extent that modern experience is characterized by meaningless mechanized situations of disrelation." On Monday, one watched six members of the Missouri delegation wandering outside the LaSalle Hotel, with wine glasses in their hands, shouting: "We're uncommitted! Who'll buy the drinks?" On Tuesday one watched Humphrey's floor leaders scurry up amphitheater aisles to squash a revolt that almost seated the entire insurgent Georgia delegation. On Wednesday afternoon, after the minority report (the "peace plank") on Vietnam was voted down, the brass band broke into a medley of martial tunes: the Air Force, Army, Navy and Marine anthems. The convention recessed for hot dogs and caucusing. New York delegates stood, joined hands, and sang *We Shall Overcome*, and the band tried to drown them out, quitting only when it realized it wasn't being paid to play at intermissions.

On Wednesday evening, while American youth was (in Senator McGovern's words) "being savagely beaten in the streets for opposing the war in Vietnam," Mayor Daley endured a public attack on his fiefdom which so flustered him he forgot what act of the charade was on and delivered Illinois to Humphrey at least two hours before he was supposed to. The New York Democratic candidate for U. S. Senator was thrown off the convention floor. Dissidents submitted to the convention the name of the Reverend Channing Phillips, the first black ever to be nominated by a major party for the presidency; he got sixty-seven votes. Lyndon Johnson's cheerleader got 1,761. Delegates pledged to other candidates and policies paraded from the amphitheater, with candles, to join at dawn the demonstrators grouped before the Hilton.

On Thursday the chairman of the New Hampshire delegation was set upon by three security guards, hustled in a headlock from the hall and arrested for having proved the electronic badge-checking devices fallible. Following a twenty-two-minute memorial film on the late Robert F. Kennedy (four years ago, at Atlantic City, there was another memorial film; they have box office appeal), delegates and alternates from California, New York, Wisconsin and South Dakota began spontaneously to sing *The Battle Hymn of the Republic*. This time Mayor Daley was prepared. He had packed the galleries with his municipal serfs; at his signal, they shouted down the *Hymn* with chants of "We Love Daley." A different hymn for a different Republic.

Senator Edmund Muskie of Maine was approved as Humphrey's running mate; and Humphrey, at length, accepted what a dispirited and fearful convention offered him. His speech, wily references to "the politics of yesterday" notwithstanding, proved principally his inability to inspire. One doubts that Humphrey could inspire bacilli to connive at anthrax.

"As in tragedy," writes Miss Sontag, "every comedy needs a scapegoat, someone who will be punished and expelled from the social order represented mimetically in the spectacle." Not Mayor Daley— for Humphrey, like George Wallace and Ronald Reagan, has absolved Daley: "We ought to quit pretending that Mayor Daley did something wrong." Perhaps, then, Eugene McCarthy? The Chicago police thought so, invading his fifteenth-floor Conrad Hilton headquarters at 5 A.M. on Friday (someone had dropped beer cans out of a window) to drag his staff from their beds and beat them. (There were no arrests; actual arrests in Chicago were surprisingly few: since the Supreme Court has so complicated police procedure with civil rights, it is simpler just to club people and leave them bleeding on the pavement.)

If not McCarthy, then it may be as Miss Sontag says: "In the happening, this scapegoat is the audience." A member of the audience, Walter Cronkite, told millions of prime-time TV watchers on Wednesday, "I want to pack my bags and get out of this city." Having been clubbed myself that night, I heartily agreed. But the following morning, TV and subversives were blamed, not the police. Stand next to someone who calls a Chicago cop a "pig," and you are provoking the cop to assault and battery.

The Democratic happening will run on until November, mixing media and meanings. Humphrey's first post-convention appearance was symbolic: in New York City's Labor Day parade, flanked by George Meany and Louis Stulberg. To such labor chieftains as Meany; to the South; to the party machinery; to a clutch of vice-presidential hopefuls; and to Lyndon Johnson he owes his nomination. Labor can no longer deliver the vote. The South will go for Nixon or Wallace. Johnson is an albatross. And the party machinery —well, McCarthy's children's crusade proved that there are no professional secrets. The machine can be beaten by amateurs. So Humphrey will seek suburbia. Like Nixon. And like Nixon, he has identified "law and order" as the crucial issue of 1968. Nixon, however, got there first, and, with the Soviet invasion of Czechoslovakia, emerges as the odds-on favorite, the experienced professional anti-Communist capable of tough talking to the Red monolith. Barring the success of the Paris peace talks in the next seven months, Humphrey looks like a loser.

A loser, too, will be the attempt to launch a new party of the Left, sponsored by Marcus Raskin of the Institute for Policy Studies in Washington. It's too late to get on the ballot in most states; and the party would suffer the additional humiliation of coming in a poor fourth behind George Wallace, who may well receive 20 per cent of the national vote. The theater is cruel, indeed.

What, then? Revolution? Were the young men and women of the McCarthy crusade sufficiently radicalized to take to the streets, to seek in "confrontation" a more promising theater, in stink bombs a more transcendent happening? I think not. Those I talked to in Chicago were determined to return to their states and cities, to work for congenial candidates on every municipal level and to apply their new expertise to the task of rebuilding the party from the bottom up. In nine months they had retired an incumbent President; inspired

the Paris negotiations; abolished the unit rule for convention delegations; and come within 200 votes of repudiating our Vietnam adventure entirely. They won the primaries; they have four years to
win the rest of the states. They, and Jesse Unruh of California and
George McGovern of South Dakota, were the real heroes of
Chicago, among the few who could retire with honor and begin the
reconstruction.

The revolutionary happening is going to be a very bad scene.
Young white radicals who think they now know what it's like to be
black in America have much to learn. Their skulls were dented, but
they lived to complain about it. There were many in Chicago's black
ghettos not so fortunate last April, in the riots following the assassination of Martin Luther King. And in Watts, Cleveland, the
District of Columbia. A technological state—with the manpower,
money, mobility, communications and counter-insurgency scenarios
of this nation—won't play games with Tom Hayden much longer,
whether Nixon or Humphrey is grand master.

Games, happenings, theater . . . I have indulged my Marat/Sade
conceit because the conceit itself is a diseased culture, a gang of
bacilli promoting moral anthrax. Institutions exist to mediate between our natural imperfections and our noble abstractions (like
justice). The mood of America may be at present anti-institutional,
anti-manipulative, anti-power, and therefore pro-happening, but
when the happening has happened, when the strobes die, all the
pieces remain to be picked up and put together again. Coherence is
as important to a society as it is to a personality, and it is achieved
by interpreting the data, checking them against the ideal, and trying
to bring data and ideal into reasonable approximation. Which means
values and work. Our whole culture is on a "value-free" binge, not
just Richard Daley and Lyndon Johnson with their Vietnam and Conrad Hilton things. Miss Sontag, Herman Kahn, Marshall McLuhan,
Andy Warhol, Timothy Leary—all have gone off on a trip into the
anti-rational; all resist interpretation of a moral, or consequential,
nature. Since interpretation is the basis of knowledge, all propose a
kind of idiocy. One side wears baby-blue riot helmets; the other is a
stylistic amalgam derived from Castro and Godard; the TV audience tunes in, not with the hope of a pity-and-terror catharsis, but
with a lust for titillation—to embrace the dark.

Whether it's Nixon or Humphrey, the next four years will mean the end of the New Deal, and of the Democratic Party as we know it. It will not mean the end of institutions, of power, of programming. The year 1972 will belong either to the young men and young women who left Chicago grimly determined to take over the institutions, or it will belong to the death merchants. Doubtless the anti-programmatic Left will reply to all this with incantations of Lord Acton's maxim. But—as John Roche once said of Arthur Schlesinger, Jr.—if power corrupts, lack of power corrupts absolutely.

(New Statesman, September 6, 1968)

The Conspiracy

Indignation may be a finite resource. Perhaps, because we've gone to the faucet so often in recent years, at last the tank is dry. The trial of the Chicago 8—accused of conspiring to embarrass the Democratic Party in August 1968—seems not to have inspired the lavish front-page coverage accorded earlier plays from the same school of farce. And yet, as Rennie Davis remarks in this paperback quickie, eight men have been arraigned before Judge Julius Hoffman in a United States District Court "on charges of crossing state lines with an unlawful frame of mind."

In *The Conspiracy* those eight men speak, along with their lawyers and Noam Chomsky, who contributes a self-indulgent introduction. Their voices are variously hortatory (Tom Hayden, Bobby Seale), thoughtful (Davis, John Froines, David Dellinger) and perverse (Abbie Hoffman, of course, and Jerry Rubin, of course). They agree on what they oppose: war, racism, capitalism and the military-industrial complex. And they appear also to agree that they will ultimately beat the "elitists," because, as Rubin puts it, "we're stealing their children."

Dellinger offers a useful "movement" history from the early civil rights campaigns through the betrayal of the Mississippi Freedom Democratic Party at Atlantic City in 1964 to the Chicago confrontation. Froines, a physical chemist, warns fellow activists that technology itself is not the enemy: "There is no reason to do without cars, electronic music, radio communication, films, refrigerators,

photoduplicators, and the like . . . What we want to do in this country is . . . to separate the knowledge we have from the dehumanized, corporate structure that now controls knowledge and the uses
to which it is put."

Davis reports on his most recent trip to North Vietnam—he was
helping arrange the release of American prisoners—with emphasis on
a visit to Vinhlinh near the DMZ. American planes have dropped
thirteen tons of bombs for every person in Vinhlinh, and Vinhlinh's
response has been to build an underground city.

Rubin wings it: "Thirty thousand people in jail in the USA because they smoke flowers!" And: "The entire school system is a crime
against young people . . . like take a baby—a baby is totally curious,
wants to touch everything, feel everything, be everywhere. The society has got to take the baby's curiosity and turn it into a machine
that works for pieces of paper—grades, money, external things."

Then there's Hoffman—Abbie not Julius. He can be funny, telling
a Walker Commission investigator that he favors the overthrow of
the government "by any means necessary. I'd prefer to see it be done
with bubble gum, but I'm having some doubts." But he bad-
mouths a lot of people, like the Mobilization and Martin Luther King.
He even bad-mouths Allen Ginsberg, which is like Dennis the
Menace bad-mouthing St. Francis of Assisi.

Finally, and of much more importance than the predictable
rhetoric of the defendants themselves, there are the lawyers. What
they have to say is straightforward and, to me at least, undeniable.
The Chicago 8 *are* being tried under an anti-riot provision of the
1968 Civil Rights Act (sometimes called the Stokely Carmichael
Amendment because it was so obviously aimed at him) which purports to read the minds of people who cross state lines and end up
participating in demonstrations permitted by the First Amendment.
Whether the anti-riot law is even constitutional remains to be seen.

Their lawyers certainly seem to have been harassed. Judge Hoffman issued bench warrants for the arrest of four lawyers, although
three had notified him that they had been engaged only to prepare
pre-trial motions, and the fourth had been released by the defendants to continue with a separate case. (The warrants for two of the
lawyers were quashed; the other two are appealing.) Their rights
under the Fourth Amendment appear to have been compromised by

the use of wiretapping and other electronic surveillance, contrary to
the 1969 Alderman decision of the Supreme Court. It is an elastic
definition of "national security," indeed, that denies the Chicago 8
defense transcripts of that surveillance while giving away, in Newark,
New Jersey, twelve volumes of Mafia eavesdropping, supposedly because of the Alderman decision.

There is no mention in this book of the binding and gagging of
Bobby Seale, presumably because it happened after the book went
to press. But the foregoing points would certainly seem to support
David Dellinger's contention that the Chicago 8—prominent radicals,
all—were arbitrarily fingered by the Justice Department (as, in a tit-
for-tat, eight Chicago policemen were chosen as scapegoats) to stand
political trial.

Oh, for the good old days of what Herbert Marcuse has called
"repressive tolerance." Herbert Marcuse, as a matter of fact, might
just as well be Attorney General. Which points up one weakness in
Jerry Rubin's argument that the dissenters are winning: the American people appear willing to suffer such a trial in silence, or approv-
ingly. Perhaps they can no longer tell the difference between Abbie
Hoffman's put-ons and Bobby Seale's travail. And that is dangerous.

(November 1969)

The Tales of Hoffman

The trial of the Chicago 8 (minus one) took five months and used
up 22,000 pages of official transcript. Two lawyers and a member of
the New York Stock Exchange have boiled those months and that
transcript down to 286 pages, to which the indefatigable Dwight
Macdonald has contributed an introduction. The result is a sometimes hilarious, often disturbing and always engrossing slice of documentary history.

There are, of course, difficulties. The editors, not without a sense
of the theatrical, choose consistently to emphasize occasions of
farce and confrontation; to indulge, as would any playwright, those
explosive instances during which Judge Hoffman, and counsel for
defense and prosecution, and the defendants and the audience re-

veal themselves in emotional dishabille. Much of the trial's substance is only hinted at. The reader never gets a clear idea of the government's case; details of that case as it pertained to individual defendants are omitted even from the summation by Assistant United States Attorney Richard G. Schultz.

Another difficulty derives from the nature of that beast, the paperback quickie, a premature child of yesterday's headlines. While it's being glued together, fresh dispatches arrive too late from the front. Thus Thomas A. Foran's cross-examination of Allen Ginsberg, alluding to homosexual elements in his poetry, seems not only immaterial (why didn't the bench say so?) but inexplicable—until we read of Mr. Foran's post-trial statements referring to "a freaking fag revolution." (Mr. Foran apparently plans to run for political office on a platform of short-haired heterosexuality.) And thus the defense's hope for a hung jury seems in retrospect a fantasy, now that we have the serialized true confessions of one of the jurors.

Nevertheless, *The Tales of Hoffman* is invaluable as the first big chunk of official transcript available for inspection, permitting us to experience for ourselves what might have been only partially perceived from reports in daily newspapers, newsmagazines, and on television. (It's worth noting that if one read nothing but *The Village Voice* during those five months, one would have had to depend on Jules Feiffer's cartoons for first-hand observation on the trial; every week, Michael Zwerin dragging himself about Europe, but no reporter filing regularly from Chicago.) We can generalize on evidence instead of ideology.

From the transcript it seems that Judge Hoffman was guilty of the original provocation. On the first day he tried to jail four lawyers who had helped the defense prepare pre-trial motions. He subsequently refused a postponement for Bobby Seale until Seale's lawyer recovered from an operation, and denied his request to defend himself. He ridiculed defense counsel, implying eventual contempt citations for them. He systematically mangled the name of a defense attorney, Leonard Weinglass, for five months calling him Weinron, Feinstein, Weinramer, Fineglass, Weingrass. He would not declare Mayor Richard J. Daley a hostile witness, or permit either Ramsey Clark or Ralph Abernathy to testify for the defense. His contempt citations before the jury's verdict, and his maximum penalties, denial of bail and (incredibly) assessment of prosecution costs after the verdict add up to something considerably less than dispassionate justice.

So far *The Tales of Hoffman* substantiates received wisdom. But what are we to make of a defense request to take a day off to participate in the Vietnam Moratorium? Of the attempt to present a birthday cake to Bobby Seale in court? Of the proposed "moment of silence" for Martin Luther King and the proposed recess on the occasion of Fred Hampton's death? Of the bathroom antics and the judicial robes? Defense attorney William Kunstler referred once to opposing counsel as "acting like a dirty old man" and another time as acting "like a little boy" running to the bench to "tattle."

Dwight Macdonald knows what to make of all this: in today's political trial, "as in the Living Theatre and other avant-garde dramatic presentations," everybody gets into the act. The Chicago trial "is the richest specimen of the new free-form trial to date, owing to the ingenious tactics of the defense (and the Judge's collaboration)." Guerrilla theater, right? Intended to demonstrate the bankruptcy of our judicial system, right? *But does it? The Tales of Hoffman* and later interviews with jurors indicate that had the defendants played it straight, they would have gotten off. And their appeal will probably succeed. What has been proved?

Now, has their conviction radicalized the nation? Apparently not. Has it exposed our courts? A circus isn't justice, and both Hoffmans conspired at a circus. There's something important at issue here—after we let historians decide how Judge Hoffman got assigned to this case; why he tried to play Abbie Hoffman's game; whether Mr. Kunstler, against his better professional judgment, was obliged by his clients to join the scrummage; what kind of Justice Department seeks such indictments; and who knows which secrets lurk in the hearts of men when they cross state lines in invisible frames of mind?

At issue is our idea of man, and therefore what system of adjudication best serves him. If we believe with Abbie Hoffman that reality is what TV shows us, or with Jerry Rubin that, somehow, computers will free us to do whatever we want, then institutions are indeed obsolete; we need only consult our senses. If, on the other hand, we suspect ourselves of demonic capacities, then institutions

(political organizations, judicial systems) are necessary to protect
not only society (variously organized) but the self (variously vulnerable and dangerous). I think even a jerk like Jerry Rubin needs more
than "free-form" protection against other people's fanged perceptions.

(April 1970)

Show Biz and Serious Biz

With *Thirty Years of Treason*, Eric Bentley has given us an absorbing but troubling book. He has edited the history of the House
Committee on Un-American Activities down to a harlequinade,
condensing three decades and hundreds of thousands of pages of
witness, entreaty, indignation, defamation and groveling to a single
volume. Because he is a Brecht scholar, drama critic and professor
of dramatic literature, Mr. Bentley's habit of mind is theatrical—
as, indeed, were the habits of HCUA—and it is natural that he
should emphasize the theatrical elements of his material. Thus there
is much about the Hollywood Ten (screenwriters, movie stars: show
biz) and nothing about Alger Hiss (serious biz), lots of drama and
not much tragedy. Instead of catharsis, emetic—just like the Living
Theatre. Our past is perceived to be a sort of metaphysical pratfall.
We laugh at it.

And yet . . . earlier this month a story appeared in the *Times*
about some victims of that very same past, that HCUA psychology,
at which it was impossible to laugh. The Board of Education is considering ways and means of reinstating thirty-one former teachers
who were dismissed from the city school system in the early 1950's
for refusing to answer questions about possible membership in the
Communist Party. All thirty-one, ranging in service from ten to
thirty years, had been discharged under laws and statutes that were
later declared unconstitutional by the Supreme Court. They are not
glamorous movie stars; they don't make good copy; still, they can't
teach in our public schools.

Not exactly a laughing matter. But then our whole approach to
the past, even the recent past, has taken on a theatrical cast, much
like *Thirty Years of Treason*. By superimposing one or another

aesthetic form on one or another misshapen reality, we "distance" ourselves from the reality. We handle it by making it "unreal." Three and a half years ago, reporting for *The New Statesman* on the Democratic Convention, I called it *"The Persecution and Assassination of the Democratic Party as performed by the Inmates of the Asylum under the Direction of Mayor Richard J. Daley,* with Hubert Humphrey as the Noël Coward of the Theatre of Cruelty." A with-it kind of cleverness; very dramatic. But did it approximate the reality of nightsticks, barbed wire, fixed bayonets and blood? It did not.

Two years ago an account of Norman Mailer's mayoralty campaign, *Running Against the Machine*, was published, full of position papers and proposals that few of us had paid any attention to during the primary. They were good proposals: monorails, Sweet Sunday, neighborhood housing banks, free bicycles in city parks, day-care centers and nurseries, no traffic allowed on the island of Manhattan except for buses, trucks and cabs, more zoos, bonuses for policemen who lived in the neighborhoods they patrolled, abolition of the Surrogate Court, locally controlled cable TV. Why hadn't we taken them seriously at the time of the campaign? Partly, perhaps, because Mailer-Breslin vaudevillified themselves in the primary; but also because we had been conditioned to take them metaphorically, not literally. We perceived it as a light show, a novel, stagecraft, "Laugh-In." Like HCUA.

A year and a half ago a paperback book called *The Tales of Hoffman* appeared, in some ways very much like *Thirty Years of Treason*. It dealt with the trial of the Chicago 8. Five months and 22,000 pages of official transcript were boiled down to 286 pages. The editors, like Mr. Bentley—and like the principals in the case, the Hoffmans Abbie and Julius—had a theatrical habit of mind. All the *Sturm und Drang* was in the book, but no clear idea of, among other things, the government's case. Details of that case were omitted even from the assistant U.S. attorney's summation. Dwight Macdonald, in his introduction, treated the whole thing metaphorically: in today's political trial, "as in the Living Theatre and other avant-garde dramatic presentations," everybody gets into the act; this trial was "the richest specimen of the new free-form trial to date." But at issue, in reality, was a law that seemed to say you can be prosecuted for crossing state lines in an invisible frame of mind. If everybody hadn't turned the trial into a guerrilla circus, we might

have tested that law. It's still on the statute books, against which we
pit jokebooks.

All the "meta" words come to mind: *metaphor* (the application
of a word or phrase to an object or concept it does not literally de-
note) *metastasizes* (transfers malignant cells to other parts of the
body by way of the blood vessels, lymphatics or membranous surfaces). Instead of *metaphrasis* (changing a literary work from one
form to another, as prose into verse), we have *metamorphosis* (a
complete change of form, structure, or substance, as in transforma-
tion by magic or witchcraft). The "work" is reality; the "body" is
the body politic; the "metaphor" is a convention of art; the "transfer of malignant cells" is the packaging of reality, the merchandising
of it as "entertainment" for conspicuous consumption, not education for change or even a simple answer to the question, What the
hell was going on?

This psychology of entertainment, of confection, of packaging,
of history as a Creative Plaything, extends beyond books to every
manifestation of social reality. Each day becomes, in newspapers and
magazines, a nonfiction novel. Yesterday gets parajournalized. Politics is street theater. We petition the media, instead of the government, for redress of grievances. The eleven o'clock eye-witless news
turns Vietnam and police corruption into *shticks*. The President
of the United States comes on like "Heeeere's Dicky!"—government
by pop-goes-the-weasel. Our vocabularies can't get into reasonable
approximation with personal sensations and public events. For the
young, everything is "like, wow!" or "you know, man," when in fact
we don't know—and, like *what?* For our leaders, "elimination with
extreme prejudice" means murder. And all the little boys have cried
Tom Wolfe so often—the hors d'oeuvres at the party matter more
than the money for the breakfast program, right?—that we no longer
believe there was an event at all, much less the little boy in the white
suit with the cap pistol pretending to report it.

A peculiar and distorting habit of mind has metastasized a salesman's sensibility on the part of the reporter, a jaded consumer's sensibility on the part of the audience. We are ravenous for gobbets of
the absurd, and retreat wildly from calcified facts, consequences for
which there are no literary or pop cultural analogues. Irony—the
irony of the observer, the voyeur—strikes an attitude like a match,
and, also like a match, in burning consumes itself. We seem to have

decided, first, that we couldn't control the modern experience (death camps, atom bombs), "a demonic comedy," as Susan Sontag described it, "characterized by meaningless mechanized situations of disrelation"; and so we postured in front of that experience. But, as Miss Sontag continued, "as in tragedy, every comedy needs a scapegoat, someone who will be punished and expelled from the social order represented mimetically in the spectacle." Who? "In the happening, this scapegoat is the audience."

Indeed. The happening. And then what? The scapegoat stops doing anything, even posturing. He becomes a screen on which the dramatist, parajournalist or director projects comic strip images of events as they have been aesthetically modified or out-takes of the recording ego it hurt too much to omit because the ego considers itself more interesting than the event. When the film strip ends, so does the energy, which came from the projector. It is a manipulation, aesthetic instead of historical, which simply stops when the lights go on. Unfortunately, reality doesn't stop. It goes on outside the cave, outside the ego, outside Lincoln Center, in the form of thirty-one schoolteachers or a political party or the voters of New York or death camps. Outside, the season's subscription is lifelong, and it is the metaphor which is laughable.

(December 1971)

Confessions of a Structure Freak

The Flower Brigade lost its first battle, but watch out, America. We were poorly equipped with flowers from uptown florists. Already there is talk of growing our own. Plans are being made to mine the East River with daffodils. Dandelion chains are being wrapped around induction centres. Holes are being dug in street pavements with seeds dropped in and covered. The cry of "Flower Power" echoes through the land. We shall not wilt.

ABBIE HOFFMAN

Richard Nixon backed into the presidency despite himself, winning only a single major American city, Los Angeles (by 48 to 46 per cent). That leaves half of America in opposition, and it's worth wondering how the opposition will express itself. For many, Mr. Nixon's ordination has inspired an existential sulk: they will suck on their alienation until their teeth fall out. For most, it means four years of surly acquiescence: waiting for Teddy. For some, it will excuse a libidinal ferocity (cf. Abbie Hoffman): guerrilla theater, the blown mind, the merchandising of the myth of a superior sexuality—even as the ghettos burn and the Mafia controls the drug trade and middle-class dropouts wearing love beads wander the white rooms of sanitaria or are found beatifically raped to death in city cellars.

Which leaves the blacks, the New Politicians and the activist Left. The blacks will take care of themselves; they have to, since their friends are habitually assassinated. The New Politicians will, hopefully, go on tinkering with institutional mechanisms—we cannot help but profit from their work. The activist Left, however—with its youth, idealism, energy and commitment; its sense of identity; its loosely affiliated communal forms; its toleration of disparate life styles and its tough-mindedness—could represent our best hope of finding out if there *is* an "alternative culture" and whether it will work. The young Leftists, like primitive Christians, might in their caves be polishing a redemptive truth to use against our thralldom to plastic. But what do they propose to do for the next four years? They propose relentlessly to CONFRONT: part sulk and part ferocity, hoping for a repression because repression invites apocalypse. Repression is *Father*.

I don't ordinarily aspire to confessional literature, but the promise of the young Left is sufficiently bright, and the prospect of permanent confrontations sufficiently dreary, to spur an exercise in reminiscence —the recorded qualms of a "structure freak." In the summer of 1967 I joined a Cambridge-based, quasi-New Left, national "umbrella" organization co-ordinating the activities of five hundred community-action groups against the Vietnam war. The action groups canvassed their local communities, collected signatures on petitions, established neighborhood study groups, staffed draft-counseling centers and worked for anti-war referenda. Our Cambridge office was a clearing house for literature and a communications headquarters. For the standard Movement subsistence wage of twenty-eight dollars a week, I handled national publicity for the effort. (The Left, like Andy Warhol, stoops obediently to service the Media Cow: the electronic udder. We learned early on to petition the media instead of the government for redress of grievances.)

They were exciting months, before McCarthy's New Hampshire, Kennedy's Los Angeles, Daley's Chicago. Grouped at midnight around the tribal drum of our mimeograph machine, among envelope flap lickers and bloody-thumbed guitarists, high on cigarettes and Cokes and miserable puns, we felt meaningful. The war *was* an umbrella under which those of various ideological persuasions and various shades of shagginess could gather: Harvard professors, clergymen, SNCC operatives, Reconciliation Fellows, rent-a-radicals leased for the summer from SDS and NCNP, and strays like me from what Michael Harrington called "the conscience constituency." There were the usual offenses against a humanist sensibility. Martin Luther King was trundled out at cocktail parties, a black saint on roller skates, to shuck the moneyed liberals for us, while behind his broad back the pygmies hissed of Uncle Tomism. We did our best to exploit the death of a young Movement man in Texas, trying to make martyrdom of what seems merely to have been misfortune. Nomenclature was debased: "war criminals," "storm troopers," "fascist pigs." (Dean Rusk speaks of "freedom"; Madison Avenue hails a "revolutionary" new miracle ingredient; John Hatchett says Hubert Humphrey is a "racist bastard"; the Central Committee of the Chinese Communist Party calls Liu Shao-chi "a traitor, renegade and scab . . . lackey of imperialism, revisionism and the Kuomintang." A gangster language is loose in the streets. Brutalize language, and you brutalize the sensations and insights it is supposed to approximate.) But at least we were *doing something.* We knew we were, because our telephones were tapped.

One incident suggests the heady atmosphere of such an operation. A colleague of mine, brought to Cambridge for his experience at raising money for Movement causes, drafted a fund appeal letter and submitted it to the steno pool. The steno pool refused to type it. When he angrily demanded to know why, the steno pool informed him that they thought it a poor letter. He replied that it wasn't their business to pass judgment on his prose; his business was to raise money; their business was to type letters. Elitism! More especially, sexism. The steno pool was composed of volunteers, not servants; most of them were Radcliffe girls; and if they didn't like his letter, they weren't going to type it. He was obliged to tear up three drafts before they were satisfied. And the radical elite, with its "participatory" rhetoric collapsed around its knees, resolved to let "the clerical staff participate in political work," which meant the women could talk to field organizers on the WATS line. The male elite never did get around, however, to joining the steno pool for an hour or two of typing. That would have been an insupportable thing to do to their *machismo*.

But as Labor Day loomed, the problems of an "unstructured" political enterprise multiplied. Our "non-leaders" could seldom be found because they were caucusing on what attitude to take at the forthcoming New Politics convention in Chicago. Our college volunteers prepared to go back to school. Our high school volunteers deserted their posts to mobilize for the march on the Pentagon. Our fund-raising program ground to a halt because the rented radicals refused to divulge their lists of philanthropic prospects; they were saving the fattest cats for a fall hustle by their own organizations. There were enervating arguments: was "middle-class organizing" worth our revolutionary wile (this when the blacks ordered all honkies off their turf; when blue-collar whites kicked around our canvassers; when our entire "constituency," with or without "conscience," was irremediably middle-class)? Was a third party worth the money and energy it would exhaust (here McCarthy, within the "system," proved more revolutionary than anyone outside of it)? Ought any sort of national office be maintained at all, smacking as it did of "centralized control" (the office was abandoned, leaving newly formed community-action groups without a national identity, a literature supply or money; but then, it was argued, if those groups couldn't "swim in the sea of the people," their revolutionary consciousness was "insufficiently developed")? There was, finally, a profound structure fatigue, a longing for the romance of the streets. It was a dress rehearsal for the disaster of the New Politics convention itself, where formlessness and guilt conspired at a rite of self-castration that might have been choreographed by William F. Buckley, Jr.: White Virgin, Black Dynamo . . . One's metaphoric retch exceeds one's metaphoric gasp.

It isn't my intention to make that summer sound comic-operatic. They were among the best people I've met in my life. They were right about the war, and the connection between adventurism abroad and neglect at home, before most of us admitted it. They forsook the industrial money teat and the monastic sanctuary of graduate school, to put their bodies where their mouths were. I saw many of them in Chicago last August, getting their skulls smashed in front of the Conrad Hilton. (It is significant, though, that the McCarthy-Kennedy forces, by retiring an incumbent President and abolishing the unit rule, achieved more in Chicago than the demonstrators did. After the agony, there were polls, and the polled approved repression.) Many have gone to jail for resisting the draft. Their courage should shame the professional indignitaries who only rarely sprain a wrist from so much petition-signing. But they are, I think, "anti-structure freaks," fetishists of formlessness. They think of their tactics as guerrilla-like, but there is no people-sea for them to swim in. If they can't convert their mothers and fathers, their own middle-class neighborhoods, how the hell do they think they're going to convert the nation? By swimming in the media-sea? It isn't a sea; it's a bank of unblinking eyes which register every extravagance of motion on the electric moonscape. Petition it all you like; what it wants is your pictorial grievance; it lacks the capacity to redress.

Confrontations make a lot of motion on the moonscape. Like the rest of us, the young Left loves a mythological representation of itself. (This magazine was not long ago bemused by the myth of Sonny Liston; *Ramparts* is presently obsessed with the Black Panthers. Liston met Ali; the Panthers have been politically co-opted. Both myths combine sexuality and terror and fantasy—sometimes media-inspired—to whose psychological seed there's not much point in penetrating here.) The mythological representation of the young Left right now is a compound of Che Guevara and Jean-Luc Godard: costumes, an infatuation with violence, a desire for the cinemascopic gesture, a lust for martyrdom (so long as there's a lawyer to defend you and someone else to raise the bail money), maidens waiting for the roan stallion of the apocalypse. This makes for good psychodrama and poor politics.

Poor politics because technology appears pretty much irreversible in its centralizing imperative. In store for us, unless we come up with some managers who know *how* to manage and are determined to do it along moral lines, are "knowledge banks" capable of blasting electronically coded messages directly into our nervous systems (bypassing consciousness itself); "genetic banks" hoarding reproductive cells for the artificial insemination of a super-race; programmed dreams; human hibernation. Reality for us *right now* is the love-nesting of the aerospace industry, the Pentagon and the relevant congressional committees. Reality is the $50,000,000,000 antiballistic missile system Nixon will approve . . . the CIA . . . Hoover and Hershey . . . the modern university . . . that overdevelopment of capital which requires a new definition of "imperialism" (the exploited country is the Mother Country—us; certainly we do not hope to steal from Vietnam a colonial profit in tin, or rubber, or betel nuts; the tax-payer at home is the well-wrung washrag in this particular bath, and the parent whose son dies for Lockheed). To that reality and that prospect, the *Berkeley Barb* responds by shouting that "the universities cannot be reformed" and summons shock troops to "ravage college campuses, burning books, busting up classrooms, and freeing our brothers from the prison of the university."

The task of the young Left should be to create parallel or *alternative* institutions—schools, city councils, courts, etc.—to propose solutions which, even if they are not adopted, stand as possibilities. The task is to build an information-retrieval system (Yes!) capable of documenting connections between business and labor and politics and education, instead of a slogan factory turning out placards. The task is to commit oneself to sustained work on almost any social level, instead of sporadic gestures contributing to nothing more edifying than a revolutionary folklore, the mythological dump of losers.

The task, in fact, hasn't changed since Paul Goodman wrote about it last June in *Commentary:* "To concentrate exclusively on 'gut' issues is to be finally irrelevant and, paradoxically, merely symbolic. Gut issues like the draft, police brutality, or rent gouging are, of course, *prima facie* and must be met; they create hot commitment and solidarity; they might have some immediate tangible payoff. But they do not address the tremendous questions of our times which will determine our fate, including the fate of gut issues: How to prevent nuclear war? How to avert ecological catastrophe? How to use modern technology? What to automate and what not to automate? What and how to decentralize? What should Research & Development policy be? What is a possible structure of mass education that will not process and brainwash? What kind of help ought to be given to underdeveloped regions? How to cope with galloping urbanization? How to weaken the nation-states?"

Young Leftists have brought back into our vocabulary the old, messy and important words—hope, evil, idolatry, personal dignity. With the New Politicians working on the inside, and the New Left on the outside, there can be a genuine alternative to Nixon and the other America he so perfectly reflects. But the alternative must be planned; the knowledge must be acquired; the power must be rationally deployed; the development must be managed. Change requires brains and work unless, like a fire, it is only to destroy. The media will cover the fires, all right. To set them is to play the media game.

(Esquire, February 1969)

P.S. The foregoing mishmash seems now by turns naïve and incomprehensible. Since it was written, there have been communes, bank burnings, bombs, women's liberation, the satanism of a Charles Manson, the Jesus freaks, Ralph Nader. Especially, of course, Ralph Nader, whose raiders represent the "information-retrieval" system I was talking about, and whose reports have managed to penetrate even the cerebellum of General Motors. Time caught up with the aerospace industry. The fate of Democratic Party reform is yet to be determined. Chappaquiddick. George Jackson. The states of Kent and Jackson. Pentagon Papers. Nixon will go to China without a wage increase. If there is a counter-culture outside of the fantasy projections of magazine editors and television executives, it has split up and gone off in two equally mindless directions, the pot-heads and the violence-heads. The young Left never even learned how to take care of its own, much less the rest of the country.

(December 1971)

James Simon Kunen's *The Strawberry Statement*
Dotson Rader's *I Ain't Marchin' Anymore*

Here's where we're at this morning: not in a real-life United States, but on a moonscape under the sign of Moloch. Stage-left stand the revolutionaries (students, street guerrillas, ghetto militants). Stage-center sits the unblinking Electronic Eye (Mother Media), scan-

ning the left-scape for movement, distraction, encephalographic blip.
Stage-right recline the children of the Eye, image-eaters, voyeurs.
The Eye and her children collaborate at an amoral witness: they
experience without risk, record without commitment, know without
caring. The revolutionaries exist to be consumed on the 11 P.M. news.

James Simon Kunen, a nineteen-year-old New Englander, and
Dotson Rader, a twenty-six-year-old Midwesterner, are revolutionaries, and it was inevitable that they should try to escape the Electronic Eye by resorting to print to explain themselves. Alas, their
revolution—the Columbia uprising of April 1968—was last year. This
year belongs to Nathan Pusey, not Grayson Kirk; to guns at Cornell,
not communes at Hamilton, Avery and Fayerweather Halls. The
Big Eye has so sapped our attention span that we can hardly remember which building was liberated last week, much less last year; and
all those commission reports—Kerner, Cox, Walker and Warren—
fade into one huge, gray, unreadable autopsy.

Thus the very readable testimony of two college radicals, written
on Band-Aids while the blood flowed, seems almost prehistoric. But
far from irrelevant. Both these books are moving, troubling, assertive
and eloquent. Taken together, they exemplify two faces of student
disaffection, two personalities and styles so wholly dissimilar that
the fact that both young men were involved in the same confrontation confounds all simpleminded generalizations.

Kunen, whose Columbia diaries appeared anonymously in *New
York* magazine last spring, is the more immediately sympathetic of
the two. He likes baseball and Eugene McCarthy. He is upset by
violence. He drifted almost inadvertently into the April ugliness,
and usually managed to escape through a commune window every
afternoon for crew practice. His radicalism began with an unexcep-
tionable intuition: "Isn't it singular that no one ever goes to jail for
waging wars, let alone advocating them? But the jails are filled with
those who want peace."

He is, moreover, an elegant writer, always seeing himself as though
through an ironic eye on the ceiling above the action, in command
of an affecting wistfulness that makes him seem a sort of politicized
Dustin Hoffman. His *Strawberry Statement* refers to a declaration
by a Columbia dean that "whether students vote 'yes' or 'no' on an
issue is like telling me they like strawberries." When Kunen con-

cludes that, because this country is 192 years old and he is only nineteen, "I will give it one more chance," the reader actually feels grateful.

Dotson Rader, on the other hand, is furious. A contributor to *The New Republic* and the *Evergreen Review*, he apparently started feeling furious in 1956, when the Hungarian revolt was crushed by Soviet troops and the United States didn't intervene. For Rader, Columbia represents the place where he stopped marching—for civil rights, for the poor, for peace—and started to fight. He declares a "civil war," with "the young and black and radical and disaffected and the homosexual and the head" against "the pigs and gangsters and generals and politicians and businessmen and liberal bullshit managers."

What is initially frightening about Rader's book is his contempt for those with whom he disagrees and his infatuation with violence. The contempt is often heaped on people like Martin Luther King, who deserve an empathetic act of the imagination of which Rader is incapable. And the violence is a mirror image of the social gangsterism he abhors: "Violence was liberating . . . a fantasy of revolution and ritual murder and the giving way to a clean violence and a final peace . . . I wanted to kill."

(This sort of *machismo* rubbish is also to be found in one of the better accounts of what happened in Chicago last August—John Schultz's *No One Was Killed*. Mr. Schultz reports the drums, the fear, the theater and rage in Lincoln Park; the mind's echo of "Seig, Heil!" with each chorus of "Peace, Now"; the rediscovery by the street guerrillas of "the ancient survival role of the hunter." His footnote admonishing the young women of the Left to remember their sex-function is preposterous enough. But his apparent embrace of primordial violence, of some prehistoric theater of turf and death, suggests a lust for the night we cannot afford again this century. Why levitate the Pentagon, only to play puppets in a bloody myth beneath it? To their credit, both Schultz and Rader admit the feeling.)

Not that fury isn't appropriate: An obscene war goes on, and poverty and racism persist. Rader is arguing that, while he knows "anger destroyed balance, and style depended on balance," violence is the only ritual left to him to define his manhood. (I don't know: maybe the thing to question, then, is our definition of manhood.) His anger is a promise: if and when the final blow-up comes, one knows Rader will be around, but one suspects that Kunen might be off on the road with his girl, or lost in graceful introspections. And the rest of us will be watching it on television.

What is scanted in both books is analysis. I suppose it is ungrateful to ask for more than two depth probes into the young radical temperament, but Kunen and Rader had an opportunity to address themselves to some of the paradoxes of left-wing activity today—in the leisure of print instead of on the Big Eye newscast. For instance, you attack the university (reminding the faculty it has exchanged substantive power for the privileges of the "tenured gentry"); attack academic affiliations with the Institute for Defense Analyses (because you are helpless to levitate the Pentagon); attack ROTC (because you are helpless to reform or abolish the draft). But if you destroy the university, what becomes of your hard-won "community"? How will you "radicalize" the next generation of freshmen? Without that sanctuary, albeit minimal, that base of operations, albeit strife-ridden, that public forum, albeit noisy, how will you plan, what can you do, who will listen to you?

(May 1969)

P.S. Now, of course, they are revolting in junior high schools. College freshmen are veterans of a thousand radical Waterloos. Mr. Kunen has gone off to write an occasional newspaper column and see his book turned into a dumb exploitation film. Mr. Rader has gone on to become one of New York's most enigmatic fellows, as likely to be found with the Warhol crowd as to turn up at a cocktail party-buffet supper given for Jerzy Kosinski by Senator and Marian Javits. Rader has also written a novel, *Government Inspected Meat.* Will he be around at the final blow-up? The trouble with getting furious when you are very young is that sometimes you are totally exhausted before you're old enough to vote. And by the time the revolution arrives, you've got a reputation in the slicks and a mortgage on a condominium.

Paul Cowan's *The Making of an Un-American*

Portrait of the Young American as an Upper-Middle-Class Idealist: Paul Cowan went to Dalton, where his grades were poor. He went to Choate, where they improved. He went to Harvard, where he was an editor of the *Crimson*. He dropped out, served some time at the London School of Economics, then drifted to the Middle East, where he worked on an Israeli kibbutz and taught English in Beersheba. He came back to the U.S. in 1962, tutored black children one summer in Chestertown, Maryland, returned to Harvard to get his degree and enrolled in graduate school at the University of Chicago. In 1964 he was a white volunteer in the Mississippi Summer Project. In 1965 he married, and became a reporter for *The Village Voice*. In 1966 he and his wife, Rachel, joined the Peace Corps and spent two years in Ecuador. Surely the résumé of a Boy Scout on the New Frontier, a can of sincerity as indigenous to America as our cans of frozen orange juice.

Yet Paul Cowan is an "un-American," a New Left activist. And his book, as Jack Newfield observes in a blurb, "is the collective biography of a generation that was born on the New Frontier, baptized on the Mississippi Delta, and educated by Vietnam." At Choate he experienced anti-Semitism; at Harvard, irrelevance; in Israel, meaningful work; in Vicksburg, Mississippi, white middle-class attitudinizing about the poor; in New York, the "Big Fiesta" of literary logrolling; in Ecuador with the Peace Corps, a cosmetized but nonetheless virulent form of racism and imperialism. "Nixonia"—our nation now perceived—inspires in him a powerful loathing.

There are ways to mount a defense against the bad news that Paul Cowan brings us. One is to attack him personally. He seems to have made a career out of his insufferability; to have bad-mouthed his teachers, employers and peers; to have sought a life style that approximates the *machismo* he is prone to fantasizing for himself. He is clearly not an Organization Man.

Another defense is to sit knock-kneed around our Ouija board invoking the spirits to punish Mr. Cowan for his ingratitude. After all, he was a child of affluence, sent to private schools, admitted to Harvard only on the intervention of "some influential faculty friends"

of his family. He was supported in his year of searching for himself
abroad. He could afford all the North American amenities while
working in a Guayaquil barrio, and, when he felt depressed, fly to
Mexico for a vacation. Even the elitist "old boy network" of which
he disapproves helped spare him expulsion from the Peace Corps.
His roving conscience was made possible by material well-being; his
capacity for moral inquiry is a kind of luxury product.

But the trouble with these defenses is that Mr. Cowan himself
supplies the data necessary to construct them. He admits everything.
One of his purposes is to trace the reticular formation of his own
elitist sensibility, his preconceptions and careerism. He earns the
right to be hard on the Peace Corps bureaucrats (and Allard Lowen-
stein) because he has been equally hard on himself. His honesty,
like his unadorned prose, disarms us.

Having disarmed us, he is free to pursue his larger purpose, which
is to convince the reader that Americans are "unable to accept people from alien cultures on any terms but their own." That "instinc-
tively, we insist on our moral and intellectual superiority." That this
arrogance, this incapacity for imaginative projection, makes for mis-
chief and immorality at home and abroad.

Thus Paul Cowan in Vicksburg couldn't understand the pride of
the black project director he nicknamed "Papa Doc." Thus Joe Rauh
in Atlantic City couldn't understand why Bob Moses and James
Forman and Fannie Lou Hammer weren't willing to sacrifice the
Mississippi Freedom Democratic Party for Hubert Humphrey's vice-
presidential aspirations. Thus Peace Corps trainees at the University
of New Mexico couldn't understand why laughing at a film of an
African carpenter who stored nails in his hair—instead of his mouth
—implied at best insensitivity, at worst racism.

Thus Peace Corps "colonialists" in Guayaquil attribute their lack
of progress to the "dirty, lazy Ekkies" (Ecuadorians) instead of realizing there can be no progress until an oligarchial grip on the land,
economy and government is loosened. Thus, Mr. Cowan argues, the
Peace Corps, AID, CIA and our embassy work to preserve that oli-
garchy against the Communist menace, all the while contemptuous
of the country they presume to help.

He supports his argument with hundreds of anecdotes, autopsies
of aborted projects, quotes from official documents. Resorting seldom to mindless New Left code words, patiently marshaling and

deploying his facts, eloquently recording his changing perceptions, he first absorbs and finally persuades the reader. There is a quality of the inevitable about his progress to "un-Americanism," his determination to redefine "my loyalties through actions," his decision to place himself in permanent guerrilla opposition to American policies in Ecuador, Vietnam, Mississippi, Watts. Which means he has written precisely the book he intended to write.

(February 1970)

P.S. Ray Mungo, Michael Myerson, Cowan, Rader, Kunen . . . their first books are autobiographies, and they're not even untrustworthy yet. Whatever happened to the first novel as a literary debut? Dienbienphu happened to it, apparently.

George Kennan's *Democracy and the Student Left*

Louis XIV once wrote a sonnet. He submitted it for judgment to Boileau, a poet who at that time happened to be Court historiographer. Boileau, after reading it, told the King: "Sire, nothing is impossible for Your Majesty. You set out to write some bad verses and you have succeeded."

George Kennan must have set out to write a bad book. He has succeeded. There can be no other explanation of *Democracy and the Student Left*. His publishers appear to have conspired with Kennan to embarrass him and exasperate the rest of us.

Impertinent? Yes. I wish I had half of George Kennan's abilities, that I could count a third of his achievements as my own. I am not an admirer of Mark Rudd, nor do I subscribe to "confrontation" as the pre-eminent form of social discourse. In fact, like Kennan, I'm predisposed to a sort of pessimistic Calvinism. Unlike Kennan, however, I conducted a brief affair with the New Left; and his perverse and patronizing essay is unworthy of him.

It is an essay divided into three parts. First is a speech prepared for ceremonies dedicating a new library at Swarthmore last December, and subsequently printed in *The New York Times Magazine*. Next is a selection of letters—to the *Times* and to Kennan—responding to the speech. And last is his 104-page rebuttal.

In his speech, Kennan contrasts Woodrow Wilson's 1896 ideal of the university ("a place removed—calm Science seated there, recluse, ascetic, like a nun; not knowing that the world passes, not caring, if the truth but come in answer to her prayer") with what he sees today ("screaming tantrums and brawling in the streets," "banners and epithets and obscenities and virtually meaningless slogans," "massive certainties already present in the minds of people who not only *have not* studied very much but presumably *are not* studying a great deal . . ."). Surveying student protest ("violent objection to what exists, unaccompanied by any constructive concept of what, ideally, ought to exist in its place"), Kennan is reminded of "the origins of totalitarianism in other countries." He doubts "whether civil disobedience has any place in a democratic society." He has seen "more harm done in this world by those who stormed the bastions of society in the name of utopian beliefs . . . than by all the humble efforts of those who have tried to create a little order and civility and affection within their own intimate entourage, even at the cost of tolerating a great deal of evil in the public domain." And he Calvinizes: "The decisive seat of evil in this world is not in social and political institutions, and not even, as a rule, in the will or iniquities of statesmen, but simply in the weakness and imperfection of the human soul itself . . ."

Because Guilt so loves promiscuous Association, it would be unfair to say that Kennan expresses, albeit more gracefully, the sentiments of Billy Graham, Grayson Kirk and the three principal pygmies presently campaigning for the presidency of the United States. It *would* be, but Kennan plays his *obiter dicta* by peculiar rules: pleading reasonableness after every provocation, bending contexts to serve a prejudice, hustling for an "order" and "civility" selective enough to inhibit the student Left while licensing, say, the Defense Department. We are not arguing about social and political institutions; we are arguing about *policies*, and what men like Kennan have done to oppose or change them.

Three themes are reiterated by the letters: (1) our Vietnam adventure abroad, black disenfranchisement at home, and the vagaries of the draft are wrong; (2) the university shouldn't be a "service station" for government and industry; and (3) traditional political processes are inadequate to accommodate dissent and to effect change. "I have," Kennan assures us, "read, pondered and made notes on every single one of the letters." But he didn't understand them.

In his long rejoinder, Kennan flails about.

Item: Are New Leftists poorer students than their non-political classmates? Kennan cites Jack Newfield's outdated A *Prophetic Minority*, while ignoring Kenneth Keniston's more recent *The Young Radicals*. Anyone in peripheral touch with the New Left must admit dismay at its reading habits, or lack of them. But are the reading habits of the non-politicals—in mind-numbing survey courses, or in seminars devoted to the disemboweling of the classics in order that symbolic entrails might be read and dreary papers written on sadomasochistic cyclothymia in Shakespeare—in any way superior?

Item: Responding to Kennan's call for a "constructive concept of what . . . ought to exist," several letters suggested printed materials outlining programs. He replies by criticizing the prose style of the SDS Port Huron Statement. It is, admittedly, wretched prose. But committee prose, excepting King James, has always been wretched. Are congressional resolutions, foundation proposals, the deliberations of academic senates, the trivia of Rotarians and diplomats any more rhetorically distinguished? He avoids the point.

Item: "A second thing that stands out in these letters is the lack of humor and of any *joie de vivre*. . . . The politics, like what one expects to be the love life of many of these young people, is tense, anxious, defiant and joyless." Nonsense. There are humorless people everywhere, of all ages. But I can't believe that Kennan has ever visited a Movement workshop, a community-organizing project, even a commune. If he had, he would have found plenty of examples of humor, a number of examples of community, and a love life that on the whole seems a little less anxious and a little more joyful than the versions of it to be found among faculty communities or in exurbia or in penthouses. Why deny the variousness of these people? The letters were responding to an extraordinarily uncharitable attack, not trying to write Johnny Carson's monologue or rewrite *Splendor in the Grass*.

Item: Why, Kennan, wants to know, are none of his correspondents interested in the conservation of natural resources? But, again, they were writing in response to an article which didn't mention natural resources. And they have expressed themselves volubly against depredations on the environment. And, besides, not much of that environment is available to people locked into big-city ghettos or off in Danang.

Item: "The speed with which the focus of student concern has switched from the Negro of the rural South to the Negro of the urban North, and then to Vietnam, and then to the disciplinary regime of the college campus, suggests strongly to me that the real seat of discomfort lies not in the objects that attract those feelings but in some inner distress and discontent with contemporary society that would find other issues to fasten to as points of grievance against the established order, even if the present ones did not exist." It suggests to me, on the other hand, that students keep getting defeated on the larger issues—partially because of such complacency as Kennan expresses—and retreat to smaller and more manageable issues. Of course, there is distress and discontent, and floundering and imprecision. There is also idealism. And the situation of the Negro, North and South, like the situation of our country in Vietnam, is an object of legitimate concern, isn't it? If Kennan is going to dabble in amateur psychologizing, he might check first with those—like Keniston and Willard Gaylin—who have already done it on a professional basis; their conclusions contradict him. Amazingly, the war *is* a radicalizing experience, especially when nobody seems to be doing anything about it.

Item: "The idea that life could be made richer, more tolerable and enjoyable, and even perhaps more useful socially, by an emphasis on the being as well as the doing, by a cultivation of the amenities, by the creation of a dignified and attractive personal environment; the recognition that if great masses of people are to be elevated out of degradation or vulgarity, it is imperative that some people should set an example of graciousness and good taste . . . all this seems quite foreign to the writers of these letters." A good deal of it, alas, seems quite foreign to me. Surely Kennan must have seen, while he was watching "the origins of totalitarianism in other countries," people setting examples of graciousness and good taste while other people went off to gas chambers. No, this isn't Nazi Germany; but men, women and children die daily in Vietnam; suffocate daily in our big cities. Napalm isn't in good taste. There is nothing gracious about rats, narcotics, joblessness and tenth-rate education; there is nothing even *vulgar* about it. And there is nothing a good example in one's "personal environment" is going to do to change it. Work is required to change it, work some people are doing and others aren't.

Item: Kennan, writing about the American Negro, says: "Aside from the distinction of his contributions to music and the drama and humor, he has an exceptionally high sensitivity to people and situations . . . When not upset by painful racial reactions or demoralized by the various strains and artificialities of urban life, he tends, accordingly, to have better natural manners than a great many American whites." Wonderful. Maybe his "exceptionally high sensitivity to people and situations" derives from his need to survive in a society that would be more comfortable if he didn't exist. Maybe his better natural manners usually manifest themselves in situations of power: then it is clear just who has to be polite to whom in order to keep a job, avoid arrest, beg a favor or be allowed to continue to entertain us musically, dramatically, humorously. *Demoralized*, for God's sake!

There is scarcely a page in this book without similar unhappy generalizations. But let's look at two final points, Kennan on the draft and Kennan on the university. Of the draft he says: "The violent resentment of the draft appears to be unmodified by the slightest trace of any sense of obligation to country or pride in the wearing of the uniform of the armed services of the United States. What in earlier decades would have carried with it at least the suspicion of cowardice or lack of patriotism is today pursued wholly without shame or hesitation." He goes on to show that the probability of a recent male *college graduate* being drafted and killed in action is not very high, and deplores "the strong streak of hysteria and exaggeration that pervades the student view." Finally, he comes down on the side of order: "The policies under which this defense [of the country] is at the moment being conducted may be ones that the draftee does not like; but they are not ones that he is fully competent to judge, particularly at his age and against the background of his experience."

Nothing here, of course, about the probabilities of the recent male high school dropout getting killed in action. But then he would probably come from the great mass of degraded and vulgar people. No joining here, either, of the argument: does a country, wearing that uniform, which does what we are doing in Vietnam deserve pride, inspire a sense of obligation? Will there ever be an end to nationalism, and commercials for it? We aren't talking here about "the

real actuarial prospects . . . for personal disaster." We are talking
about moral issues. They can be argued, but not ignored. And there
are questions about the very mechanics of the draft that should be
raised. What about its use as a punitive device (General Hershey's
October 26 memorandum to local boards asking that college students
demonstrating against the draft be reclassified 1A, subject to immediate call-up)? The iniquities of the deferment system itself? The
existence of 4,000 different draft boards with 4,000 different sets of
rules? Hershey's refusal to allow lawyers to appear before draft
boards because of the "delays" their appearance would cause? Local
boards unrepresentative of their communities (how many Negroes
on draft boards in the South?)? Quadruple jeopardy from ages nineteen to twenty-five? And so on. The draft is a mess, the morality of
the war it feeds is in question, and we are past the point where argument ends by the exercise of an authority whose internal workings
we are not permitted to examine.

As for the university, Kennan wants it to be calm and detached.
I agree. Those on the Left who wish it to be an instrument of their
convictions are as short-sighted as those on the Right who wish it to
be *their* instrument. (Remember *God and Man at Yale?*) But what in
fact *is* the university today? Have we learned nothing at all from
Columbia? According to James Ridgeway in his forthcoming *The
Closed Corporation,* more than two thirds of university research
funds come from the Department of Defense, the Atomic Energy
Commission and NASA. Eighty per cent of MIT's funds come from
the government, 50 per cent of Columbia's and Princeton's. Federal
contract research centers, located in and around universities, give
money to the universities while the professors operate on a shuttle
system from classroom to research center. Biological and chemical
warfare research goes on at a dozen major universities. Universities
own ball parks, hotels, ships, forests, airlines, magazines, ant poisons,
spaghetti factories, as well as mortgages. University officials sit on
the boards of one fourth of the largest corporations in America. A
dean of students at Kennan's own university recruits for the CIA.
Universities maintain lobbyists in Washington; and faculty members
perform as lobbyists for corporations. All this adds up to something
less than detachment. The university becomes increasingly a voca-
tional training school for managers, just as the ghettos are service
pools for white society. Full professors contract themselves out, and

they are more often on the road than they are in the classroom. The
university is no longer half as interested in the pursuit of truth as it is
in the pursuit of the dollar. And when students ask for changes, Kennan tells them to leave it if they don't like it.

Mr. Generation, meet the Gap.

(September 1968)

P.S. I went on at such frenzied length in this article on Mr. Kennan's book—and have added clarifications here for which there
wasn't space in *New York* magazine then—because the book seemed
then, and still seems now, characteristic of the intelligent, established, eastern, government-academic liberal's confusion when faced
with the young people who wouldn't shut up in the last half of the
1960's. The draft situation has changed drastically as a result of
the lottery system, through no help of Mr. Kennan's and as a direct
result of the considerable pressures and noises of students. The university situation has changed somewhat, with professors finding they
could learn something even from the babble. I doubt whether Mr.
Kennan's sort of elitism will ever be expressed again in such a naked
form; I doubt whether he himself would want to express it in such a
form. He saw the Hun at the gate; most of the Huns were his own
children; the other Huns—the ones who hate all civilization, however imperfectly realized, because they haven't made that garden,
that "personal environment," themselves—are another matter, but
no excuse for books full of nonsense.

Margaret Mead's *Culture and Commitment*

Ross Macdonald, in his most recent novel, *The Goodbye Look*, has
his detective Lew Archer tell a young woman: "I don't believe people know everything at birth and forget it as they get older." Raymond Aron, in his most recent book, *The Elusive Revolution*,
observes: "A professor would have to be very ignorant indeed to be
more ignorant than his students, particularly in their first years at
university." Margaret Mead, in this slim volume of shining intelligence, sees the situation from a less comfortable point of view. The
young, she says, know something the rest of us refuse to admit. They

know that "there are no adults anywhere in the world from whom they can learn what the next steps should be." What the next steps should be . . . a deceptively simple and ultimately frightening formulation to describe that most notorious of holes, the Generation Gap.

For the dissident young, writes Dr. Mead, "the past . . . is a colossal, unintelligible failure and the future may hold nothing but the destruction of the planet." One needn't subscribe wholly to such a feverish vision, it being the nature of many young men to build Taj Mahals of anguish around an uncertain sex life, of many young women to conceive of themselves as Antigone, of the combination to confuse a campus skirmish with Götterdämmerung.

But something is going on in the United States, Latin America, France, Germany, Czechoslovakia and Japan that can't be sloughed off as glandular irregularities, or explained away by ritual invocations of that dastardly triad: Spock, Leary, Marcuse. Dr. Mead suggests that the something is a new world culture, which she calls "prefigurative," conspired at by transistor radios, space satellites and hydrogen bombs, but based on a profound revision of authority roles, the nature of dependency and the "location of the future."

Her concepts are perfectly straightforward. In a "postfigurative" culture—primitive societies, small religious and ideological enclaves—children learn primarily from their forebears. Authority derives from the past, from grandparents who, because change is almost imperceptible, "cannot conceive of any other future . . . than their own pasts." In a timeless culture, the oldest among us is the inevitable model; the youngest, the child, is a palimpsest on which a role is pressed.

In a "cofigurative" culture—such "great civilizations" as our own, incorporating change—both children and adults learn from their peers, playmates, fraternity brothers, colleagues. The grandfather, hopelessly anachronistic, has been wheeled off to the nearest Gerontion Garden for figs and estrogen. The father often abdicates his authority to a surrogate: the teacher, the employer. Caste wars with assimilation. The past is irrelevant. People, after a certain amount of use, are obsolescent.

"Prefigurative" culture is what is happening to us. The young, in their apprehension of "the still unknown future," assume new authority; teach us by asking questions we were too busy to worry about; require of us a nurture, an environment, that, rather than pressing roles and forms upon the child, instead invite his limitless inquiry. Accustomed as we are to being thumped on the head with slogans—"the collapse of the family, the decay of capitalism, the triumph of a soul-less technology"—we may resist Dr. Mead's quiet and commonsensical notion that the pace of change has so accelerated that traditional forms of culturally incorporating it are insufficient. We would be foolish to do so.

Her methodology is as straightforward as her concepts. She has not ransacked dead civilizations in search of edifying shards. She has, from a lifetime of anthropological investigation, concentrated on those cultures—post-, co- or pre-figurative—that coexist today, whether in Polynesia or Spain or Pakistan or Cambridge, Massachusetts. One of her principal contentions is that these cultures converge, primitive and sophisticated, on a relocation of the future to "Now." Which means tension.

It is impossible to do justice to her weaving of fine details into this persuasive tapestry—Mao employing the Red Guards to re-establish a postfigurative authority (grandfather) over a cofigurative deviation (father goes bourgeois); adult behavior as "the most flexible and complex part" of the cultural system, and therefore responsible for discovering "prefigurative ways of teaching and learning," ways to open instead of "replicating" the system—but one must suggest the wisdom, the pithy distillations, of this book. We require, says Dr. Mead, a biological and ecological model of our world which repudiates "the old calculus of gain and loss," which substitutes a model of "negative entropy," the mutuality of gain by interreaction in a single environment.

She is optimistic, and so embarrasses those of us who have tended lately to go about mongering gloom. A gloom-monger would propose to Dr. Mead that youth, dissident youth, at times seems as much constituted of louts, frauds, fascists, zombies, careerists and dilettantes as the Gerontions. Dr. Mead was herself rudely treated, and witnessed greater rudeness and stupidity, at the annual meeting of the American Association for the Advancement of Science last week in Boston. Are these the children who will lead us? To what debauch? They were as disgusting as she is admirable. One hopes that her postfigurations will prevail.

(January 1970)

Raymond Aron's *The Elusive Revolution*

Raymond Aron is that ultimate inconvenience: the man who stays sober at your saturnalia, and who will afterward give everybody else an intellectual hangover. He is an ambulatory reproach. Thus he observes that in May 1968, "once again the French people, obsessed by their memories or the myths of their past, mistook riot and disorder in the streets for a Promethean exploit." Thus he refuses to believe that university revolt, student communes, barricades, workers' occupation of factories and a not-quite-general strike add up to a "revolution." They add up instead to an "ideological debauchery" and a "psychodrama." "Everyone of us," he writes, "indulged in role-playing. . . . I have told you that I played the part of Tocqueville, which is not without a touch of the ridiculous, but others played Saint-Just, Robespierre or Lenin, which all things considered was even more ridiculous."

Tocqueville, a liberal who was accused in his day of being a reactionary, is a hard part to play. Yet Mr. Aron has been playing it for years, albeit ironically. In 1955, with *The Opium of the Intellectuals*, he broke decisively with the French Left over Communism. Ever since, either from his chair at the Sorbonne or in columns for *Le Figaro*, he has had to contend with Sartre on one flank and with De Gaulle on the other.

His colleagues apparently expected him to approve the French student revolt. He had, after all, proposed university reforms for fifteen years, and was known to oppose the cult of personality that is Gaullism. But his colleagues seem not to have read him very carefully. His dismay over "the events of May"—recorded here in newspaper articles and a long conversation with Alain Duhamel—are of a piece with all he has said before about liberal institutions and modern industrial society.

First and foremost, Mr. Aron appreciates the fragility of liberal institutions, as must any Frenchman who isn't mainlining on abstractions. Since he also cherishes those institutions, any "revolution" that attacks and immobilizes them without defining an alternative inspires his disdain, especially one that gets called off after a three-minute speech by le Grand Charles.

He disdains as well the intellectuals who abetted the binge, re-marking their lust for apocalyptic situations that are thankfully untainted by Stalinism (tyranny, bureaucracy). He considers these traumatized refugees of the Old Left wars no better than the film directors who complain about a "consumer society" from behind "the wheels of their Ferraris. . . . If people genuinely find that their privileges and material possessions are a real embarrassment, there are many ways open to them of giving them up."

Which leads to Mr. Aron's second principal objection to the rhetoric and details of the May uprising. "When all is said and done at times I am tempted to turn Beotian and state that every society is subject to the constraints of fact—the need for organization, for a technical hierarchy, the need for a techno-bureaucracy and so on. French intellectuals are so subtle that they end up forgetting the obvious."

Among the "constraints of fact" are that "a professor would have to be very ignorant indeed to be more ignorant than his students, particularly in their first years at university," meaning that there's an inherent inequality in the teacher-student relationship that no amount of communion can abolish.

Finally, he is clear that after the moment of transcendence (from boredom, from history), which even participants in "pseudo-revolutions" experience, there is the messiness of creating new forms or reviving old ones, and the risk of an insupportable anarchy in the interim, yielding inevitably to one sort of repressive authority or an-other. If, he suggests, the French Communist Party had not been tacitly in league with Gaullism; if the party had thrown all its ener-gies into a general strike, the regime would have fallen, and another round of musical republics would have ensued.

These are hard truths, but truths nevertheless, and admirably articulated. Aesthetes and Luddites do seek in "the cult of violence" a dangerous kick, just as the guilty Left seeks redemption in an "ex-istential" free-for-all, a shuffling and dealing of symbols—like the barricade. Political freedoms are too vulnerable to be played with mischievously. And there is the paradox of a Gaullism triumphant, even without De Gaulle, after all that bombast and those paving stones.

But one point troubles me. "Language," says Mr. Aron, "is far less important than people's emotional state." Yes. And aren't

"emotional states" partially what contemporary student rebellions
are about? "Someone who has enjoyed . . . a reprieve, however
brief," wrote Susan Sontag of France in May 1968, "from the inhibi-
tion on love and trust this society enforces, is never the same again."
Of an American version of the same thing, Benjamin DeMott noted
"a frozen world unblocked . . . young and old speaking seriously to
each other, perceiving freshly the shortness and preciousness of the
life adventure." There is an element of celebration in these events,
meaningful emotionally, afterward, whatever the reassertion of
bureaucratic authority. Woodstock might, somehow, substitute for
the cult of violence, but even if it can't, we must confront the need
of people for a shared affirmation, a rite of togetherness. That rite
can take on ugly forms, but it seems so desperately, humanly necessary, that to oppose it altogether is to ensure that it will be ugly.
Reasons will be so much fallout from the explosion.

(November 1969)

Raymond Aron's *Marxism and the Existentialists*

It was less a love affair than a doomed flirtation. The Marxists and
the existentialists went hand in hand to every postwar Popular Front
in France. But between fronts there were spats about purges, slave
labor camps, personality cults, Hungary. And the principals (and
principles) were philosophically incompatible: on the one side, crude
materialists convinced of historical inevitability; on the other, Pas-
calian drunks who kept trying to carry on a dialogue with the non-
existence of God. The Marxists saw in Jean-Paul Sartre and Maurice
Merleau-Ponty a chance to get intellectually respectable. The existentialists saw in Communism an opportunity to escape from alienation, to connect the "useless passion" of Self with the hated Other in
an orgasmic "rendezvous with truth," the "perfect moment" of
communal violence which is Revolution. Alas, for all their ingenuity,
intellectuals like Sartre have intermittent moral compunctions; and
"perfect moments" have a way of turning into Politburos.

Raymond Aron tells all about the tryst in this latest volume from
the "World Perspectives" series. A hardheaded social democrat,
Aron parted company with Sartre over the issue of Communism af-

ter their comradeship in the Resistance. There is a sense in which he forgives too much what is and looks too bleakly on what might be; a sense, not of smugness, but of an informed pessimism so resolute that it's sometimes difficult to distinguish it from complacency. However, he was there; he makes the arcana intelligible; and what he says is immediately pertinent.

So we have existentialism: the idea of personal authenticity, of taking responsibility for yourself, your heritage, your talents—plus the idea of reciprocity, of seeing the Other, respecting him, helping him to fulfill himself. (No historical dimension.) And we have Marxism: man in history, at once subject and object, knowing and acting —plus the inevitability of degenerate capitalism and triumphant socialism. (No personal dimension.) The anti-determinists try to make it with the determinists, and they spawn manifestos.

We have the spectacle of intellectuals longing for a holocaust in order to resolve their abstract paradoxes. Of Sartre trying to convince Thorez that a dialogue with Nothingness is superior to dialectical materialism as a philosophical basis for revolution. Of Merleau-Ponty reversing himself between *Les Aventures de la dialectique* and *Humanisme et terreur* without realizing it. Of petit bourgeois theoreticians lecturing everybody on the burden of historical consciousness, the "true intersubjectivity," of the proletariat. (Whatever happened to the proletariat? In this country the Georges—Meany and Wallace—were what happened.) We have, finally, the obsolescence of *Das Kapital* today. No one alive can have failed to learn profitably from Marx, as from Freud. We know more than they did, but as T. S. Eliot said, they are that which we know. Still, a lot has happened, enough to justify regretting the brilliance Sartre wasted trying to pump some life into Communism's sacred text.

Capitalist societies developed in unforeseen ways. The first "Marxist" revolution took place in a country with none of the prerequisites. Lenin substituted the party for the proletariat; Stalin, the general secretary for the party. Collectivization of agriculture failed. State ownership of the means of production hasn't liberated anybody. The abolition of "scarcity" probably won't rid us of alienation. The concept of "work" is itself almost outmoded. Technological processes inflict upon us new psychological patterns we haven't willed and don't want and can't even understand.

In other words, we need new texts, not rubber patches on an old historical wheel; new analyses as rich in documentation as *Das Kapital*, but analyses concerned with the twentieth instead of the nineteenth century. And it is here that Raymond Aron's study of the doomed flirtation is especially useful. There is, he argues, no "scientific" reading of history that "proves" something—such as that social contradictions lead spontaneously to a classless society. If, then, victory for a vanguard is not inevitable; if it might lose; if the future might not belong to it, then the justification in futuristic terms of present, sometimes ugly, actions has no meaning. We are stuck not with the nobility of our intentions but with the sum of our acts.

A terrible prospect. But one to which existentialism—without Marx or Lenin or Stalin or Mao—*is* relevant. The young Left today has obviously been influenced by Sartre. They seek to define themselves in action, to connect with the Other (each other, all of us) through gestures so extravagant as to be undeniable, to find a community in "perfect moments" of concerted action. The moment fades, but in the momentary light it is possible to see one another in various states of emotional and spiritual nakedness.

If, then, they and we are prepared to be the sum of our acts and prepared to accept the consequences of those acts, there's hope. Raymond Aron writes: "For history to be comparable to a dialogue in which Reason has the last word, it is necessary that the questions be as reasonable as the answers, that the situations created by past answers or the things themselves be as reasonable as the questions." It may be that no such dialogue is going on at all; that Reason hardly ever speaks, much less has the last word. And certainly it's a heavy load of historical consciousness to put on a Columbia communard or a corporation executive or a think-tank systems analyst or even a Congressman. But that's where we are: we have to operate as though it were possible. Otherwise, nothing is.

(July 1969)

Odyssey of a Friend: Letters from Whittaker Chambers to William F. Buckley, Jr., 1954–61

More drivel has been written about Whittaker Chambers than about almost any other contemporary American fantasy-figure with the

possible exception of Jacqueline Kennedy Onassis. Some men need
to hate Chambers. If they can't Cooke the facts or Jowitt them away,
they will Zeligsize or Cruise O'Brien over them. Or object to his
metaphysical bravura, his appearance, the number of inflections he
ascribed to a Russian noun, his failure to sell the proper panaceas at
the approved ideological pharmacy. Why? After what Mary Mc-
Carthy called our "prurient avidity for the details of political deflora-
tion," do we compensate with an all-American resentment against
the tattletale? Are only men of the Left permitted to be complicated?
Might one indulge one's own capacity for Zeligsizing, and blather
on about traumatized left-wing sensibilities projecting their collective guilt on the accusatory Other?

No. We are uncomfortable with characters out of Dostoyevsky.
Chambers, whose *Witness* is one of the great autobiographies, was
such a character. His excess makes us nervous, as would a rehabili-
tated Fyodor himself, going on about God and Mother Russia.
Chambers with his sweet fatigue was an embarrassment—morally,
politically, personally. "Such peculiar birds," wrote Arthur Koestler,
"are found only in the trees of the revolution."

"History," wrote Chambers to William F. Buckley, Jr., in his last
letter, "hit us with a freight train. History has long been doing this
to people, monotonously and usually lethally." He reveals himself,
though, as more than just a casualty of history. He was a man of surpassing tenderness, that tenderness which perhaps derives only from
the most pessimistic of intuitions: "Would that we could live in a
world of the fauves, where the planes are disjointed only on canvas,
instead of a world where the wild beasts are real and the disjointures
threaten to bury us."

Tenderness? Chambers? Depending on your preferred form of
assassination, you whet your ax or polish the telescopic sight on your
Mannlicher-Carcano. Yes, he translated *Bambi*, but . . . but didn't
he confuse himself with Lazarus and Don Quixote? (No. With
Gerontion: "Not good company this side of the Styx.") Aren't his
letters long-winded? (Yes, like Yeats's. Both were postponing serious
work.) Wasn't he sunk in pernicious mysticism? (No. He told
Buckley, "You tend to take off from a mainland of established verities. I am the horrid brat of historicity. . . . Faced with almost anything my first questions are: how, why, from what cause through
what lines of development [in flux] to what effect [in flux]?")

Extraordinary letters. And I despair of proving it, because there isn't sufficient space to sample them, and who would believe my assertion of value? Everybody has already decided about Chambers. Should I say that he loathed Joseph McCarthy; supported the right of Alger Hiss (and Paul Robeson) to a passport; explained to Buckley the incompatibility of capitalism (which innovates) and conservatism (which clings); urged the Republican Party to embrace the civil libertarian cause . . . would it zipper up your yawn of incredulity? But it's true.

Or: These letters illuminate an intramural squabble at *National Review*. (Chambers resigned because the editorial board didn't like Nixon.) They indicate that Buckley saved Chambers from a literary failure of nerve. They suggest that Chambers, like Koestler and Malraux and Manes Sperber, conceived of the "counterrevolution" as something transcending the defense of property rights; it had to do with the individual soul. A man might be murdered meaninglessly, said Chambers, and "this reality cuts across our mind like a wound whose edges crave to heal, but cannot. Thus, one of the great sins, perhaps *the* great sin, is to say: It will heal; it has healed; there is no wound; there is something more important than this wound. There is nothing more important than this wound."

He worried about the meaning of life and death. Odd. And oddly this spiritual preoccupation, this sense of the distance between an individual and history, this messy groping for reasons, this intuition of impotence, this longing for deliverance by the technological wheel, this reluctance to give up on ravished values, this gloomy determination to accommodate man as he is known and the mysteries as they are suspected, is much closer to the mood of our youth today than the social engineers are willing to admit. Chambers anticipated our material abundance and our spiritual aridity; he also anticipated our inability to cope with it.

His poets were Rilke ("every angel is terrible") and Lorca ("on awaiting, with a little patience, the black angel"). His city was Venice. His habit of mind was a worrying of paradoxes: "It seems as if, by the fretting of raw edges, there arises a peculiar music: we do not know how." His humor was dark: "Mr. Dulles was in Peru (what on earth could have taken him there—hints from the Incas on how to lose an empire?)." He was, of course, neither a saint nor a monster—but he could write.

I cannot subscribe to this man's life-view: Oedipus should never have gone on to Colonus, really; and Job *did* get a run around from God. But I envy Mr. Buckley for those mornings when these letters arrived in the mail; and hope, for Chambers's sake, that Camus was right—"*Il faut supposer Sisyphe heureux.*"

(January 1970)

Arthur Koestler's *Arrow in the Blue* and *The Invisible Writing*

First, let me don a penitential sackcloth. Like cowards, reviewers try to kill the thing they love with an apothegm instead of a sword. Thus, commenting some months ago on a collection of essays, I said of Arthur Koestler: "On the twentieth-century grid, he is the ultimate waffle." How fearlessly inadequate! Macmillan's reissuings of the Koestler *oeuvre* in the handsome, uniform Danube Edition constitutes an enormous reproach. I had managed to forget that Koestler had taught my generation what we needed to know about the century that grilled him. On the evidence of his novels, essays and four volumes of autobiography, he is the West's pre-eminent journalist. That he is equally uncomfortable with monogamy and ideology may account for his awe-inspiring vagabondage.

By journalist I mean no slur. If his autobiography lacks the literary elegance of Malraux's *Antimemoirs*, it is more specific and engrossing; nor does K. wrap himself in the Gaullist sheet of "I Am a Historical Enigma." If novels like *Darkness at Noon* (the Purge trials), *Thieves in the Night* (Palestinian terrorism) and *Arrival and Departure* (portrait of the revolutionary as a Jung man) are *romans à thèse*, they are still infinitely to be preferred to a bilious *roman à clef* like Simone de Beauvoir's *The Mandarins*, which did a disservice to K., Camus, Sartre and even Nelson Algren. If *The Ghost in the Machine* and *Drinkers of Infinity* suggest a lamentable lust on K.'s part for material proofs of his metaphysical raptures, at least he seeks proofs, instead of foaming at the mouth about lapwings and absolutes.

Two of the four autobiographical volumes, *Dialogue with Death* and *Scum of the Earth*, were written immediately after a stint in a

Franco prison during the Spanish Civil War and a stint in a French concentration camp two years later. They are time-bound. But *Arrow in the Blue* and *The Invisible Writing* deal with K.'s first forty years recollected in as much tranquillity as such a man will ever permit himself. They add up, as he says, to "a typical case history of a member of the educated middle classes of Central Europe in the first half of our century," one of those refugees for whom a new word had to be coined: "Stepmotherland." Anger, anomaly, irony and tragedy abound.

Here is K. as a child in Budapest, precocious and paralyzingly shy; an engineering student in Vienna, torn between political action and contemplative sloth; a twenty-year-old Zionist emigrating to Palestine; a Mideast correspondent for the Ullstein newspaper empire; a science editor turned Communist in Berlin at the moment of Hitler's ascendancy; the only reporter on a marvelous Zeppelin expedition to the North Pole. To be followed by K. traveling in the Soviet Union during the famine years of the early 1930's; working in Paris as a propagandist for the Willy Munzenberg *Apparat*; seeking in Spain evidence of German-Italian collaboration with Franco; finding in Spain "the reality of the third order"; renouncing the Party, settling in England, writing his novels, surviving . . . unlike almost all of his friends, who die throughout these thousand pages at the hands of Hitler and Stalin.

Whether he is brooding about language (he went from writing in Hungarian to German to English, not to mention Hebrew and Russian) or attitudes ("The mystic of the nineteen-thirties yearned, as a sign of Grace, for a look at the Dnieper Dam and a three per cent increase in the Soviet pig-iron production") or justice ("a concept of ethical symmetry, and therefore an essentially natural concept—like the design of a crystal") or English prisons ("It was nice to know that you were at a place where putting a man to death was still regarded as a solemn and exceptional event"), K. is superb.

His inferiority complex, as Otto Katz told him, may have been the size of a cathedral. And, as Orwell said, "The chink in K.'s armor is his hedonism." But he was always where the action was, always scribbling, usually indignant. If his Cassandra-like cries embarrassed his friends, they deserved to be embarrassed. (Just this month a magazine whose brows are not quite high enough to let it see much, so wholly misses the point of Whittaker Chambers that Chambers,

Koestler, Manes Sperber, Gustav Regler, Victor Serge and André Gide might just as well have recorded their qualms about Communism in Quechua.)

As for that rapture, that "reality of the third order," it occurred to him while under a sentence of death in a Spanish prison. (Nothing like a sentence of death to focus the mind.) Its logic begins with Euclid's demonstration that, in the climb up a numerical series of prime numbers, we shall never discover a "virgin"—the highest prime. Therefore, K. concludes, "a meaningful and comprehensive statement about the infinite is arrived at by precise and finite means." Should one object that such statements refer only to a man-made, not an infinite scheme, one must still cope with K.'s gallivanting after ESP as an anti-materialist proof. Mysticism: the last refuge of an infirm mind?

No. K. rejects any variety of determinism, and had we lived his life, we would, too. But isn't it possible to believe in choice without subscribing to the theistic swoon? Freud, a year before he died, granted K. an interview. Freud had never experienced the "oceanic feeling" or seen "the invisible writing." Says K.: "I wondered with admiration and compassion how a man can face his death without it." I submit, with admiration and compassion for the invaluable K., that we must most of us face our deaths without it, learning somehow to swim through what the existentialists have called a "vertigo of possibility." We have to take the rap for our own freedom.

(June 1970)

VARIATIONS ON VIETNAM

Townsend Hoopes's *The Limits of Intervention*

Townsend Hoopes's extraordinary book about "how the Johnson policy of escalation in Vietnam was reversed" suggests that we are in for a decade of self-laceration after a decade of blunders. The lacerating will focus on Vietnam because Vietnam exemplifies our conceptual and institutional disarray. The concepts—honor, consensus, the American mission—will get it for their imprecision and misapprehension. The institutions—Pentagon, State Department, White House, Congress—will get it for the vagaries of policy making. First up are the participants: Schlesinger, Galbraith, Roger Hilsman, George Ball, Mr. Hoopes. (Dean Rusk may be writing his book; Walt Rostow is probably writing Lyndon Johnson's book.) They will be followed by the critics of the participants. (David Halberstam is a year away, but on the evidence of his *Harper's* article about Mc-George Bundy, it will be a critique of terrifying intelligence; Joseph Alsop, of course, has been writing his novel serially for years.)

How useful are such autopsies? In this instance, very useful indeed. Townsend Hoopes was with the Defense Department from 1965 through 1968, ultimately as Undersecretary of the Air Force. His book, part memoir and part historical reconstruction, supplies excellent thumbnail sketches of the men around the President and how they sought to influence him; documents the demoralization of many high-level advisers during Johnson's last two years; and suggests, perhaps inadvertently, that Johnson's March 31 speech—announcing a partial bombing halt and his own retirement—may not really have been intended to get us to the conference table after all.

Moreover, Mr. Hoopes does his reconstructing gracefully, with a decent reticence about his own role. His hero is Clark Clifford, Mc-Namara's replacement as Secretary of Defense, whom he credits as the crucial figure in changing Johnson's mind: "It was one of the great individual performances in recent American history." Dean Acheson, Douglas Dillon and Cyrus Vance are also praised for revising their earlier positions; and Paul Warnke, Paul Nitze, Richard Steadman and others appear to have become convinced of the bankruptcy of our Vietnam policy after the Tet offensive.

What appears to have happened during the early months of 1968 was a cracking-up of the American system. Trapped in a land war on the Asian continent, committed to selective bombing up North and "search and destroy" missions in the South, and faced with a "pacification" program in shambles, Johnson and the Joint Chiefs of Staff still believed in a "strategy of attrition" and imminent military victory. Mr. Hoopes makes it clear that few others shared this belief. There was division in the country: the President was persona non grata in big cities and on college campuses. There was division in his party: two Senators challenged his renomination. And there was division in his own Administration: people were prepared to resign. What's more, they were prepared to resign with a bang of protest instead of whimpering off to the Ford Foundation or the World Bank. From Mr. Hoopes's account, every time the "doves" thought the President was listening to them, he would fly off to the Middle West and end up Alamoting. (Why, incidentally, was Abe Fortas writing Johnson's Vietnam speeches while sitting as an Associate Justice of the Supreme Court? Will Judge Haynsworth, if he's ever confirmed, write Richard Nixon's civil rights speeches?)

New Hampshire delivered its message. Scouting reports from Wisconsin predicted disaster. Agreeing to the additional 206,000 soldiers General Westmoreland requested—a 40 per cent increase in our commitment—would have promoted domestic pandemonium. In this atmosphere, the Administration "doves" went to work. Allies like Mr. Clifford and Mr. Acheson were indispensable. The March 31 speech, which seems to have gotten more peaceable in tone and substance with each new draft, was the result.

What about that speech? Mr. Hoopes notes: "To Washington's surprise, North Vietnam responded quickly and affirmatively to President Johnson's new call for negotiations, accepting the half loaf of a partial bombing halt as an adequate basis for preliminary talks." Why was Washington surprised? Perhaps because many hands were involved in the speech's preparation; and most of them were aware that the 20th Parallel plan was indeed half a loaf; and not a few believed the speech they were shaping would be addressed more to Wisconsin voters than to Hanoi. It is important to remember that none of the speech writers expected the President to renounce his presidency; their purpose was partially, and in some cases wholly, political. Even Secretary Clifford didn't know about the trick ending until the last minute.

Yet Hanoi responded within an incredible sixty hours. Could it be that the President and the Pentagon and Mr. Rostow and Mr. Rusk actually didn't expect the North Vietnamese to respond favorably? Could it be that the President's retirement, tacked on at the end, actually had no strict bearing on the diplomatic intentions of the United States? That the escalation stopped, but the "strategy of attrition" is still subscribed to? That we are trapped in negotiations that we don't really want? One of the perils of electronic diplomacy is that you may be taken seriously. Embarrassing.

Answers will have to await other lacerating texts. Meanwhile, the concluding chapter of Mr. Hoopes's fascinating book is the most compelling argument I have seen for announcing our total withdrawal from Vietnam, and letting General Thieu and Marshal Ky accommodate themselves to that timetable. And the book in its entirety is the best account of decision making at a time of crisis since Robert Kennedy's *Thirteen Days*.

(November 1969)

P.S. Questions, as Wallace Stevens once said, are remarks, especially in a daily *Times* book review. You are supposed to keep your personal political opinions in your pocket, where, like Lenny and his mouse, you can twist their heads off. But you are permitted to insinuate those opinions by putting question marks on the end of statements, and letting the reader hang by them. Actually, two members of the Foreign Service, one of whom had worked on the March 31 speech, told me a month before my review appeared that Washington was flabbergasted by Hanoi's response.

The lacerating, of course, goes on. Mr. Hoopes himself has been accused of being a war criminal by people so innocent of institutions and of policy making that they couldn't organize a withdrawal from the breakfast table. They don't write books; they Xerox their indignation. For some appreciation of what really went on, outside of the Xerox-heads, we have to read Don Oberdorfer's *Tet!*, Anthony Austin's *The President's War*, Richard Hammer's *The Court-Martial of Lt. Calley* and the Pentagon Papers. Halberstam still hasn't finished his book. Richard Nixon is writing his re-election, on the assumption that so long as not too many American boys die in Vietnam, the American public won't care how many Vietnamese go on dying.

Willard Gaylin's *In the Service of Their Country*

All right, what happens to you if you chance to feel that the Parrot's Beak and the Fishhook aren't worth dying for? If you can't quite bring into reasonable approximation the rhetoric of Mr. Nixon and the reality of Southeast Asia? If you choose three to five years in prison instead of killing Vietnamese? As Dr. Willard Gaylin says, "This was a politically volatile subject, war resistance; in a sociologically vulnerable area, the prisons; conducted by a questionably respectable researcher, a psychoanalyst." Wrong. At least on the last count: Kenneth Keniston, Robert Coles, Robert Jay Lifton and, of course, Erik Erikson stack up as a library that—for respectability, intelligence and pertinence—makes most recent sociology look like comic books written by computers. Dr. Gaylin belongs on their shelf. At some length, over a considerable period of time, he interviewed young men who refused induction into our armed services; who chose instead to go to jail. In the process, he learned a great deal not only about prisons and the draft, but also about himself. A significant "counter-transference" occurred, leading him to ask crucial questions about psychoanalytic theory and therapeutic practice, as well as the war.

First, the young men. Twenty-six of them agreed to talk into Dr. Gaylin's tape recorder; twenty-two were white; twenty-one were the first sons in their families. Many might have escaped military service for reasons of religious conviction or physical disability. Few had been political activists. A representative six have chapters to themselves, their individual personalities leaping off the page as vividly as characters from Tolstoy. Not one of the twenty-six was a draft *dodger* (decamper to Canada) and not one will be the same sort of person after his experience of this particular "sanctuary."

Next, the prison: two prisons, plus an affiliated work camp. Forget, if you can, the possibility of a conscientious objector's getting
gang-raped because he comes on like a nice guy. Forget the fact that,
as Dr. Gaylin documents it, Jehovah's Witnesses get paroled and
CO's don't. Forget a warden's reluctance to give "work-releases" to
CO's and his indifference to the censorship of their mail and his—
let's be charitable—flexibility about job assignments. Forget the
judges who go hard on blacks and "political deviates"—Dr. Gaylin
is enraged, but he keeps his indignation on a leash—and the judges
who interpret the law according to the ideological sirocco, and the
families ashamed of sons who seek a premature withdrawal.

Which leaves the "stress" situation of the cage we call "rehabilitation" or "deterrence." Which leaves an individual's conscience subject to the severing by slide rule (pump, slice) that ensues without
the extenuation of belief in a Supreme Being. Which leaves an
analyst, an associate professor of psychiatry at Columbia, an ad-
junct professor at the Union Theological Seminary, wondering how
many fingers on one hand he would be willing to sacrifice for a year
of his youth, a year of his life. Dr. Gaylin invents an arbitration process called "gonk," in which warring tribes each put forward fifty
young girls, the lot to be tossed into a pit of crocodiles, the winning
tribe to be declared on the basis of the last maiden devoured. He
asks then whether "gonk" is any less sensible than that arbitration
process whereby each tribe sends 500,000 young men against the
other, until one side is destroyed.

But we know, don't we, that prisons are dreadful places? (Like
schools, they are places where we send those who, for a variety of
reasons, inconvenience us.) That political prisoners get worse treatment in jail than mere thugs do? That fathers insist on their sons
winning all the wars the fathers lost? Death, the Mafia, taxes and
General Thieu are inevitable, so what else is new from Dr. Gaylin?

Only, finally, that his introduction to psychoanalytic terminology
is succinct and sensible. Plus the fact that he writes uncommonly
well. In addition to which he makes perfectly clear that "displaced
rebellion against the father figure" doesn't explain away all the young
men who refuse to kill Orientals—after all, most of the astronauts
were the oldest sons in their families, too. Not to mention his throwaway line: "The war resister becomes victim not only to the nation's

pride, but to his own conscience." (Was there any political utility to their sacrifice? Weren't they compromised by their "co-operation" with prison authorities? Didn't their pacifism, and/or their Christianity, and/or their innocence, undergo an insupportable erosion during the heavy rains of penance, of persecution?)

Dr. Gaylin tells us that psychiatrists and psychologists are inevitably concerned with "value judgments"—"by defining an act as healthy or sick, as desirable or undesirable, as to be retained or abandoned." He tells us that social, political and moral conclusions emerge from a psychological investigation. He tells us that the non-directed, open-ended interview, and the recognition of the patient's repertoire of defenses, and dream-interpretation and "transference" are very fine so long as we assume the situation is sane and the patient is messed up. If the situation isn't sane, the psychiatrist, psychologist, psychoanalyst becomes a warden, hacker, screw: the guy with the ax who lops off all the excesses, the misshapenness, that makes us ill fitting (not *unfit*). Better, then, to change the situation, which should at least be large enough to accommodate some moral excess.

If you can read this book, and not feel that there's something wrong with sending these young men to prison, then I give up.

(May 1970)

A Nation of Veterans

(1) "The rapid deployment and support of a force of over one quarter of a million men to an area 10,000 miles from our shores clearly demonstrates that our logistics system has that capability. Never before has this country been able to field and support in combat so large a force in so short a time over so great a distance."

(2) "The war is far from over, but the future is much brighter and the record shows that it was tactical airpower, U. S. Air Force style, that gave our ground troops the edge they needed to break up the VC drive and turn the tide of battle in our favor."

(3) "There are no greater patriots than those good men who have been maimed in the service of their country."

(4) "The assumption is that war is a kind of game on which nations embark after consulting a computer to see who would come out ahead."

Of these four quotations, three come directly from *Militarism: U.S.A.*, by Col. James A. Donovan, United States Marine Corps, retired. They were uttered, respectively, by Robert S. McNamara (1966), *Air Force* magazine (1966) and Napoleon (somewhat earlier). The fourth quotation is from an article by I. F. Stone, and is included because I think it represents an important point on the compass of Colonel Donovan's argument.

Colonel Donovan believes that American servicemen were deployed in Southeast Asia simply because we had the capacity to do so, and not because the national interest warranted it. Vietnam gave the Army a chance to test its counter-insurgency doctrines; the Air Force a chance to perfect its tactical and strategic bombing strikes; the Marines a chance to try out amphibious coastal attacks and mobile air–ground "inkblot" operations; and the Navy a chance to play in-shore counter-infiltration patrol and riverine-delta warfare games.

He further believes that the bombing of North Vietnam was a "hoax." By October 1968, we had dropped almost 50 per cent more bombs on Vietnam than in both Europe and the Pacific during all of World War ii—2,948,057 tons to 2,057,244 tons—at a cost of about fifty cents a pound of bomb, or $3 billion. "Never," he says, "were more money and effort wasted with less results to show for it." By July 1969, according to Gen. John P. McConnell's testimony before the Senate Armed Services Committee, everything was operating in North Vietnam "very nearly as if it had not even been touched." And, adds Colonel Donovan, "a small underequipped army of irregulars [has fought] to a bloody standstill the finest and best-equipped expeditionary force America has ever fielded."

Colonel Donovan attributes the impasse both to faulty strategy (we are an air/sea power and shouldn't have gotten ourselves trapped in an Asian land war) and to faulty psychology (the idea that we can police the world, and that there are military solutions to every political problem). He offers a number of specific proposals for cutting back military manpower and reducing defense appropriations, none of which I am qualified to review. But the design of *Mil-*

itarism: U.S.A., which grew out of an *Atlantic* magazine article by Colonel Donovan and Gen. David M. Shoup, is much broader than just one more critique of our Vietnam war policies.

Several chapters are devoted to the history of the American military establishment from the Spanish-American War to the Safeguard ABM system. Much of this material is familiar, but the incidental facts are fascinating and disturbing. For instance: 2,072 retired senior military officials are employed by defense industries. The Department of Defense owns $195.5 billion worth of property. L. Mendel Rivers's Charleston congressional district got quite a few defense plants, submarine bases, Air Force bases, supply depots and military hospitals after Mr. Rivers became the chairman of the House Armed Services Committee. The cost-efficient Mr. McNamara took over a defense budget of $44.7 billion a year, and left a defense budget of $80 billion a year.

More important are the chapters dealing with our acquiescence to demands by the military for tax monies at home and adventurism abroad. Colonel Donovan believes that the reasons for this acquiescence go deeper than any conspiracy theory about military-industrial complexes. "We are," he says, "a nation of veteran military and naval professionals": 14.9 million World War ii veterans, 5.7 million Korean veterans—most of them conditioned by training to respect military codes of honor, patriotism, sacrifice; most of them associated with veterans' groups; many of them (3,182,141 in 1967) receiving compensation and pension benefits. Every American President since Franklin Roosevelt has tried to shore up his image with the personal popularity of generals and admirals, excepting, of course, Dwight Eisenhower.

This is dangerous territory, not really dealt with in Morris Janowitz's *The Professional Soldier* (1960) or Samuel P. Huntington's *The Soldier and the State* (1964). Colonel Donovan goes over it with the same thoughtfulness he brings to ROTC (he wants liberal arts majors in the armed services to counterbalance the professional warriors) and military careerism (reminding us of Tocqueville's observation that "an officer has no property but his pay and no distinction but that of military honors," and so military professionals may desire war "because war creates vacancies"). He is matter-of-fact, almost as matter-of-fact as a "vacancy."

(July 1970)

Telford Taylor's *Nuremberg and Vietnam*
Mark Lane's *Conversations with Americans*

Telford Taylor, who was chief counsel for the prosecution at the Nuremberg trials twenty-five years ago and who is today a professor of law at Columbia University, undertakes the elucidation of a dark paradox: "It has come to this: that the anti-aggression spirit of Nuremberg and the United Nations Charter is invoked to justify our venture in Vietnam, where we have smashed the country to bits, and will not even take the trouble to clean up the blood and rubble. None there will ever thank us; few elsewhere that do not see our America as a sort of Steinbeckian 'Lennie,' gigantic and powerful, but prone to shatter what we try to save."

Mr. Taylor is painstaking. He begins with a survey of historical precedents in defining "war crimes" and establishing tribunals to judge the accused. He considers such notions as "just," "unjust" and "aggressive" wars; "the principle of chivalry"; "superior orders" and "reprisals." He examines the Hague and Geneva Conventions, the U. S. Army Field Manual of 1956 and the 1863 Lieber regulations on treatment of prisoners during the American Civil War. He tells what actually happened at the Nuremberg and Tokyo trials of Germans and Japanese. (The Japanese fared worse than the Germans. Gen. Tomoyuki Yamashita was condemned to death by hanging "for failure properly to control the conduct of Japanese troops under his command in the Philippines.")

It's a messy business, trying to decide what's permissible on a battlefield. "No rules to restrain the conduct of war will ever be observed if victory seems to depend upon the breach of them," warned Lowes Dickinson. Guerrilla insurgencies complicate the picture: the Vietcong do not subscribe to the Geneva Convention. And yet, as Mr. Taylor insists, literally millions of lives have been saved because most nations observe at least a few of the "rules" we have agreed on to protect ourselves from what we are capable of doing. By exploring the thinking behind those rules, Mr. Taylor qualifies himself to look at what Americans are up to in Vietnam—not as a polemicist but as a lawyer.

He doesn't like what he sees. He doesn't like "reprisal" attacks by mortar and aerial bombardment, the Songmy massacre and our treatment of prisoners, which he calls "war crimes" by any definition. The case of Lt. James Duffy, who executed a Vietnamese prisoner, is instructive. Lieutenant Duffy's defense was that his action was consistent with official policy, considering the Army's emphasis on a "high body count." The court was sufficiently impressed by this argument to revoke its own verdict of premeditated murder (mandatory life sentence) and convict him instead of involuntary manslaughter (six months). "The crime," says Mr. Taylor, "was made to fit the punishment."

But if the Duffy defense has any logic whatsoever, it leads upward —to the policy makers. "The ultimate question of 'guilt' in the trials of the Songmy troops is how far what they did departed from general American military practice in Vietnam as they had witnessed it," says Mr. Taylor. In this respect, it is not only instructive but appalling to read Mark Lane's *Conversations with Americans*, edited transcripts of his interviews with American servicemen, some of them deserters, some of them honorably discharged, some of them still in our armed services. Mark Lane is his own credibility gap, but editors at Simon & Schuster have listened to the tapes, many of the veterans use their real names, and the weight of specific detail is enormous.

According to the thirty-two servicemen Mr. Lane talked to, the following were common practices in Vietnam: American soldiers and Marines snipping off enemy ears and wearing them in their hats or preserving them in jars of alcohol . . . torture of suspected Vietcong by bamboo splints under the fingernails, amputation of fingers, electrical wiring from field telephones attached to the genitals . . . prisoners dropped from helicopters . . . the gang-raping of Vietnamese nurses, followed by GIs shoving hand flares into the women's vaginas, which exploded their stomachs. In its attention to the details of sadism and murder, *Conversations with Americans* is a sickening book, a kind of pornography, the livid flip side of Mr. Taylor's legal brief. But the cross-references and eyewitness testimony and, in many instances, personal confession make it horrifyingly convincing.

General American military practice in Vietnam—then who is to blame? Mr. Taylor cites the Yamashita precedent, which we as a nation established. He stops just short of calling for a "war crimes" trial of American policy makers. He does not believe the courts can declare this war illegal—treaties like the Geneva Convention have no more binding legal effect than congressional statutes; the latest statute supersedes the previous ones; Congress determines the national "acceptance" of a policy—nor that any policy maker will in fact be tried. But he throws some names into the hopper to help us think about Songmy: Lt. Gen. Robert E. Cushman, Gen. William C. Westmoreland, Gen. Creighton Abrams, Lt. Gen. William B. Rossen, Adm. Ulysses Grant Sharp, Jr., and the Chiefs of Staff in Washington. "It is on these officers that command responsibility for the conduct of operations has lain."

(November 1970)

p.s. A month after this review appeared, I had left the daily *Times* for the Sunday *Book Review*. Neil Sheehan delivered an article to us on Mark Lane that opened the "credibility gap" so wide the book disappeared into it, never again to be advertised by Simon & Schuster. Sheehan was much abused by opponents of the war for having made Lane look unreliable. God, not Sheehan, did that. A remarkable example of high-mindlessness: if you don't believe everything awful everyone says about American conduct in Vietnam, you must approve of Americans conducting themselves in Vietnam. Sheehan, of course, didn't approve. He had seen enough on his own tour of duty in Southeast Asia, and brooded enough afterwards on what he had seen, to make him wonder about war crimes. He simply wanted them authenticated. He would subsequently write a 7,000-word review of the evidence for the *Book Review* that got national attention. (He would also come into possession of the Pentagon Papers.) But, again, some people were thinking with their stomachs, and were willing to eat any old garbage fed to them in hardcovers. Knowing Lane, I should have known better than to swallow anything he said without checking it out more thoroughly than a couple of telephone calls to Simon & Schuster. I suppose I wanted to believe it, too: the snipped-off ears, the gang-rape, the electrical wires on genitals. A show-biz pornography, easier to get angry about than Mylai, which numbs the mind. Sex is the least of war, but a more manageable reality.

Mylai, or Songmy, was what Telford Taylor was worried about. It goes on, our Calleys enjoying the sympathy of our President, Calley's senior officers excused from the Yamashita precedent, our Colonel Herberts gagged and disgraced by the Army they tried to warn, a country refusing to think about it. It may be that Nuremberg and Tokyo were bad precedents, victor's justice. That the outrage of a Telford Taylor and a Neil Sheehan over what we've done, unprecedented in a nation that *hasn't* lost a war—hasn't, in fact, stopped fighting it—is somehow a credit to our democracy. But if democracy amounts to nothing more than a highly permissive noise level, and no substantive reform, screams and no accounting . . . I can't think of a way to finish this sentence.

John Kenneth Galbraith's *Ambassador's Journal*

Were one to construct, from the glass bricks in these diaries, an architectural idea of John Kenneth Galbraith's ego, it would be a cathedral the size of a subcontinent. Beneath each icon would lie a mirror and one of his books. Above each arch would be nailed the stuffed head of a State Department mountebank. In each apse would be a bar, a groaning board and two or three beautiful women. He admits to imperfections—his fishing is indifferent, his sinuses are poorly, his "Uzbek is shaky," Krishna Menon reduced him to conversational impotence and the actress Angie Dickinson refused to accompany him to Honolulu—but on the whole his self-esteem is awesome. And he gets away with it. He is large enough to bear the weight of his own charming arrogance. He is, to use his favorite adjective, "agreeable." Admit it. Most of us would like to be John Kenneth Galbraith as much as John Kenneth Galbraith likes to be himself.

His diary begins a month after John Kennedy's election to the presidency and ends four days after Dallas. In between are his stints as ghostwriter on the New Frontier; his years in India as our imperial presence; his jet stops in Geneva, Rome, Washington and Cambridge, Massachusetts; his cable writing, speech giving, partygoing and personal letters to the White House. (What letters! Imagine writing to the President: "A few weeks ago one of our aircraft carriers brought 12 supersonic jets to Karachi where they were unloaded with all the secrecy that would attend mass sodomy on the BMT at rush hour.")

We learn little in these pages that is new about Kennedy, Dean Rusk, Nehru, Kashmir, Vietnam. Nor—except for a fine account of the China-India border crisis, the story of the Boharo steel plant and the presidential letters—do we get much substantive examination of foreign policy issues. But the day-to-day life of an American ambassador and his family is delightfully recorded. So is the dreariness of working with the State Department. (Dealing with one high official is "like playing badminton with a marshmallow—you don't know whether he is going to stick or bounce.") And for tourists of the subcontinent of Galbraith, he is his own engaging Baedeker.

He is, moreover, a compulsive wit, aphorist and anecdotalist. On presidential appointments: "On all honorific boards and bodies, it is imperative to be either a Republican or Ralph McGill." On pragmatism: "Politics is not the art of the possible. It consists in choosing between the disastrous and the unpalatable." On the Indian parliament during the border war: "There was some heckling and a great deal of highly original military advice from the back benches. The arming of elephants was not proposed but only because no one had thought of it." On embassy food: "It takes some skill to spoil a breakfast—even the English can't do it. But our cook can. His bacon was what turned Islam against pork." On academic honors: "My rule on honorary degrees has been to always have one more than Arthur Schlesinger Jr." On Senator Frank Lausche, who abstained when the Senate confirmed Galbraith's appointment as ambassador: "In 1968, Lausche was defeated for renomination. Asked to comment, I hazarded the guess that it was the result of the lingering resentment of the people of Ohio over this action. The explanation was not widely accepted." Or, finally, eavesdrop on Nehru's remarks after having met Gov. Nelson Rockefeller: "A most extraordinary man. He talked to me about nothing but bomb shelters. Why does he think I am interested in bomb shelters? He gave me a pamphlet on how to build my own shelter."

We watch Mr. Galbraith's growing concern with events in Vietnam, as confided to his diary and the President. We come to understand how much of an ambassador's time is squandered on social functions, on waiting for the State Department to reply to his queries, on balancing domestic (political) and careerist (personal) considerations, on fighting off the military and the intelligence agencies. We approve his escape into the "McLandress Dimension" fantasy, even as lesser men escape into the sports pages. We sympathize with his Byzantine arrangements for the Jacqueline Kennedy visit. We are in excellent company.

It is company, however, a trifle disdainful of most of the world. The sins of the mountebanks are not nearly so well documented as his biting commentary on the sinners. Perhaps the slight disappointment of the book, like the thinness of his novel *Triumph*, might be accounted for by his disinclination to imagine other people's "realities," to project himself into their minds and shoes. On himself, and on abstract ideas, he is incisive and absorbing. Other people, though, seem only to move in fixed orbits around his confident sensibility: a sort of Galbraitho-centric view of the universe.

But perhaps I am being ungrateful. Wit, grace, intelligence, dedication—they are *almost* enough. He sums up himself and his post: "The job itself is amusing and interesting and one for which I have four considerable qualifications—a grasp of the economic situation, considerable ease in written and spoken communication, some knowledge of politics and an unquestioned willingness to instruct other people in their duty."

(October 1969)

Running Against the Machine

Oh, yawn, Mailer-Breslin . . . City of New York . . . Democratic Party primary . . . ego-moonshot . . . (Yes, Virginia, there is a reserve clause.) Begin with the effrontery—how else to begin when this book is as much a package of heart, brains and garbage as was the campaign itself?—and do a lot of snorting. They *are* crybabies. The press didn't take them seriously, the electorate was out to naked lunch, the competition came prefab from Zombies, Inc., and the city is a cancer ward. Because too few listened to these noisy patients, they retired to suck on eggs of sulk and write articles for *Life* magazine on astronaughtiness and, in a thrombotic snit, permit this anthology of their misdemeanors to be published.

Fifty-first state, indeed. (As though Albany would let its tax base go; as though Congress would allow us a couple of extra trouble-making Senators.) Power to the neighborhoods, wow. (As though that would take care of Con Ed, corporate unionism, mass transit, legal and medical services, etc.) "Free Huey Newton, end fluorida-tion . . . compulsory free love in those neighborhoods which vote for it along with compulsory church attendance on Sunday for those neighborhoods who vote for that." (As though the exchange of privacy and hard-won individual freedoms-under-the-law for hetero-doxies of self-constituted fiefdoms was some kind of libertarian bar-gain. The politics of kindergarten.)

Having yawned, snorted, as-thoughed; having observed that if Mailer lost half his vote to Herman Badillo the final week of the campaign, the other half might also have gone to Badillo had the Pulitzer Prize winner pulled out; having complained that Gloria Steinem's ultimate reticence took most of the political sophistica-tion and all of the physical beauty out of the campaign; having ob-jected to the unconscionable repetitiousness of *Running Against the Machine*; having decided to ignore the sobering similarities be-tween William F. Buckley, Jr.'s adventurism in 1965 and Mailer's in 1969; having asserted that Mailer-Breslin got more attention than most splinter-party candidates and quixotic insurgents, so why whine about it and where are you now . . . ?

Having, in other words, said all the obvious, what more is there to say about this freeze-dried autopsy of a book? In fact, a great deal. (Here comes that reserve clause.) Sandwiched in between the stale parajournalism are position papers that have more to say about transportation, air pollution, schools, crime and municipal economics than any of the floorwalkers campaigning right now on television are giving us. Astonishing sensible position papers. Moreover, we wouldn't need a fifty-first state to try them out.

And there are actually ideas. Admittedly, they are dropped like popcorn into the ideological frying pan, but attention should be paid. Forget the jousting tournaments, the Muhammed Ali resolu-tion, Mario Procaccino as Official City Greeter, the World Series of stickball. Forget turning Coney Island into a Las Vegas East—a drag ball for gangsters? But monorail, community colleges, Sweet Sunday, neighborhood housing banks . . . Free bicycles in city parks, day-care centers and nurseries . . . no traffic allowed on the island of Manhattan except for buses, trucks and cabs . . . More zoos, bonuses for policemen who live in the neighborhoods they patrol . . . abolition of the Surrogate Court . . . locally controlled cable TV . . . These are proposals that can't, and shouldn't be laughed off.

No amount of casuistry is going to explain away Norman Mailer's performance at the Village Gate as anything other than the disgrace it was. No amount of bitterness is going to alter the fact that one of America's finest writers was one of her worst mayoralty candidates, in instinct and in practice. No amount of statistical legerdemain will change the fact that his candidacy wounded the liberal cause this year. But wounds heal. Sometimes we need them, especially in the self-esteem; the scar tissue can make us tougher, more knowledgeable, street-wise. More important questions were asked during the Mailer-Breslin light show last spring than I, for one, realized. (Which is partly my fault, and partly the fault of the media for not taking the thing seriously, and mostly the fault of Mailer-Breslin for vaudevillifying themselves in such a way as to make it almost impossible to take them seriously.) And now, after the speeches, papers, clippings, memos—after the witty articles by Noel Parmentel and Jane O'Reilly reprinted here—one more question nags. Where are all these people? Having lost their first political skirmish, will they with their righteous silence add to the smog, the plague, the frug of the fantoccini now oppressing us in the person of Mr. Procaccino? Is there any more heart?

(October 1969)

Who Killed John F. Kennedy?

American Grotesque, An Account of the Clay
Shaw–Jim Garrison Affair in the City of New
Orleans, by James Kirkwood

A Heritage of Stone, by Jim Garrison

Bad vibrations.

New Orleans District Attorney Jim Garrison arrested New Orleans
businessman Clay Shaw, charging that Mr. Shaw conspired to as-
sassinate President John F. Kennedy. Mr. Shaw was acquitted by a
jury. Mr. Garrison then had Mr. Shaw rearrested on two charges of
perjury. Mr. Shaw is suing Mr. Garrison, and a host of others. The
judge at Mr. Shaw's trial has since been arrested in a motel room
where stag movies and loose women are alleged to have exhibited
themselves. The principal witness against Mr. Shaw has since been
arrested for burglary. Mr. Garrison has since been accused of molest-
ing a thirteen-year-old boy at the New Orleans Athletic Club, which
is interesting because Mr. Shaw allegedly had links with the New
Orleans homosexual underground.

No, this is not a fiction by Gore Vidal. It is a serialized novel on
the front pages of our daily newspapers. Maybe that explains why
novelist James Kirkwood—*Good Times, Bad Times*—got obsessed
with the subject. Mr. Kirkwood met Mr. Shaw, and believed his story,
and so wrote a sympathetic article before the trial (published by
Esquire) and an indignant article after the trial (rejected by
Playboy) and this tome-stone of a book (troubling the reviewer).
Did Clay Shaw know David Ferrie and Lee Harvey Oswald? Is Jim
Garrison paranoiac about the federal government? One wishes the
whole business were a fevered invention.

It isn't. Mr. Kirkwood argues in *American Grotesque* that Jim
Garrison used Clay Shaw to try the Warren Commission report;
that Garrison scraped the bottom of the barrel for variously sick
and variously intimidated witnesses to smear Shaw; that Garrison's
guerrillas sought a jury of sub-par intelligence to bemuse with bloody

fantasies; that, having impaneled such a jury, they were so upset
by the acquittal that they added the insult of "perjury" to the injury
of "conspiracy" accusations. Unfortunately, Mr. Kirkwood is so conscientious in his reportage that one wonders *why* so many people
claimed to have seen Mr. Shaw with Oswald and Ferrie. Were they
all mistaken or lying?

To be sure, conspiracy wasn't proved, and the state embarrassed
itself with surreal incompetence. But "conspiracy" is no longer the
charge against Shaw; perjury is. We have only Mr. Kirkwood's emotional word on innocence to go by. Such a word isn't conclusive, not
even in a book reviewer's court. Mr. Kirkwood's loyalty to a friend
is admirable; his taped interviews with all the principals in the first
Shaw trial are fascinating; his attention to trivia is in the best
parajournalistic tradition—the little boy who cried Tom Wolfe. But
legitimate questions about John Kennedy's assassination aren't answered according to the buddy system.

Which brings us to Jim Garrison's *A Heritage of Stone*. The District Attorney of Orleans Parish argues that Kennedy's assassination
can only be explained by a "model" that pins the murder on
the Central Intelligence Agency. The CIA could have engineered
Dallas in behalf of the military/intelligence/industrial complex that
feared the President's disposition toward a détente with the Russians. Mr. Garrison nowhere in his book mentions Clay Shaw, or
the botch his office made of Shaw's prosecution—surely an extraordinary omission! He is, however, heavy on all the other characters
who have become familiar to us via late-night talk shows on television.
And he insists that the Warren Commission, the executive branch of
the government, some members of the Dallas Police Department,
the pathologists at Bethesda who performed the second Kennedy
autopsy and many, many others must have known they were lying to
the American public.

Frankly, I prefer to believe that the Warren Commission did a
poor job, rather than a dishonest one. I like to think that Mr. Garrison invents monsters to explain what was really just incompetence.
But until somebody explains why two autopsies came to two different conclusions about the President's wounds, why the limousine
was washed out and rebuilt without investigation, why certain witnesses near the "grassy knoll" were never asked to testify before the
commission, why we were all so eager to buy Oswald's brilliant

marksmanship in split seconds, why no one inquired into Jack Ruby's relations with a staggering variety of strange people, why a "loner" like Oswald always had friends and could always get a passport—who can blame the Garrison guerrillas for fantasizing?

Something stinks about this whole affair. A *Heritage of Stone* rehashes the smelliness; the recipe is as unappetizing as our doubts about the official version of what happened. (Would then-Attorney General Robert F. Kennedy have endured his brother's murder in silence? Was John Kennedy quite so liberated from cold war clichés as Mr. Garrison maintains?) But the stench is there, and clings to each of us. Why were Kennedy's neck organs not examined at Bethesda for evidence of a frontal shot? Why was his body whisked away to Washington before the legally required Texas inquest? Why?

(December 1970)

P.S. This was my last review for the daily *Times*. It appeared as written above in the first edition of December 1, under the headline "Who Killed John F. Kennedy?" In all subsequent editions, the review ended after the sentence, "I like to think that Mr. Garrison invents monsters . . ." And there was a new headline: "The Shaw-Garrison Affair." A night editor in the bullpen at the *Times* had taken it upon himself to decide that the questions which followed that sentence were my own private political opinions, and not properly a part of a book review. So he cut them, without consulting me. They were not, of course, my own opinions; they were questions raised by the books; and deleting them deformed, if indeed it didn't reverse, the judgment expressed in the review. A year and a half later, I still receive a letter every other week from a graduate student or researcher who has discovered the discrepancy between the first and last editions of the newspaper, since both versions of the review are on microfilm. The letters want to know what happened, and I tell all.

This was the only time during my year and a half as a *Times* reviewer that such a thing occurred—although once I was asked to change a phrase which described John Lindsay as "like a younger brother or a clubfoot; we are stuck with him."

BAD DREAMS

The Ultimate Folly, War by Pestilence, Asphyxiation and Defoliation, by Congressman Richard D. McCarthy

Just last week President Nixon came out against most germs and some gas. To many, it will seem that a bad dream has been called off on account of common sense, a dream of chemical and biological weapons on which the Army alone has spent $203.8 million since 1963. Plague, anthrax, tularemia, psittacosis, botulism, Rocky Mountain spotted fever and Venezuelan equine encephalitis are no longer to be considered legitimate extensions of statecraft. The Senate is prepared, only forty-four years late, to ratify the 1925 Geneva Protocol, binding us with over sixty other signatories in one of those agreements by nations to pretend to be civilized. Haven't we therefore abolished the dream by executive order? Is it really necessary to ponder Representative Richard D. McCarthy's angry, disquieting, fact-filled book?

It is necessary. *The Ultimate Folly* is part history: Sir Jeffrey Amherst in the French and Indian War giving away smallpox-infected blankets to Indian chiefs, deliberately causing an epidemic; the United States in 1962 contemplating gas warfare against Cuba. And part journalism: why those 6,400 sheep in Utah died from nerve gas; which Government agencies, universities, research institutes and industrial organizations engage in CBW activity. And part moral inquiry: asking the questions that went unanswered in Mr. Nixon's directive last week.

That directive promised that *we* would never use germs in combat, that we would use incapacitating chemicals only in retaliation (the common cold war), and that our biological arsenal would be destroyed. Tear gas and defoliants of the sort employed in Vietnam were exempted from the presidential order.

Yet the New York Representative demonstrates that CS tear gas, a "super" variant which attacks the lungs instead of the eyes and is moisture-resistant besides, is used in Vietnam in a lethal way: to flush enemy soldiers and civilians from buildings and caves in order to kill them with air and artillery strikes (contrary to most interpretations of the Geneva Protocol). He also demonstrates that the defoliants, attacking rice crops as well as jungle, might have dangerous long-term effects on Vietnam's ecology. (Defoliants and ecology were unanticipated by the protocol draftsmen.)

Beyond the specifics of Vietnam are all those unappetizing ethical generalities. We apparently abandoned our pursuit of a CBW capacity not because anyone thought it was evil, but because there was no way to test it; and smaller, poorer nations might develop it as a substitute for the hydrogen bomb; and no one could figure out how to keep a contagious disease from crossing the wrong border; and domestic transport of the stuff was a hazard. (Even so, the Joint Chiefs of Staff opposed Mr. Nixon's directive to the last yawp.)

In addition, Mr. McCarthy points out that only five Congressmen, unknown even to their colleagues, are sufficiently briefed and privileged to slip funds for such projects—CBW, CIA, Green Berets —into appropriations bills. He alludes to the moral responsibility of the bureaucrats, scientists and businessmen who kept the very hairy ball rolling toward a possible "pandemic." He wonders how much even a President knows about the sort of "commitment" that begins as a feasibility study and ends as an autonomous process, self-justifying and all-liquidating.

The only aspect of this ugly business unexplored by the admirable Congressman is why we experiment with such stuff only on Orientals, rioting blacks, and young white demonstrators. Is it so very paranoid to speculate that we only spray upon those whom we wish didn't exist?

(March 1970)

Let Them Eat Promises, The Politics of Hunger in America, by Nick Kotz

This savage, eloquent, fact-filled book seems a sort of Unhappy Birthday card to Martin Luther King. Dr. King proposed the 1968 Poor People's March on Washington less than a week before his assassination, and *Let Them Eat Promises* is partly a body count of that abortive engagement. It's as though our national conscience were a cement block, and Nick Kotz resolved with a sledgehammer to drive spike after spike of reproach into it until it crumbles or is shaped into something not quite so ugly. No more sophistry, he insists: "The poorest Americans who have been buried in the Deep South, the Indian reservations, the barrios of the Southwest, and the big city ghetto did not fail to make it in America because they lacked ambition or ability. The plantation system, the migrant system, the Indian welfare system, the mining system all created long odds against a man's breaking out of a cycle of abject, dependent peonage."

We have officially admitted that some sixteen million Americans go hungry. Richard Nixon is perturbed about it: "Something very like the honor of American democracy is at issue," he said. Yet while they hunger we persist in quibbling: Which federal agency should feed them, and how; does "hunger" mean "starvation"; is malnutrition a consequence of ignorance or lack of income?

Mr. Kotz, a Pulitzer Prize-winning Washington correspondent for the Des Moines *Register,* paints an appalling picture of political persiflage, bureaucratic ineptitude and moral obtuseness. His is investigative reportage of the highest order, telling us what we need to know about a congressional seniority system that elevates and perpetuates satraps like Jamie Whitten; Orville Freeman's floundering at the Department of Agriculture; the indifference of Lyndon Johnson to anything but Vietnam and inflation; the ethical callousness of the food industry; the anxiety of the white southern Establishment to drive blacks off the land and up North before blacks vote the Establishment out of office; and the arrangement by which liberals buy a little food for the hungry by voting for farm subsidies.

What about malnutrition? Mr. Kotz demonstrates that (1) it retards the development of mind and body; and (2) the poor, according to an Agriculture Department study, "actually make *better* use of their nutritional dollars" than do the rest of us.

What about the food industry? He informs us that food technologists have developed inexpensive synthetic or fortified food products —e.g., the corn, soy and dried milk concentrate called CSM—containing all those proteins and vitamins missing from a poor man's diet. While such products are available to underdeveloped countries, they aren't available to Harlem or Appalachia or Mississippi, because then they would be competing with established commercial staples. Meanwhile, the industry takes iodine out of salt, iron out of bread, vitamins A and D out of milk, and compensates by putting more fat into frankfurters.

What about national priorities? Despite Mr. Nixon's perturbation, ABM and SST went sailing through budgetary review, and all the other programs had to scramble for any loose change left over: "Education was pitted against welfare, which competed with mass transit, which vied with air pollution, which competed with food programs." We have, notes Mr. Kotz, a Gross National Product of $900 billion. We pay farmers $3 billion a year not to plant food. Each family has 1.2 cars and 1.3 TV sets. There are eight million pleasure boats in the Great Society . . . and seven million children don't have enough to eat; we feed them pieties.

There isn't an aspect of this "dismal story" that Mr. Kotz neglects: the food stamp and commodities programs; the "cost benefit ratio" of feeding a child versus what we will eventually have to pay in welfare, hospitalization and other expenses for neglecting him originally; the inadequacy of the hot lunch program for schoolchildren; the names of the lobbyists involved and synopses of their rationalizations; the absence of overall economic planning; the wretched coverage Resurrection City received from the mass media; the penitence of Ernest Hollings.

His conclusions are compelling. Some kind of income maintenance or guaranteed annual wage is inevitable, he argues, but while we argue about it, the food stamp and commodity distribution programs should be reformed "to supply adequate nutrition at minimum cost to all poor families." We must expand the school lunch program, require the enrichment of food staples, encourage the development of synthetic and fortified products, and transfer jurisdiction over federal food aid projects from the Department of Agriculture to the Department of Health, Education and Welfare.

Finally, Mr. Kotz touches on a dimension of "the politics of hunger" that should excite whichever ethical faculties in us remain unatrophied: statistical morality. He quotes a doctor: "If the infant mortality rate [in the United States] was on a par with modern European countries, 50,000 children would not die unnecessarily in this nation each year." In other words, if Norway can do it, we should be able to. And if we don't, are we not, as a nation, collectively guilty of the murder of 50,000 children? It is only one question in this excellent book of questions and answers, but it hurts the mind.

(November 1969)

Nader's Raiders, The Ralph Nader Study Group Reports on the Food and Drug Administration, Air Pollution, and the Interstate Commerce Commission

"I grow daily to honor facts more and more, and theory less and less," wrote Thomas Carlyle to Ralph Waldo Emerson in 1836. "A fact, it seems to me, is a great thing—a sentence printed, if not by God, then at least by the Devil." What Ralph Nader and his cadres of young lawyers and graduate students have provided for us is a swamp of facts, mostly printed by the Devil, about our federal regulatory agencies. The reader is bound to get lost in this swamp, stopping here amazed, there outraged, without a compass (that is, a theory) in a world of rapacity, incompetence, collusion and criminal negligence. The reviewer wonders how to manage the facts, how to make the swamp into something comprehensible: a stockyard or a sewer.

We heard last year from Nicholas Johnson on the Federal Communications Commission, in *How to Talk Back to Your Television Set*. We also heard from Mr. Nader, Edward F. Cox, Robert C. Fellmeth and John E. Schulz on the Federal Trade Commission, re-issued this month as a $1.25 Grove paperback. Now there are Nader reports on the Food and Drug Administration, the National Air Pollution Control Administration and the Interstate Commerce Commission, published simultaneously in cloth and paper by Gross-man, with the promise of three more such reports this fall.

White papers, black books, bills of indictment: Do they add up to anything generalizable? It seems to me that they add up to an ac-cusation that the New Deal failed. On the evidence of these books, agencies established to protect the consumer (whether he is consum-ing food, air, advertisements, transportation services or electronic images) from corporate venality and physical and/or psychic poison-ing do no such thing. Those agencies take as their client not the consumer, but the very industry they are supposed to regulate. The laws are inadequate. Their enforcement is lax. Research budgets are pitifully small. Research priorities are poorly conceived. Political ap-pointments compromise professional integrity and staff morale. And there appears to be a two-way street of careerism between "regulator" and "regulated"—eighty-three FDA employees left for jobs in the food industry in 1964 alone—just as there is between the Pentagon and the defense industries.

James S. Turner in *The Chemical Feast* reports that the food industry spends 18 per cent of its annual $125-billion gross in-come on promotion. And yet Coca-Cola and Dr. Pepper are not obliged to admit that they contain caffeine; Lipton's Beef Stroganoff avoids a Department of Agriculture requirement of 45 per cent beef by dividing its product into three subpackages, only one of which measures up to the rules (the whole is 20 per cent beef, and 25 per cent soy bean meal); and frankfurter makers don't have to acknowledge their fat content, which was up to 33 per cent of average weight in 1969. The FDA is very good at burning all the books of Wilhelm Reich, but failed to act on cyclamates for twenty years, denies there's any malnutrition in America, can't do anything about monosodium glutamate in baby foods, or make anybody com-ply with legislative guidelines on content, processing or labeling.

Etcetera. One wants to keep saying etcetera as the horror stories accumulate. John C. Esposito in *Vanishing Air* reports that General Motors in three years spent $40 million for research on a "low-polluting" automobile engine—a whopping "sixteen hours of gross revenue for the corporation"—and concluded it wasn't feasible. Manufacturing contributes $450 billion a year to the Gross National Product, but also contributes 58 billion pounds of air contaminants (300 pounds per person); the public must absorb the more than $40 billion a year it costs to clean up after that manufacturing, while waiting for the next "temperature inversion" to kill people, as it has in Los Angeles, Chicago and New York in recent years. Monsanto, the chemical company, markets an anti-pollution system it won't use in its own St. Louis plant.

Do we need any more etceteras? Robert Fellmeth, back from his wars with the FTC, argues in *The Interstate Commerce Omission* that the ICC is "an elephant's graveyard for political hacks"; the public is excluded from the decision-making process; important studies of commission functions and transportation problems have been suppressed; railroad mergers are rubber-stamped; passenger rail service is being allowed to die; conglomerates cheat the customer; truck-driving safety regulations are unenforced; home-moving firms overcharge; rate bureaus encourage "monopolistic" price-fixing . . .

Facts, literally a million of them. A few, of course, have gotten into newspapers and magazines, since the Nader reports are released to the media before they are published for the general public. But, after throwing away the newspapers and magazines, the public forgets, as it forgets what the American Committee for Information on Brazil had to say about *Terror in Brazil*, or what the Twentieth Century Fund Task Force had to report on *Electing Congress: The Financial Dilemma*. I can't think of any concerned American—whether he or she writes editorials, works for the government, subscribes to *National Review*, or does whatever passes for planning whatever pass for policies on the New Left—who shouldn't wade through the Nader swamp of facts and, Carlyle to the contrary notwithstanding, perhaps form a theory of what they mean. Meanwhile, we require a kind of "institutionalization" of Ralph Nader, to keep the heat on, file the legal suits, write the books and drag us by our tin ears into the swamp.

(July 1970)

The Politics of Ecology, by James Ridgeway

In last Thursday's New York *Times*, E. W. Kenworthy reported from Washington that representatives of ten environmental and consumer organizations were refused permission by the Department of Commerce to attend a meeting of the National Industrial Pollution Control Council. The council was established in April by President Nixon to advise the government "on environmental programs affecting industry and on industry's proposals for dealing with the pollution it causes." The members of the council are top executives of major companies and industry associations. Not only were representatives of the conservation groups kept out, but they were also told that no transcript of the meeting would be provided and that no press conference would be held afterward. If you want to know why the President and the Department of Commerce prefer to be advised on pollution, in secret, by the people who do the polluting instead of the people who protest being polluted, read James Ridgeway's *The Politics of Ecology*.

Mr. Ridgeway, a contributing editor to *The New Republic* and co-editor of the radical weekly *Hard Times*, has muckraked before, admirably, in *The Closed Corporation*, an account of academic profiteering on weapons research and counter-insurgency programs. *The Politics of Ecology* sets out to prove that the principal polluters of our environment—the industrial burners of coal, gas and oil—have taken over the ecology movement in order to control our natural resources and dominate "the world energy markets." There is also money to be made in pollution-control systems, a potential $25-billion market, but only so long as the polluters continue to pollute, passing along the cost of control systems to the taxpayer.

Begin with sewage. Mr. Ridgeway teaches us the difference between "primary" treatment of sewage (storing it temporarily in tanks, allowing solid matter to settle into sludge, pouring liquid into streams and rivers, carting off the sludge) and "secondary" treatment (a form of filter that permits bacteria to feed on organic waste before the effluent gets into a waterway). The trouble is that, of the 280,000 manufacturing businesses in this country, all but 25,000 discharge into municipal sewers, already overburdened handling civic waste and storm overflow at the same time. And industrial waste contains inorganic pollutants (metals, phosphorous) that biological "secondary" treatment leaves unaffected.

Politics enters in at every level. Industry pays ridiculously small fees to use municipal sewers, as it pays ridiculously small fines for polluting the air and water. Federal guidelines, where they exist, are unenforceable, and federal grants for sewer systems are awarded as "pork," mixed up with the tax-exempt municipal bond racket. The public land itself is exploited by the major polluters—Lyndon Johnson tried to balance his budget by selling oil companies the right to drill on the continental shelf, thus occasioning the oil slicks at Santa Barbara and off the coasts of Florida and Louisiana.

Which brings Mr. Ridgeway to the "energy" combines, the petroleum companies that all but monopolize our natural resources via a network of tax breaks (the oil depletion allowance), import quotas (foreign oil is $1.25 a barrel cheaper than domestic crude) and political clout. The petroleum companies already control our oil and gas production; now they are moving into alternative sources of energy, like coal. Gasoline can be produced from coal; the Germans fueled their airplanes with such gasoline in World War II. Our government gives oil companies the right to work vast public lands for coal, at minuscule fees. The companies proceed to squat there, doing nothing.

Thus, while oil and natural gas go from Alaska to Japan in huge disaster-prone tankers, while oil tides wash Santa Barbara, while coal isn't turned into gasoline, while quotas keep foreign oil from reaching our shores, while we are suddenly faced with an artificial "energy shortage," the polluters attend meetings of the National Industrial Pollution Control Council, knowing full well that pollution-control policy is directly related to natural resources policy.

"The source of pollution," says Mr. Ridgeway, is "concentrated corporate power." He recommends abolishing economic incentives for oil companies; ending oil import quotas; no more drilling on the outer continental shelf; federal laws on pollutant levels, with injunctive power to close down plants that violate them; divesting oil companies of their chemical, coal and uranium subsidiaries; developing a steam or gas-turbine engine for automobiles; and making industry foot the bill for cleaning up all that it has dirtied.

Having said all this, Mr. Ridgeway does some polluting of his own, of an ideological sort. It is true that most pollution is caused by technology and industry, not by overpopulation. But to leap from this fact to the conclusion that birth-control programs are only a means of advancing American corporate interests is simpleminded. And to look the gift horse of Ralph Nader's consumer-interest study groups in the mouth, and to decide that what it's really all about is a power grab by a new "elite" of lawyers, is preposterous. Otherwise, *The Politics of Ecology* is a fine, tough and indispensable book.

(May 1970)

The Real Majority, by Richard M. Scammon and Ben J. Wattenberg

Ah, *The Real Majority.* What's a reviewer to do? John P. Roche, who once played Chingachgook to Lyndon Johnson's Natty Bumppo, growled out loud a month ago in the Washington *Post* about "the credentials and orientation" of critics likely to comment on this book. Mr. Nixon is known to have recommended it to his janissaries. Mr. Agnew is reputed to be acting on its substance. The syndicated columnists, Evans and Novak, suggest that it has contributed to the "purge-Galbraith" mood of the Democratic National Committee. Mr. Scammon, one co-author, is a public opinion consultant for *Newsweek,* which quotes him constantly. Mr. Wattenberg, the other co-author, has gone to Minnesota to assist in the rehabilitation of Hubert Humphrey. Thus *The Real Majority* is a genuine pseudo-event. Reviewing it is like trying to use a smog-ball as a punching bag, while all the boys at the National Press Club Bar go hee-haw.

Mr. Scammon and Mr. Wattenberg purport to acquaint us innocents with *psephology,* which is either the study of elections and voting behavior or counting the bumps on your own political head. It is their contention that the "tide" of American votes, as distinguished from parochial "waves," flows these days toward a "Social Issue"—disapproval of crime, racial unrest, campus nihilism, drugs, sexual license. This is because 70 per cent of American voters are "un-young, un-poor and un-black." The Middle Voter is a "middle-aged, middle-income, high-school-educated, white Protestant, who works with his hands," or "a forty-seven-year-old housewife from the outskirts of Dayton, Ohio, whose husband is a machinist." Such Middle Voters seek a political "centrist"—not a Barry Goldwater or a Robert Kennedy—and the party that fails to supply one is doomed to disaster.

Add *quadcali*, a hypothetical quadrangle of voters extending on the East from Massachusetts to Washington, west and northwest to Illinois and Wisconsin, including New York, plus California, and you've got the presidency, Kevin Phillips to the contrary notwithstanding. Provided, of course, that the presidential candidate says that, "When students break laws they will be treated as lawbreakers," and, "I am going to make our neighborhoods safe again for decent citizens of every color" (if he's a Democrat) or, "The American workingman is the backbone of America; we must help him help America" (if he's a Republican). Vietnam doesn't count; neither, presumably, does the Middle East.

One might jab at the smog-ball. Scammon and Wattenberg light candles before the Wisdom of the American Voter, and yet dismiss preferential primaries as "beauty contests." They explain election results after the fact, on the basis of carefully selected polls before the fact. They compare voting figures in off-year local elections with voting figures in national presidential elections. They assume, as few would, a relationship between democracy and the present way we select delegates to a national party convention. (Blacks? Women?) They cherish the role of party affiliation in determining voting patterns, and yet poor-mouth John Lindsay's plurality last fall in New York. Now, was Sam Yorty a "centrist"?

But flicking the Left at a smog-ball only makes it wobble. *The Real Majority* is the Johnson-Humphrey-Roche-O'Brien-Meany version of *The Prince* by St. Franklin; in fact, a scenario for inflicting Mr. Humphrey or Mr. Muskie on us in 1972. And someday perhaps their Prince *will* come. But do Scammon and Wattenberg really imagine that Robert Kennedy was unaware of the machinist's wife in Dayton, or Mayor Daley in Chicago? That Eugene McCarthy didn't play games with gun control during the Oregon primary? That any presidential condidate *wants* to lose Massachusetts, New York, Pennsylvania, Illinois, Michigan and California? Kevin Phillips exists because Richard Nixon exists; there would be no need for a Kevin Phillips if Richard Nixon hadn't invented himself with so little of the country in him.

No. What the whole discussion hangs on is whether the appearance of the "center" is the same as the reality; whether the voter three polls later will discover the difference; whether the "center" itself shifts according to the gravity of events; whether the pollster realizes that he's so much flotsam on the tide of tentative opinions; whether the politician decides to lead (by example, by media, by inadvertence) instead of following; whether personal honor, animal magnetism and, God help us, TV stunts, have anything to do with public popularity; whether enough waves—in the soul, in the pocketbook —eventually conspire at a "tide; whether, finally, campaign organization works and voters actually listen to the candidates who so philanthropically volunteer themselves for power; whether decency is perceived and vibrations felt. Even the Weathermen know you need blue collars along with longhairs, the poor, the black and the Galbraith. Is it permissible to wonder about "the credentials and orientation" of Messrs. Roche, Nixon, Agnew, Evans, Novak, Scammon and Wattenberg? May they eat Heisenbergers and come down with Uncertainty Poisoning.

(September 1970)

COMMISSION REPORTS—
A BRIEF SELECTION

The History of Violence in America. A Report to the National Commission on the Causes and Prevention of Violence, edited by Hugh Davis Graham and Ted Robert Gurr

The only problem with this sea of words—350,000 words—is that, having dropped into it like a salvage diver, one undergoes the dislocating raptures of the deep. Speculations of every size and shape press upon the eye and bend the mind: J-curves of "relative deprivation," statistical balloonfish, squids of fact. You learn so many facts —between 1882 and 1903, 1,985 Negroes were lynched; there are more murders per year in Manhattan (population 1.7 million) than in England and Wales combined (population 49 million)—that you somehow lose your grasp of the particular and the significant. Violence is dematerialized, becoming part of what Julio Cortazar has called "the ordinary routine of buses and history."

Which is not to say the authors haven't done a stupendous job. The general survey of American labor violence by Philip Taft and Philip Ross is alone worth the price of the book. Equally worthy are Richard Maxwell Brown's history of vigilante movements; Morris Janowitz's "Patterns of Collective Racial Violence"; Ted Robert Gurr's cross-cultural comparison of civil strife; and Bernard J. Siegel's extraordinary analysis of "defensive withdrawal," the non-violent adaptations by minority groups (Pueblo Indians, Amish, Mormons) to a dominant culture threatening their identity.

And they have articulated the challenge and paradox of the American situation: those characteristics of which we are most proud are also responsible for the divisiveness that now paralyzes us. We are an immigrant society based on liberal-bourgeois principles, but the Anglo-Saxons have forced upon that society a consensus which obliged the minorities to enter a violence-breeding status scramble, pitting group against group for Establishment favor. We avoided the ideological strife of nineteenth-century Europe, but the twentieth-century black man is 1789 at last.

Even the frontier experience which defined our individualist tradition was compounded as well of vigilantism and genocide. The industrial revolution which brought us prosperity also caused the mass migrations to our cities, overcrowding, labor and racial conflict. The technological revolution which made us the most powerful nation in the world also rendered our Puritan work ethic irrelevant and our children powerless and soulless.

But I wonder how lawmakers will react, if at all, to these essays, tables, charts, conclusions. They are told that we have always been a violent people, but that other peoples are violent too, even the English (Luddites, Chartists). That we are more strife-torn now than other Western democracies (France?), but the turmoil, lacking popular support, doesn't threaten the state itself. That violence is not some primitive regression, some aberrant abscess in the body politic, but an inevitable part of the political process. And that we must endure a clumsy dialectic between concession and coercion, a sex act between the shy and the brutish, taking polls to determine how repressive we can be this week.

How to escape this trap of armed sloth, of institutionalized greed, when every accession of knowledge seems only to deepen our gloom and certify a sort of biologic recidivism? Will the children of Cain ever grow up? How, when every bit of evidence indicts us, can we sustain our cartoon version of the Enlightenment's dream of man's perfectability? Three essays speak—inadvertently—to this issue.

First is Louis Hartz's "Comparative Study of Fragment Cultures." Professor Hartz has always celebrated (1) America's lack of a feudal past because it finessed class animosity, and (2) our liberal Locke-in because it exempted us from ideological gang-war. Now he revises himself: the "aborigine," whether Afro or Australo or Inca, threatens the consensus culture of the European "fragment." We either exterminate or accommodate that aborigine; and if indeed the United States Supreme Court exists because of a "notion that there is enough moral agreement in the political world to permit the adjudication of even its largest questions," surely we will accommodate. Extermination would shatter any possible consensus.

In "Violence in American Literature and Folk Lore" Kenneth Lynn first argues that a "dream of peace" coexists with the violent images in our literature, then admits the "tragic hopelessness" of Melville's *Benito Cereno*, Twain's *Pudd'nhead Wilson* and Wright's *Native Son*. And yet the dream, and the loneliness, of the best American writers also expresses a desire for community, for racial reconciliation. Our writers are another kind of "aborigine": like young Indians, they destroy themselves to testify. Surely their witness can be transmitted in our colleges as the best sort of social criticism.

Finally, Charles Tilly's "Collective Violence in European Perspective," after demonstrating that violence is international, defines evolving forms of protest: primitive (brawls without political purpose); reactionary (demonstrations against the state, on behalf of old threatened life styles); and modern (associational, future-oriented, asking the state to reform). A new protest form presages a fundamental political rearrangement. The persistent ideological protest of our young may be a new form telling us "that something important is happening to the political system itself."

Our hope, then, must derive from the inability of any "consensus" to survive another genocidal enterprise; the witness of our writers to the alternatives of death and reconciliation; and a new constituency of radicals (our children, our future). Pessimism, though conservative, need not be complacent; reform, though reluctant, need not be hypocritical; community must consist of souls, not color-coded labor units. At worst, we have to pretend that it will work.

(July 1969)

The Politics of Protest, A Task Force Report Submitted to the National Commission on the Causes and Prevention of Violence under the Direction of Jerome H. Skolnick

Welcome once again to the Guilt Machine. The Guilt Machine is a perpetual motion Angst-converter. It grinds up white liberals, reconstitutes their qualms into sausage links of reproach or pellets of rhetorical corn, wraps the product in Cellophane and sells it to us for conspicuous consumption. As penance. To be cursed and unforgiven. The sins of the founding fathers shall be visited on their institutions, yea, unto Mark Rudd.

In other words, another report to the National Commission on the Causes and Prevention of Violence has appeared. The question is, who will consume it, besides book reviewers and other compulsive penitents? Who will have the appetite to consume, specifically, this particular report? For a task force has bitten the hand that commissioned it. *The Politics of Protest* is no sobersided sociological extenuation. It is a brief against the war in Vietnam, racism at home, the university, the judiciary, the police and the government. Will Strom Thurmond let Richard Nixon read it?

Jerome H. Skolnick is a resident at Berkeley's Center for the Study of Law and Society. He and his staff—including Frederick Crews and Irving Louis Horowitz, consultants—set out to analyze "Violent Aspects of Protest and Confrontation." Their conclusions aren't going to startle anyone with much experience of the Guilt Machine— that is, anyone who reads and worries—but because those conclusions are rooted for the most part in fact, and sensibly organized, attention should be paid.

Skolnick et al. conclude that there's been relatively little violence associated with contemporary demonstrations and group protests; that what violence there has been is often on the part of the authorities; that the protests themselves are related to "crises in American institutions." They see the protest "movement" as essentially dependent on the stupidity of college presidents and government policy makers; black militants as rejecting "Western cultural superiority";

white radicals as becoming more aggressive to "prove" themselves to blacks and working-class young people.

Of special interest are the two chapters on "The Police in Protest" and "Judicial Response in Crisis." The task force is worried about police slowdowns, strikes, political activism, lobbying and challenges to departmental and civic authority. (New York's own John Cassese gets a special mention, along with the "right-wing" Law Enforcement Group within the Patrolmen's Benevolent Association.) The courts are found to have tolerated inadequate legal representation for defendants after urban riots; to have indulged requests for bail so high it amounts to preventive detention; and to have behaved more like "an instrument of social control" than seekers of justice.

Along the way, *The Politics of Protest* takes a hard look at political violence in this country as it manifested itself in other minority struggles—Indians, Appalachian farmers, white Southerners, working men seeking union recognition. There is a fascinating catalogue of New Left rationalizations for "confrontation tactics" (e.g., "The experience of resistance and combat may have a liberating effect on young middle-class radicals") and a useful history of the civil rights movement from the Reverend Dr. Martin Luther King's bus boycott to the failure of the Mississippi Freedom Democratic Party's challenge at the 1964 convention.

Since I wouldn't be a white liberal if I didn't have qualms, I should list some. Why are student radicals exempted from psychoanalysis, and accepted at face value as wholly issue-oriented, while their opponents get the old "status anxiety" treatment and are measured on the "F" (for fascist) authoritarian personality scale? (Psychologizing about group behavior is usually as much fun as it is usually balderdash, but fair's fair: balderdash everybody if balderdashing is your game.) Why, on the task force's only day of hearings on black militancy, were no black militants around to testify? What will happen when black students find that black studies programs on college campuses are just one more shuck, a pedagogical tranquilizer, keeping them from acquiring skills to market in a technological society that's going to go on being technological no matter how much radical rhetoric blues the air? (Okay, open admissions. Okay, black studies. But not a dime for day-care centers. Is it possible that open admissions and black studies are a form of social control, getting young blacks off the streets, where they might be politically dangerous?

Blacks are eventually going to decide that college is a place to master disciplines and develop skills that are important to their communities, at the same time whites have decided college is a place where my pampered soul can't be saved and therefore tear it down. And so the campus will become just like the city.)

Finally, the authors seem to be in sympathy with the radical proposition that "the war might be a natural result of the bureaucratic welfare state, with its liberal rhetoric, its tendency to self-expansion, its growing military establishment, and its paternalism toward the downtrodden." The sausage links turn into chains; the liberal writhes. War, rhetoric, the expanding of nations, military establishments, and even paternalism antedate the welfare state, don't they? And then there's the paradox: It is precisely to that liberal, bureaucratic, paternalistic welfare state that this report is addressed. Are the resources of that state exhausted? Would, for instance, Hubert Humphrey have made the same decisions regarding ABM, school desegregation, medical grants, Judge Haynsworth, Dean Burch, etc., as Richard Nixon? Are we asking the state to wither away? How many states ever have? Kerner, Cox, Walker, Warren, Skolnick . . . What happens to these reports? And the Guilt Machine grinds on, fine as dust.

(September 1969)

Soulside, Inquiries into Ghetto Culture and Community, by Ulf Hannerz

The poor must now fend off not only policemen and welfare workers, but anthropologists as well. Vine Deloria, in Custer Died for Your Sins, observes that despite the number of anthropologists who have inflicted themselves on the American Indian and the enormous amount of money spent to fund their projects, the situation of the Indian keeps on deteriorating. In some instances, the foundation moneys that sustained the anthropologists might have saved a reservation school or medical clinic. But defining a problem is intellectually more satisfying, and personally less dangerous, than trying to solve it.

Still, like everybody else, anthropologists want to be relevant. The Oscar Lewis game is all the rage. Explicating "the culture of poverty" has become an exercise as popular as dilating on kill ratios, nuclear sufficiency, guerrilla theater and electronic tribalization. To this debate on the culture of poverty Ulf Hannerz addresses himself in *Soulside*. Is culture to be defined as a transmission belt for images and precepts, a package of "norms and aspirations," a system of "situational constraints"? Does "ghetto-specific behavior" add up to a culture? If so, is that culture "change-resistant" or a process of adaptation?

From August 1966 to July 1968, Mr. Hannerz—a blond, blue-eyed Swedish social anthropologist—lived on a ghetto street in Washington, D.C. His stay was financed by the Carnegie Corporation through the Urban Language Study of the Center for Applied Linguistics. He drank wine in the alleyways with the "street-cornermen," went to parties with the "swingers," sat in on conversations with what he calls "the mainstreamers," endeavored to be unobtrusive, and took notes.

Since much of Mr. Hannerz's argument is with other social scientists, there are inevitable lapses into Dread Nomenclature: "matrifocality," "negative valence," "symmetrically schismogenetic interaction," etc. He acknowledges that, since "Winston Street" appears to be more of a neighborhood than many ghetto areas, his conclusions might not apply specifically to Harlem or Chicago's South Side. And he admits that his inquiry, dependent on the good will of the men who tolerated his omnipresence, had of necessity to concentrate more on male than on female behavior—a handicap, what with all the flapdoodle about matrifocality. Yet it's hard to quarrel with his findings:

"Female household dominance; a ghetto-specific male role of somewhat varying expression including . . . toughness, sexual activity and a fair amount of liquor consumption; a relatively conflict-ridden relationship between the sexes; rather intensive participation in informal social life outside the domestic domain; flexible household composition; fear of trouble in the environment; a certain amount of suspiciousness toward other persons' motives; relative closeness to religion; particular food habits; a great interest in the music of the group; and a relatively hostile view of much of white America . . ."

His notion that ghetto-specific and mainstream cultures coexist on Winston Street—the one a kind of consolation prize and defense mechanism against the difficulties of achieving entrée into the other—seems sound. Unlike Oscar Lewis, he resists calling unemployment, low wages, chronic cash shortages and crowded quarters "features" of a "culture of poverty," since they are obviously the poverty itself, nothing else. (The white social scientists are going to have to fight it out with the Black Aestheticians to determine whether the resulting "culture," which seems to be "situational," is a product of deprivation or a triumph over it or somehow, miraculously, an anomaly immune to historical and economic contexts. Individuals, black and white, argue with and abuse one another; people, mostly black, suffer ghetto-specifically.) And one wants to share his hope that black power "can serve as a symbolic basis for group cohesion while the group is in strenuous economic and political movement," that "soul" can be mobilized—even as one imagines blacks grinding teeth to sharpen them for the next visit of the anthropological missionaries.

Don't we know most of these things? At least we've been told them, and by more powerful, authoritative books than *Soulside*—books by Claude Brown, John A. Williams, Ishmael Reed and, of course, James Baldwin. Isn't it time that Myrdal and Moynihan and Glazer and Singer stop arguing about whether ghetto-specific culture is a "pathological distortion" of mainstream culture, or, contrarily, an "ethnogenesis on American ground"—and face up to the fact that unless white America provides black America with decent housing, education, employment, health services and all the rest, our "mainstream" is going to dry up and our cities are going to burn down? One might even mount a pretty good case for the idea that "matrifocality" came about as a consequence of an insane welfare system that penalized the family with a man around the house, instead of going as far back as the plantation system for an explanation.

Mr. Hannerz is most useful in his refusal to romanticize Winston Street. Romanticizers in the social sciences and in the black power movement lay on the rhetoric with a trowel; it doesn't alter the fact that when people riot they are unhappy. And arguments about culture and subculture, in the light of that fact, are useful only insofar as they challenge the fantasy some white Americans still indulge: Let's get raped by any old Apocalyptic horsemen happening by. To project our private libidinal and political hopes and fears on an underclass; to seek redemption or scourging in a sociological psycho-drama; to employ the poor, as Michael Harrington has put it, as actors in a middle-class morality play—is to trivialize their pain and delude ourselves painlessly, at least until the horseman actually arrives. Such presumption, lurking unarticulated behind the methodologies of some social scientists, and implicit in the bombast of some radical theoreticians, is more pathological than anthropological.

For, finally, as Mr. Hannerz does mention, anthropological elaborations of a "culture of poverty" can and do harden into excuses. They can be used to suggest that ghetto dwellers, because of their poverty-culture conditioning, are ill equipped to enter the mainstream even when given the opportunity; that deprivation gives stunted birth to life styles that ensure failure. A dangerous cop-out, that. When the fire comes to Winston Street, all the anthropologists in the world aren't going to be able to extinguish it by slapping at the flames with tomes and textbooks. That scene will be schismogenetic with bells on.

(November 1969)

INTERPRETERS OF BAD DREAMS

Love and Will, by Rollo May

Rollo May's extraordinary book was ignored by this column when it first appeared three months ago, for which some of us should have our space-bar thumbs chopped off and fried for hors d'oeuvres. It is wise, rich, witty and provocative: a meditation rather than an apocalyptic seizure; a text on consciousness as well as an approach to psychotherapy; an argument for the fashioning of a set of values appropriate to our biological, historical and individual selves, as we apprehend them in the fitful modern gleam; an escape from determinism. It should not only have been reviewed; it should have led any list of important books published in 1969. Therefore, both as an act of penance and because we are about to stumble into a new decade requiring people like Dr. May, I want to devote today's box and tomorrow's to a vain attempt at synopsizing *Love and Will.*

Cartographing the human personality is a risky business. There is no "where" for ego and id; nor do they "do" anything as such. We must infer from symptoms. Dr. May begins with symptoms before moving on to remedies, or "values." Thus we must first agree—I think it indisputable—that there is a crisis of love and will, an emotional and spiritual impotence, upon us. On the one hand, joyless promiscuity: "alienation from the body . . . separation of emotion from reason . . . the use of the body as a machine." On the other, man's political helplessness: "Even if he *did* exert his 'will'—or whatever illusion passes for it—his actions wouldn't do any good anyway."

Such an agreement secured, we can grapple with Dr. May's conceptual apparatus, which is tripartite. First, "eros"—a meta-sex within and outside us, drawing us toward possibilities and ideal forms, eliciting our capacity to reach out, to mold our own futures. Next, "the daimonic"—our biological underground (lust, rage, power), which is either integrated "on the personal dimension of consciousness" or destroys us. Finally, "intentionality"—"an assertive response of the person to the structure of his world," "awareness of our capacity to change," "our means of putting the meaning surprised by consciousness into action."

Consider love. Freud and contraception combined to unbuckle the Victorian straitjacket, and sex was liberated. Into what? "Into," says Dr. May, "an unbounded and empty sea of free choice [which] does not in itself give freedom, but is more apt to increase inner conflict." Into a "New Puritanism": God will not punish you; therefore you have only yourself to blame. Into a machinelike series of casual copulations, without "the experience of giving feelings, sharing fantasies, offering the inner psychic richness that normally takes a little time and enables sensation to transcend itself in emotion and emotion to transcend itself in tenderness and sometimes love."

Time: "dependability," "lastingness," the kind of commitment that complicates and deepens a human relationship. Instead, we have "short order sex," playing it cool, why-notness?, the cult of technique: efficiency experts seeking orgasm, not man and woman seeking intimacy. Alienation: "We go to bed because we cannot bear each other; we go to bed because we are too shy to look in each other's eyes, and in bed one can turn away one's head."

Orthodox psychoanalysis sometimes encourages such friction-proof boudoirism. That's why Dr. May quotes half-approvingly the quip by C. Macfie Campbell: "Psychoanalysis is Calvinism in Bermuda shorts." By thinking of sex as a tension to be reduced, and the body and the self as mechanisms requiring gratification by way of faceless objects (casual partners), we wound men and women in their transcendental capacity, their variousness.

Part of this was Freud's fault and part the fault of his epigones. Freud for two thirds of his life tried to reduce love to libido, as though like Helmholtzian physics it could be quantified. When at last he had to face the fact that the pleasure principle was self-defeating—aspiring to tensionless sloth, to death—he came up with a revamped Eros and a brand-new Thanatos. The epigones found this autumnal formulation too pessimistic, and settled for dispensing optimism cookies to their clients; Fromming at the mouth: adjust, slay "the daimonic," climb off your three-wheeled Oedipal-cycle.

So love was made banal, trivialized into proximate spasms, robbed of duration, imagination and even tragic gloss. So, as in all declining cultures, Eros was stripped down into Cupid. All motion, no feeling. We've hit robot-tom. The dynamic movement of nature, the polar movement of positive-negative, male-female, *process*, has been made into a universal joint, which we might as well smoke since "turning on" (as in a TV set) is our ultimate admission of passivity.

Is there a way out? "Loveliness," says Dr. May, replying to Euripides in the affirmative, "shall be loved not because of infantile needs, or because it stands for the breast, or because it is aim-inhibited sex, or because it will make us happy—but simply because it is lovely. Loveliness exercises a pull upon us; we are drawn to life by love."

That's Eros. Tune in tomorrow for the daimonic, intentionality, and Dr. May's gentle, convincing synthesis.

To resume. Yesterday was banal love. This morning we consider crippled will. Merry Christmas! As a matter of fact, Dr. May has a Christmas message: "the mythos of care," care being the opposite of apathy, and an aspect of Eros, and (in Heidegger) the source of will. "It is a state," writes Dr. May, "composed of the recognition of another, a fellow human being like one's self; of identification of one's self with the pain or joy of the other" and an awareness of complicity, responsibility, community.

It's a better message than most, for it implies some risk of self. Dr. May belongs to the "existential" school of psychology (Binswanger, Maslow, etc.); whatever the risk, he participates in the life situation of the patient. Thus love is a "falling," a seeking of rebirth and new patterns, even though the gamble is on self-destruction. That such love is related to death, that it flirts with an exhaustion of the "I" in the impossible attempt at union, doesn't frighten him. After all, we are the only animals who procreate face to face, vulnerability to vulnerability. Wanting to know is our blessing and our curse.

We are also, as Nietzsche noted, "the only animal who can make promises." We have a future tense and sense. Dr. May subsumes that tense-sense under "intentionality," our push toward a direction for action. We can't know reality unless we are engaged in making our meaning as we perceive. Conception precedes perception. (We need a word or a symbol for something before we can actually *see* it.) Consciousness creates in a continuous reciprocity between subject and object—a kind of perceptual sex—and each meaning has within it a commitment, an *intention*. Our acts reveal us and, because an act always involves responding, the actor is responsible for the consequences of the act.

Have I driven everybody to the wassail bowl? I apologize for me; Dr. May needs no apology. The fault is not in Dr. May, but in your reviewer. Dr. May has taken on all the tough epistemological questions Descartes botched. He proposes, instead of "I think, therefore I am," a process of experiencing identity which abolishes the mind-body dualism: "I conceive—I can—I will—I am." Between "I can" and "I will," identity, or at least the possibility of it, is forged, in action.

Getting rid of this *Descartes blanche* which has paralyzed Western epistemology for a couple of centuries involves getting rid of compartmentalization—of the personality and the society. Dr. May is up to it, and the best of *Love and Will* is his graceful dispatch. Begin with a comprehensive way of "knowing" reality (St. Augustine, standing on the shoulders of Arabic philosophers). Proceed to the constituting of that reality, by our understanding of it (Kant, of course). Leap, then, to Franz Brentano's notion that consciousness is defined by the fact that it *intends* something, points toward something outside itself: it intends, specifically, the perceived object. Note that Freud (one of Dr. May's intellectual fathers) and Husserl (a grandfather who gave birth to Sartre) were both students of Brentano. Conclude that "intentionality" gives meaningful contents to consciousness.

Now: A psychotherapist must begin his critique with his own discipline. Dr. May does. The "radical inconsistency" between psychoanalytic theory (arguing an inexorable determinism) and therapeutic practice (an effort to "liberate" the patient into a world of choices), indicates to him a failure of theory. The "ego" analysts excite his disdain; how can the ego be autonomous? "The ego is, by definition, a *part* of the personality; and how can a *part* be free?"

Nor are Wittgenstein, the positivists and the behaviorists allowed to retire with their reduction of the world to objective facts. " 'I can,' " says Dr. May, "is part of the world."

All right. Given tension, how to deal with it outside of a context of tropism? How to end it except by death, an id impulse leading through gratification to satiety, aspiring ultimately to an integral sloth, an inorganicism, that aborts the whole evolutionary adventure?

We can never return to the breast, argues Dr. May. Once consciousness has asserted itself—beginning with the ability to say "No" —warm reunion with the universe is impossible. The meaning of life will thenceforth reside in the human emotions of "pity, loneliness and love." Grief and compassion are our only trumps against death's stacked hand. "Care"—not sentimentality, which is the satisfaction we take in recognizing an emotion, in thinking about it; but rather the genuine experience of the object of that emotion—is the only base upon which to build our ethical skyscrapers. Care is ontological, referring to a state of being; one must do something, make decisions. Thus love and will are joined. Name the daimon, but don't kill it, for it is a creative source if it can be integrated. Employ the Word, which partakes of symbol, which yields myth: "It is the symbolic meanings that have gone awry in neurosis, and not the id impulse." Seek "mutuality," those "others" who, added to our calculation, help convert wishes into a willed future. Share as best we can another's "meaning matrix," involving a mutual experience of human history and language as well as the particular predicament.

From sex, to Eros, to Philia, to Agape—it's difficult, but the only game in town.

(December 24, 25, 1969)

P.S. I never did get around to explaining "the daimonic," did I? Nor how one goes about integrating it. The rivers and streams of the mind are, these days, polluted with psychological theory and therapeutic contradictions. Mr. Skinner would have us abandon our illusions of freedom and dignity, and submit to a state laboratory of stimulus and response, of conditioned "goodness" by way of positive reinforcement; the state laboratory would, presumably, be constructed along the lines of the nineteenth-century, small-town American imagination—up the work ethic, off the licentiousness! Mr. Laing, who is understandably more popular with the young, has decided that madness is a proof of grace; the family and the society are insane; the only sane response to an insane social situation is to go personally insane; and from there to Kingsley Hall. The Esalen freaks have rediscovered the sandbox, the bathtub and the massage parlor as therapeutic tools. The existential analysts have been ultimately vulgarized in the person and precepts of Martin Shepherd, who wrote one book wondering whether the doctor shouldn't get involved with his patients socially and sexually; then wrote another saying that the doctor should, and it works wonders; and now has written a third saying that he, Shepherd, did start making it with all his patients and it's *wonderful!* As for Dr. May, well, he could be accused—as, more interestingly, Laing has been accused—of ignoring, or scanting, the social context (war, racism, poverty, etc.). In Laing's instance, it's a question of following the logic of your own argument: if society's so rotten, why don't you *do* something about it, turn your critical guns on the broader issues? In May's instance, it's a question of the utility of "care" in a bureaucratic world, a world in which the daimonic and the machine have been wed, their children bloody: what if we can't get from "I can" to "I will" because, in fact, we "cannot" because of—pick your determinism, the State, capitalism, anal-retentive science, ethological pre-programming, etc.? I liked May's book so much, not because it *proved* anything, but because, like poetry, it systematized a set of perceptions so persuasively—a function of language as much as perception—that I wanted to believe it was true. An act of faith on Christmas morning, faltering as such acts are. Down at *Commentary* magazine they grumble about people like Robert Coles, Kenneth Keniston, Robert Jay Lifton, people who are said to represent the slipshod idea that Politics Is Health. Well, part of politics *is* health, in the state and in the individual. Dr. May's idea of health would, I think, contribute more to healthy politics than hating the young because they don't remember what you remember; or rediscovering Natural Law just when you need to stake out some territory a little to the right of *The New York Review of Books.* As for the critique from the Left—that these people aren't changing society, even when they notice what society is doing to their patients—I can only say that the division of labor has been with us always; Laing, May, Keniston, Coles, Lifton, etc., are worried about children, marriages, schizophrenia, death. Their energy, their moral and therapeutic imaginations, are an accession of goodness in a time when goodness is in short supply. Erik Erikson would not be profitably employed as a conscript in the battalion of shamans who tried to levitate the Pentagon. When we do as much as these people do, perhaps we will be qualified to suggest what more they might have done. Anyway, the politicizing of psychology raises more problems than I'm capable of having opinions about, much less solving, as the next review demonstrates.

The Freudian Left, Wilhelm Reich, Geza Roheim, Herbert Marcuse, by Paul A. Robinson

"There is, first, the question of whether psychoanalysis should be considered a scientific psychology or an imaginative metaphysics. . . . There is also the question of whether psychoanalysis was the final product of nineteenth-century positivism, or an early manifestation of the revolt against positivism with which our century began. . . . Finally, there is the issue of rationalism versus instinctualism— Freud the loyal son of the Enlightenment, struggling to uphold the values of reason and humanity and to defend the embattled ego against the assaults of instinct and conscience, versus Freud the doctor and sometime apologist of the passions, who portrayed man as licentious and murderous, the victim of unconscious impulses, truly himself only in his most childish and irrational moments."

Very good questions, indeed. Paul Robinson, a twenty-nine-year-old assistant professor of history at Stanford, raises them in the preface to his crisp and contentious book, only to subsume them immediately under a "larger dichotomy": "Did Freud's theoretical achievement imply a revolutionary or a reactionary attitude toward the human situation?"

Mr. Robinson thinks revolutionary, in both politics and sex. He has no use for the ego psychologists (a little bit of spiritual uplift, please, so we can detach the traumata). He chooses to illustrate the revolutionary tendencies in psychoanalytic theory by examining the thought of three men who entered the mind of Freud and emerged, after much heavy breathing, with a critique of capitalism: Wilhelm Reich (orgone energy); Geza Roheim (anthropology); and Herbert Marcuse (philosophy).

The problem is that, for all his "meta-historical" speculations, Freud was a pessimist, and pessimism is essentially conservative. If culture is necessarily repressive, if we survive our destructive impulses only by the "aim-oriented" sublimation of libidinal rages, then psychoanalysis finds itself charged with somehow patching up the individual psyche to make it "operative," while leaving socio-economic theory to the socio-economic theorists.

Wilhelm Reich tried hard. From Freud he borrowed the hydraulic or economic notion of psychic energy, adding to it the idea of the orgasm as "the natural regulating mechanism of the closed energy system called man." Neurotics are sick because of a genital disturbance: their inability to achieve a satisfactory orgasm. Ideology is internalized in the character of the individual by his family, reflecting the political myths of a previous era. (For instance, lower-middle-class family life on a Weimar Republic farm, in which the father, "employing" his sons, had both economic and paternal authority. Reich blamed the sexual and political tyranny of capitalism on patriarchy.)

Mr. Robinson rescues Reich's reputation from the disgrace of those last Orgone Energy Accumulator years. The relationship between the sex life of a worker and his function as a labor unit is important, especially in an age of regimented leisure. Unfortunately, Reich made a bad "Freudo-Marxist" because he didn't believe in either the class struggle or the death instinct.

So on to Geza Roheim, never terribly political but radical enough when it came to relating psychoanalysis and the anthropological interpretation of various cultures. Roheim borrowed more than he acknowledged from Otto Rank (separation anxiety), but his idea that in each culture a child experiences a characteristic crisis, typical of that culture's dominant economic, political and religious preconceptions, was significant.

Roheim's special service was his attack on the anthropological "functionalism" of Boas and Malinowski, a cultural relativism that made cross-cultural comparisons and abstract generalizations (and, therefore, significant political change) impossible. He spent far too much time looking for Oedipus complexes, and he was capable of such absurdities as attributing the development of herding societies to Oedipal reduplication (Agriculture as incest with Mother Earth, the plow as symbolic phallus), but he manfully resisted the idea that cultures must simply be adjusted to, not changed.

Marcuse, of course, came late to Freud. His greatest contributions were the notions of "surplus repression" (an equivalent of Marx's "surplus value," the *quantitative* measure of exploitation: society may always be based on repression, but certain historical forms are more repressive than is necessary); and the "performance principle" (like Marx's alienation and reification, a *qualitative* characterization of existence under capitalism).

In *Eros and Civilization* Marcuse argued that technology might release man into a re-sexualizing leisure, polymorphous perverse instead of just genital. He also reinterpreted the primal crime idea: father was the capitalist entrepreneur; brothers were the European proletariat; guilt derived from the proletarian realization that its post-Oedipal totemistic religion merely re-established a paternal morality instead of going revolutionary whole-hog. Nonsense.

And Marcuse was subsequently to decide that technology worked the wrong way; that tolerance could be repressive; that establishmentarian apologists didn't deserve the same political freedoms enjoyed by Herbert Marcuse. He didn't, like Norman O. Brown—in whose mystagogy there is a despairing biological determinism—abandon politics; but started his flirtation with death that the New Left doesn't understand because the New Left has stopped reading books. The New Left collects identification tags, chapter headings, fitful clauses snipped from contexts, and incants them, as though from a comic book or the thoughts of Chairman Mao.

Mr. Robinson has written a sophisticated brief for the revolutionary implications of psychoanalytic theory; it is a brief that occasionally strains—one strains to bring one's own political perceptions into an approximation of what one knows about a discipline one respects —but it nevertheless enlightens. If such theoretical constructs as primal crime, separation anxiety, death instinct remain as unproven as the inevitability of socialism—when Marxists predict, they are usually wrong; Freudians can't predict at all—they have a way of bending one's angle of vision, to suddenly sight new perspectives, even as those scientists in their laboratories trying to figure out the mechanisms of the brain and the nervous system discover an almost terrifying beauty in materials which don't need to be proved because they exist, don't need to be changed because they are already changing and demand only to be understood.

(July 1969)

FIXERS OF BAD DREAMS

Life on Man, by Theodor Rosebury

How can I persuade every literate man and woman to buy Dr. Rosebury's delightful book? It is sane, elegant and informative: a joy to read, making intellectual ripples that go on widening long after the words have dropped into the mind. Several subterfuges suggest themselves. It is, for instance, a book about Shakespeare and Jonathan Swift; Luther and Freud; Darwin and Lenny Bruce; the origin of life and TV commercials and magic and toilet training and sociology and scatology. It covers some of the same ground Norman O. Brown roamed over in *Life Against Death*, but with much more wit and much less hyperthyroid waffling. It says pertinent and provocative things on language, religion and science. But Dr. Rosebury is a bacteriologist, and *Life on Man* is basically about microbes—*our* microbes, the furious spirochetes and vibrios, the corkscrewlike spirilla, the clusters of bacilli and cocci that have colonized *our* bodies. And Dr. Rosebury is rather fonder of microbes than he is of deodorants and mouthwashes.

He begins, properly, with Anthony van Leeuwenhoek, the seventeenth-century Dutchman who looked through a microscope at his own feces and discovered ". . . animalcules a-moving very prettily; some of 'em a bit bigger, others a bit less, than a blood-globule; but all of one and the same make. Their bodies were somewhat longer than broad, and their belly, which was flat-like, furnisht with sundry little paws . . ." And so man learned that he was not alone, not even inside himself.

Flashback. Dr. Rosebury cites recent experiments indicating that a chemical evolution preceded the biological one. For ten billion years, organic compounds accumulated in a sort of reservoir, awaiting the electric spark (a primeval thunderstorm?) that synthesized the energy-producing and self-perpetuating thing we call life; which primordial form—perhaps the great-grandfather of a parasitic microbe—then began its twenty-billion-year climb up the scale of organization to man. "If," he says, "we think of the whole process in a scale reduced to one year, we have been around for about an hour."

Back to our microbes. We are their environment, as earth is our environment. A complex interrelationship obtains. A fetus in its mother's body is microbe-free, but on surfacing is immediately assaulted. It is a necessary assault, helping to develop antibodies against infection, helping to develop the walls of various tracts. Dr. Rosebury isn't in favor of cholera, Typhoid Mary, yellow fever or bubonic plague, but he demonstrates that there are good as well as bad microbes, and we can't get along without the good ones.

His ultimate purpose, however, is broader. Why, when we are told that the average adult each day excretes 100 trillion microbes, are we appalled? What is there about this subject that distresses us? Such questions launch him on an absorbing investigation into social mores and personal obsessions: the excremental and the erotic through history, from the Lascaux caves to Roman gods to husbandry to Elizabethan theater to Puritanism to Joyce. He challenges our definition of obscenity and he props up many of Freud's formulations with hard data.

When he gets around to modern times, he is scathing. "Once we worshipped Sterculius; now he has joined Lucifer, and in his place we have erected a god of plumbing." The history of the bathroom is recapitulated, to hilarious and telling effect. Antiseptics and deodorants and skin oils and hair sprays and suppositories are dismissed as mostly worthless. Even perfume is questioned: "Maybe we ought to stop at times to wonder why we like to smell like flowers or coconuts or little Asiatic deer or the guts of a sperm whale; couldn't we learn to love the smell of healthy men and women?" This leads him to some sensible suggestions on child rearing, personal hygiene and education; to a qualified approval of youthful revolt, against cosmetics as well as other things; to a rage against the sterilizers and the hucksters of sterilization; to a crucial distinction between "filth" and "disease."

What makes *Life on Man* rather more reliable than Brown's *Life Against Death* is that Dr. Rosebury doesn't fall into the fallacy of blaming man's hang-ups on that very "sublimation" that enables us to explore the nature of repression. He is under no illusion, either, that science itself is an unconscious manipulation of symbolic excrement, a projection of our anal disturbance on the cosmos. Science is knowledge, yielding control; it can be as liberating as art or psychoanalysis, depending (like them) on its employer. He asks for adulthood, not infantilism.

And what makes *Life on Man* required reading for literate people is that it teaches us about an important discipline; it challenges us with constructions based on our biological and historical past; it brightens with wit; and it is a splendid indictment of those who would turn us into plastic for their personal profit. "Is it you who 'offend,'" he asks, "or the adman who offends against you? Is it the healthy body . . . or the exhalations of automobiles and smokestacks? Is it the 'obscenities' hurled by unarmed civilians, or the swinging nightsticks and billowing nausea gas of helmeted and masked police? Is it normal microbes or perverted men?"

(June 1969)

The Future of the Future, by John McHale

Like many a useful thinker, John McHale sat at the feet of R. Buckminster Fuller, tapping the great man's knee with a rubber-headed hammer and getting kicked in the preconceptions. From Fuller he borrows the liberating idea of "Spaceship Earth," a closed energy system in which man is the instigator of vast dislocations for good or ill. From Fuller he also borrows the optimistic premise "that the sum total of human desire to survive is dominant over the sum total of the impulse to destroy." I hope so. If we embrace the most poetic image of our species—children of a dying star, expressions of organic processes transcending themselves, alone, aware and vulnerable— we must at the same time recognize the grotesque cartoon of that image: those children standing knee-deep in their own garbage breeding like fruit flies, eating up all the energy inside their biospheric envelope, flirting with an extinction that might be deemed tragic were anybody ultimately around to do the deeming.

Mr. McHale, variously a director at various academic centers devoted to environment and technology, begins with a consideration of the idea of the future. Like so much of our intellectual baggage, it's a Greco-Judaic legacy. For the static fixities of Egypt, Persia and the East, the Greeks substituted a vision of the city of man and the

Jews a promise of earthly utopia, both based on individual ethical responsibility. Christ "concretized" the Judaic conception, and the result was a world view happily in accord with economic interest. Labor was part of conduct; not only utopia but survival depended on work; and a postponed utopia made for good business.

Technology has changed all that. Mr. McHale does not subscribe to demonological apprehensions about technology. Whether he is talking about the ecology of the earth, the energy system that is man, the acceleration of change or the space program, he keeps drumming away on the notion that utopia has only to be willed: our information processors and systems methodologists will then deliver it.

Yes, the population explodes. Our resources are finite. Our air and water are polluted. Our cities, our wars, our souls—all those exponential curves appear to form a huge black hole into which the species will disappear. Technology has a life of its own, a momentum we must ride and can't steer. But Mr. McHale suspects those curves. Men aren't fruit flies. In the past the curves flattened out into "take-off plateaus" for human intervention. Besides which, technology has so accelerated change that past curves can't predict the future. A "social telesis" based on information input, feedback and self-correction will save us if we can agree on our goals and do some integrated planning.

For instance, new efficient methods of energy conversion are available. Microbial colonies, "chicken batteries" and biosynthetic combinations of bacteria, algae and turnips are potential new food sources. Man in space represents (1) a heartening convergence of disparate disciplines on a single task, showing what we can do when we want to; (2) an escape from the envelope and a new perspective on global interdependence; and (3) a model, with the portable "earth environment," of a self-cycling, self-sustaining, waste-reprocessing "closed ecological system," under human control, with consequences for city planning, health management and integrated design.

Mr. McHale's principal point is that technology is the way man is evolving, a sort of machine biology. We are born dependent, with unspecialized computers (digital/analog) for brains. Because of our dependency, we are from the beginning social animals. Language was our first great tool, permitting us to store information and exchange its symbols. Machines are not merely our extensions, but our children.

They are already replacing parts of our bodies and doing most of our work. And the greatest tool since language, the most promising child of man, is the computer. Computers will rescue our decision makers from the incapacitating storm of variables; will redeem our historians from hindsight, gloom and exponential curves; will release the rest of us into a revitalizing leisure—no longer labor-slaves, but service-demanding consumers and (in Marshall McLuhan's phrase) "nomads of knowledge."

Again, I hope so. Mr. McHale supplies us with an enormous amount of information and an exciting vision. Surely he is correct in observing that the very nature of communications, transportation, health, weather and food supply obliges us to think and plan globally. If he scants the problem of new sources of energy once the minerals have been exhausted, the scanting is probably inadvertent, and he would go on about the atom—fission and fusion—or solar reflectors or some as yet unimagined "take-off" stumbled on by accident in basic research. But isn't the ultimate and elusive variable man himself? We may have to live together, but we die alone, and it is in our privacy that we experience our most vivid sensations, perceptions, meanings. There is a natural solipsism that resists politics—thinking and planning even regionally, much less globally— because politics ultimately proposes abstractions, contracts among strangers, concessions and controls; planning is an invasion of privacy. And where is a *social* character-input to come from? Can we develop a self-cycling and self-supporting value system predicated on the survival of the *species*, not just on the duration of a single human life (the other, unacknowledged, legacy of the Greeks as a measurement of value)? Are there chicken batteries, duckweed colonies, microbial populations breeding away in the dark that can supply us with a moral protein, a cultural pep pill? Can we biosynthesize sanity?

(August 1969)

NO MORE PRIVACY

The Death of Privacy, by Jerry M. Rosenberg

Maybe an exploding technology makes for an imploding psychology. During World War II, when physicists with their "big machines" created Hiroshima, America belatedly discovered that knowledge is power—instead of, or in addition to, being Sin. Government immediately invested in the knowledge industry, and off we tore on a federally subsidized technological binge, a lost weekend that lasted twenty-five years. The hang-up is the hangover: We've never been a nation of philosophers, and our big machines do no philosophizing at all, and thus we may have neglected a corollary to the "knowledge is power" proposition. If intellectual activity has physical consequences, it is likely also to have moral implications. If every accession of knowledge is itself an "act," altering the observed object and the observer, then technology (applied knowledge) is going to alter psychological and social contexts, is going to fiddle around with our notions of ourselves as well as our notions of the universe. Inside of, rather than on top of, the big machine, we can't be sure whether it's a womb or bomb, and don't have much to say about it, anyway. In an age of computerized defense systems, electronic journalism, automated factories, information processing and biological refabrication, identity crisis is a "spin-off"—not just alienation from one's role or one's work or one's family romance or one's God, but from the very idea of what it *should* mean to be a human being, that conceptual cluster of possibilities, energies, renunciations, atonements, *actes gratuit.* Old questions are reopened: How much should the individual cede to the state, in exchange for what? And new questions yawn: Is the individual capable of understanding a social contract rewritten every other day by systems analysts strung out on cost effectiveness?

Dr. Rosenberg, an industrial psychologist and management consultant, attacks one aspect of our technological thralldom in this book—the threat to privacy posed by government and industrial computers. His particular concern is the proposed Federal Data Bank, where comprehensive files on every individual in the United States would be stored, as electrical impulses on magnetic tape, for the edification of strangers.

He examines the origins of the data bank proposal and the arguments for its efficiency. (We love statistics when they can be employed punitively; but when they relate smoking and cancer, holidays and auto deaths, or when they document hunger, educational inequality and substandard housing in America, we aren't interested.) He explores the role computers already play in our lives: credit rating, law enforcement, medical diagnosis, airline reservations, banking, motivational research, etc. He sketches computer history from Babbage's Difference Engine to microprogramming and lasers. He speculates on a future when computers will apply their own "inferential" logic to various behavior patterns.

And he is properly worried. For already, anyone who wants to can buy our arrest records, credit reports and tax returns. Already there are over 30,000 "investigators" on the federal payroll. Already the Bureau of the Census can force us to answer personal questions that would have outraged Thomas Jefferson. Putting all this into one centralized memory bank not only subjects us to possible blackmail, to the abuse of confidential information, but also tends to lock us into our mistakes. Who puts the data into the bank, and in what form? Who will evaluate the data, and for what purposes?

Because he believes that privacy guarantees a "personal autonomy," necessary for people to stay sane in modern society, and because he suspects that a Federal Data Bank is inevitable, Dr. Rosenberg proposes strict legislation. We should know what our file contains, how it is protected and who has access to it. We should be able to review it and challenge its accuracy. An ombudsman should oversee the operation; computer personnel should undergo security checks; technical systems should be regularly tested to prevent accidental leakage; and all files should be exempt from court subpoena. In other words, we need somebody watching the people who watch us.

The Death of Privacy is a troubling, convincing and necessary book. It serves also as a launching pad for mind probes of the technological moon. Most of us live on installments, as numbered markers and symbolic work-units on the great credit grid. It is easier to fight City Hall than the Diners' Club. For permission to borrow from our own future, we may have given up something more than just privacy. If we are considered to be the accumulation of our errors, statistical likelihoods established by computers on the basis of axiomatic principles of behavior, then we need a new definition of freedom. Neither an orthodox Christian nor an "existential" definition will do, since we will not be forgiven and cannot make ourselves anew. The "I" so laboriously fashioned from experiential transactions is no longer indivisible, but merely a killer smog of data. If we can be predicted, then we don't exist.

(June 1969)

The Second Genesis, The Coming Control of Life, by Albert Rosenfeld

Faster than a streptococcus, more provoking than locomotor ataxia, able to leap tall theories in a single bound—it's . . . Albert Rosenfeld, Super Science-Writer! No joke. Mr. Rosenfeld, science editor of *Life* magazine, performs heroic public service with this book. He has looked long and hard at the biological and medical sciences, at what they can do right now (a great deal) and what they hope to be able to do shortly (almost everything). He has, with lively intelligence and a gift for the apposite metaphor, made the arcane accessible to everyone. No more slogging through swamps of subordinate clauses, through thickets of obscurantism. Mr. Rosenfeld goes flat-out, telling us exactly what the biomedical engineers are up to and exploring the social, political and ethical implications of their work. What results is a totalitarian vision of the future so cineramic that it almost overwhelms the author's optimism.

Consider the body. It dies because it is diseased or because certain indispensable components wear out. But if we define death as the cessation of electrical impulses from the brain, there are machines that can maintain a form of life, if not a form of sentience, indefinitely. "Incurables" might be stashed away in freezers to await a medical breakthrough fifty years from now. Transplants of animal, human or artificial organs might be employed to replace malfunctioning parts and to create "chimeras." Substitute organs might be grown from laboratory cell-tissues.

Consider the embryo. Sperm banks could eliminate the need for sex (except as recreation). Artificial wombs could eliminate the need for pregnancy (the ultimate labor-saving device). An aspiring mother might walk into "a commissary, look down a row of packets not unlike flower seed packages," select a "frozen one-day-old embryo" according to her specifications, "drop it off at the bottling works and pick it up when ready." Manipulative geneticists could introduce deliberate mutations, and life itself might be synthesized in a lab. (Dr. Daniele Petrucci kept *something* alive for twenty-nine days in a glass.)

Consider the brain, that "enchanted loom where millions of flashing shuttles weave a dissolving pattern," as Sir Charles Sherrington described it. The brain has been pretty thoroughly cartographed; the application of electrodes to certain areas can elicit predictable responses of pleasure or pain, hunger or fear. Drugs of an astonishing variety can alter perceptions and emotional states and physical capacities. Sophisticated instruments can record the fact that we are dreaming, or agitated, or enraged. Individual brain cells can be isolated, and the effects of the learning process on those cells can be measured.

Patiently and lucidly, Mr. Rosenfeld brings us up to date on the state of research in all these fields. He speculates along with the scientists whose work he summarizes. And he asks crucial questions. In an age of molecular manipulation, uterine implants, packaged sperm, psycho-chemical control of perception, man-animal-machine chimeras, what does "life" mean? Can a "soul" be synthesized in a laboratory—is it a by-product? Are we "parents" if we pick up a baby from a breeding tank? Can there be a legal definition of "death"?

The question marks are waiting like scythes on every page of his book, to hack away at preconceptions and mental sloth and our habitual acquiescence in processes whose logic and combustion we have decided are inscrutable. If Mr. Rosenfeld is describing the possibility of immortality, he is also describing the possibility of an environmental control so exact, so all-encompassing, so total that it could make the modern police state look like Disneyland.

We may console ourselves by saying that the human engineers don't know everything yet. They can't explain memory, and they don't have the slightest idea how the brain operates as an integrated whole, how decisions are made (to move a finger, to fall in love), how language is learned, how a statistical determination is made of the meaning of a pattern of depolarizing neurons. They can't tell us what makes some men good and others evil—despite the recent ad campaign on behalf of the outlaw chromosome. But they, and we, *are* standing on the threshold of fabricated life. Mr. Rosenfeld's noble enterprise is to acquaint us with the imminence of that awesome fabrication. The first genesis may have been, as he says, the result of some "final energizing stroke, perhaps a powerful burst of cosmic radiation," that roiled the waters of the "primordial earth-soup" and formed the first self-replicating molecules. Or it could be, as Eddington suggests, the tragic consequences of "a lack of antiseptic precautions on the part of the cosmos." The second genesis, however, will be our fault.

(June 1969)

NO MORE ANYBODY?

Anti-Ballistic Missile: Yes or No? A Special Report from the Center for the Study of Democratic Institutions

ABM, An Evaluation of the Decision to Deploy an Antiballistic Missile System, edited by Abram Chayes and Jerome B. Wiesner

These two books seem to me to be transmitting a desperate subliminal message. Perhaps not. Perhaps the authors are wholly absorbed in facts. But surely there must be a psychological curve, plotted according to our decent instincts and our legitimate hopes and whatever remains of our respect for life, that will at some point intersect with the technological curve of the defense establishment. Beyond the quantifiable, beyond systems and statistical probabilities and money and megatonnage, there must be a moral universe, and we have merely mislaid the co-ordinates that would enable us to locate it. For we appear to be trapped in two disastrous assumptions. The first was described by I. F. Stone in *The New York Review of Books* as "the assumption . . . that war is a kind of game on which nations embark after consulting a computer to see who would come out ahead." The second was suggested by Robert Rothstein in *The New Republic*: the military, whose business it is to defend the nation, refuses to believe that there is no real defense against nuclear attack, and so assumes that there must be "technological solutions to strategic problems." Not to mention diplomatic and moral problems.

    Anti-Ballistic Missile: Yes or No? is based on a symposium sponsored last November by the Center for the Study of Democratic Institutions—a kind of mental gymnasium for liberal heavy-hearts in Santa Barbara. Events have overtaken it. The discussion between proponents and opponents of ABM deployment was predicated on Lyndon B. Johnson's proposed thin-line Sentinel defense of major population centers. Mr. Nixon has, of course, changed the name of the system to "Safeguard," as though to deodorize it; and changed the proposed deployment from American cities to Minuteman installations and bomber bases.

Thus the argument by Donald G. Brennan, former president of the Hudson Institute, that ABM deployment would reduce American fatalities in the event of a Soviet first strike "from something in the range of 80 to 100 to 120 million down to perhaps 20 or 30 or 40 million" is no longer politically relevant. (It was always about as ethically relevant as counting the number of rapists in a gang-bang.) The argument of Gen. Leon W. Johnson, U.S.A.F., retired, is more interesting: "Do you want small and insignificant nations seizing our ships upon the high seas?" General Johnson is impatient with the balance of terror because it inhibits the United States in our role of world policeman; he wants us to have more terror than anybody else. A small and insignificant book reviewer wants to sink him in his high rhetoric.

Because the arguments against the ABM advanced by Jerome B. Wiesner and Senator George McGovern at the symposium are developed at greater length in ABM, I want to pass on to the second book. But not before noting what one participant in the Center colloquy, Harvey Wheeler, said: "We are coming to the point where true legislative processes are occurring in the realm of science policy rather than in the halls of the legislatures. This is a key problem—how to bring matters that involve complex technology and difficult scientific questions into what might be called the realm of the Constitution. How do you constitutionalize science?"

How, indeed? One way is to have more books like ABM around. Edited by Mr. Wiesner and Abram Chayes, ABM is a series of essays by scientists, scholars and statesmen (all of them very Establishmentarian) attacking Sentinel/Safeguard deployment on every conceivable level: technical and economic feasibility, strategic soundness, diplomatic and psychological consequences. The study was initiated by Senator Edward M. Kennedy, who contributes an introduction, and it represents a significant step towards involving all of us outside the government in decision-making processes having to do with our survival.

Moreover, it is convincing. We are reminded of our present four-to-one missile superiority over the Soviet Union, and our diversified means of "delivering" those missiles. We are reminded that the original justification for ABM was based on faulty intelligence about Russian activity; that it was then said to be a protection against China; that it's now supposedly a bargaining tool at arms control conferences. We are shown that it will cost at least three times as much as Defense Secretary Melvin R. Laird has estimated, and that it will be obsolete before it is operational.

The despairing part of the whole debate over ABM deployment is that, while public outcry might scuttle the system, the system itself isn't nearly as important as the MIRV's (multiheaded missiles) we are already deploying. MIRV's multiply the number of warheads per missile by three to ten times. The warheads can then be fired off in different directions. Neither reconnaissance flights nor satellite surveillance will be able to detect how much megatonnage is being readied for delivery by any offensive or defensive system. The Russians are certain to develop a similar capacity soon, and what happens then to arms control treaties?

But who wants arms control? We spend $80 billion a year on defense. Adam Yarmolinsky points out in a chapter of *ABM* that of the $44 billion in contracts let last year for weapons purchase, only 11 per cent was awarded through formal advertising and competitive bidding. The top 100 defense contractors employ 2,072 retired military officers. On the evidence of *ABM*, and the ever proliferating defense system, death has a lobby in Washington.

(June 1969)

SOCIOLOGY (1): UP AGAINST THE WALL, FUNCTIONALISTS

The Coming Crisis of Western Sociology, by Alvin W. Gouldner

Most Americans don't think much about theory, and about sociological theory, they think not at all: Those who can, do; those who can't, theorize—about Kant. One measure of Alvin Gouldner's extraordinary achievement in this book is that he proves that what we do depends to a large extent on our willingness to accept the prevailing theoretical notion of the way things should be done. Another is that he demonstrates that the prevailing American social theory is full of holes. A third is that he makes the history of ideas read like a detective story: from the Utilitarianism of the eighteenth century to the Positivism (and Marxism) of the nineteenth to the Functionalism (and Stalinism) of the twentieth; from Saint-Simon to Comte to Durkeim to Weber to Pareto to Talcott Parsons, along one line of development; and from Marx to Lenin to Lukacs to Marcuse to Roger Garaudy and Adam Schaff, along another line, on the Eastern European socialist express.

Because Dr. Gouldner—Max Weber Professor of Social Theory at Washington University in St. Louis—has written the most important book in this field since C. Wright Mills's *The Sociological Imagination,* I want to spend today and tomorrow on it. In vain, for to synopsize its argument is simply to thump the reader on the head with its bare bones, lacking the meat of supportive detail, the taste of graceful expression. Still, there's room in his "reflexive sociology," or "sociology *of* sociology," for student radicals, black liberationists, Third Worlders, traumatized liberals and unaffiliated anomie-siacs to group-grope.

First, Dr. Gouldner argues that "academic sociologists" refuse to do unto themselves what they persist in doing to others, i.e., interpret their own behavior in terms of personal sentiments, "domain assumptions," careerist self-interest, institutional bias, manipulative tendencies and elitist rationalizations. When a sociologist resorts to theory against the empirical facts, or rides a methodological mono-rail to "truth," all the while crying *value-free, value-free,* he de-ceives himself as well as others: "As in the realm of physics, where there is no quality without some quantity, so in the social realm, there is no reality without value . . ."

Next, Dr. Gouldner establishes the existence of an "unemployed self," the consequence of a Utilitarian perception of man in terms of his "usefulness: as a work-unit, exchanging labor for material gratification." While bourgeois production may consist of things that have "exchange-value" rather than "use-value"—what sells instead of what's useful—the bourgeoisie share with the Marxists a modern in-dustrial society in which the state legitimatizes itself not by invoking superior moral sanction (God), but by distributing more gratifica-tions (GNP) than our immediate "adversary."

Dr. Gouldner then employs Talcott Parsons's "Functionalism" as an example of theory gone wrong. A man who escaped the incon-venience of the Great Depression, a Harvard elitist with a wretched prose style, an anti-Marxist who never read the early "alienation" manuscripts, proposes an all-inclusive social theory that leaves out sex and economics. (Seduce my wife, betray me as a friend, and I must divorce her and/or feel sorry for myself; steal my hat, and the state will throw you in jail. Property! That it can be inherited makes notions of "equality of opportunity under the law" nonsensical. Offi-cial morality and social reality deny each other.) The example suggests—

A sociology that rents itself out to whatever industrial society re-quires priests and bureaucratic plumbers; a profession, pampered by university perquisites, that seeks to conserve whatever system re-wards it, to oblige "the gods of the city" of whichever city subsidizes it, to excuse any variety of authoritarianism in the name of "order," for in "order" is the preservation of the priesthood. Police state (re-pressive apparatus) or welfare state ("manipulation of the techno-logical fruits by income allocation")—who cares?

The crisis of Western sociology enters its second day. Next month, almost as though the professors had been reading Alvin W. Gouldner's book, Harvard will re-establish an independent department of sociology, ending twenty-four years of interdisciplinary group-grope (sociologists, psychologists, anthropologists) under the "social relations" umbrella. One reason for the change, as reported by Robert Reinhold in the New York *Times*, is that American sociology is shifting its emphasis away from "micro-scale" analyses of individual behavior, toward urban and racial problems instead. Sociologists will thus have more in common with economists and political scientists than with psychologists and anthropologists.

Presumably, graduate students have been nipping at their heels. And yet, as Dr. Gouldner says, the growth of the welfare state makes such a shift inevitable. Parsonsian Functionalism took the social system (with its existing power arrangements, property relationships and institutions) as a given, and took "equilibrium" (order, stability) as an ideal. So long as citizens conformed to an agreed-upon moral code (divine sanction, caste niche), or so long as they got a sufficient number of gratifications (consumer products, prestige symbols), there was no reason why the social system wouldn't last forever. Power had a way of becoming "authority"; authority was somehow always "legitimate."

Alas, the system has proved in many respects to be "dysfunctional." The Great Depression required a lot of tinkering with the social machinery to keep those gratifications rolling off the assembly line without altering basic power arrangements and property relationships. A black minority threatens to bring the ideological wars of nineteenth-century Europe to twentieth-century America. A psychedelic "counter-culture" lacks respect for authority. Women want to be liberated and students refuse careers and farm workers live brutish half-lives and too many citizens derive no pleasure from either their work or their regimented leisure and a war goes on and on because no one knows how to stop it.

For sociologists, one result of this dysfunctionalism was an impulse to pump a little Marx into their paradigms. Dr. Gouldner documents the "convergence" of academic sociology and Marxism in recent years, even as he sketches in various recent departures from Parsonsian theory (Erving Goffman's "dramaturgy," Harold Garfinkel's "ethnomethodology," George Homans's "social exchange"). A sense of *precariousness* is loose in the land, which perhaps explains

the substitution of "games" theories for the old hydraulic model of
an input-output social system.

Another result is that sociologists have been hired by the welfare
state to fix things. The federal government spent $200 million on
social science research in 1964, and the subsidy goes up each year.
Washington's assumption that it can do something specific about
civic turmoil, if only sociologists will tell it what to do, almost directly opposes the Parsonsian assumption that, since "everything
influences everything else," adaptive mechanisms will emerge "spontaneously" to restore equilibrium. The theory had to change, then,
not only to accommodate the fact of disorder, but to accommodate
the men with the money as well.

And so a new Rent-a-Professor agency opened with headquarters
in the nation's capital, to which sociologists on credit cards and consultants' fees and tax deductions shuttled from their college campuses. Leaving aside the binge of counter-insurgency and riot-control
scenarios such shuttling inflicted on a luckless world, is there anything wrong with sociologists trying to solve social problems, instead of just studying them?

Dr. Gouldner argues convincingly that there *is* something wrong
if . . . if the sociologist hides behind a mask of "objectivity" to
avoid seeing facts about power arrangements and property relationships that would inspire a moral qualm or two; if he conceives of his
methodology, ever so scientific, as a substitute for values with discrete weights; if his theory is simply procedural, uninformed by a
private vision of what *ought* to be; if he refuses to face up to his own
complicity in a system of university and government rewards and
punishments; if he is merely "the liberal technologue who produces
information and theories that serve to bind the poor and the working classes both to the state apparatus and the political machinery
of the Democratic Party . . ."

"Theory," he says, is really just "an effort to make sense of one's
experience . . . to locate and to interpret the meaning of what one
has lived." He proposes a "reflexive sociology," necessarily radical:
"Radical, because it would recognize that knowledge of the world
cannot be advanced apart from a sociologist's knowledge of himself
and his position in the social world, or apart from his efforts to
change these. Radical, because it seeks to transform as well as to

know the alien world outside the sociologist as well as the alien world inside of him. Radical, because it would accept the fact that the roots of sociology pass through the sociologist as a total man, and that the question he must confront, therefore, is not merely how to *work* but how to *live*."

Not the least of the marvels of Dr. Gouldner's exciting book is that what he says of sociologists is true of all of us. We need a reflexive humanity.

(June 1970)

Policy I, for Freshmen

"Pedagogy," said Lionel Trilling, "is a depressing subject to all persons of sensibility." Mr. Trilling said so some years ago, long before the appearance of hundreds of "education" books exhorting the pedagogue to save our souls and solve our social problems—*How Mama Sincere Reached the Recalcitrants, Absolute Truth for Breakfast, Happiness Is a Warm Professor*—the polonaise, the clair de lune and the ritual fire dance of the radical reformers. Even Mr. Trilling didn't know how depressing the subject could become.

Depressing: because schools and/or universities are no more capable of saving a soul than the Army, the Rotary Club, the Rolling Stones or *The New York Times Book Review*. Depressing, too, because the university ought ideally to be a place where people who know something teach what they know to people who don't know it, in an agreeable fashion. It should not be a place where the teacher contracts out to the messianisms either of the Defense Department or the Student Society for an Unobstructed Id.

Alas, the times are perceived to be hard, and in hard times knowledge for knowledge's sake looks like self-indulgence. The pedagogue isn't going to be permitted to do *his* own thing. According to the new dispensation, he has to do that thing which is most ardently desired by the most ardent of his students. If he lusts for their approval (and he does, shamelessly), he must be relevant. Being relevant means solving problems instead of just describing them. The pedagogue, a good liberal, knows that problems are complicated; but how is he to dramatize the complications to Mama Sincere and the

Absolutely Truthful without whoring after that exemption from culpability which all good liberals ultimately desire?

Oddly enough, a partial answer is suggested not by the radical reformers but in two recent books by, respectively, a doctor of philosophy and a professor of social administration. Daniel Callahan, former executive editor of *Commonweal* and director of the Institute of Society, Ethics and the Life Sciences, is the doctor of philosophy. Richard Titmuss, chief adviser to the British Labor Party on welfare policy, is the professor of social administration. They have both written books about "problems" which are, in fact, superb essays on the formation of *policy*.

Daniel Callahan began his book, *Abortion: Law, Choice and Morality*, opposed to abortion. He ends it—after a staggering amount of research and long chapters on the medical and psychological reasons for (and hazards of) abortion; the fetal situation; the various legal codes, statistical experience and ethical perceptions of Eastern Europe, Latin America, Scandinavia, Africa and Japan; what philosophers, biologists, Roman Catholics and liberated women have to say on the subject—believing that the state has no right to refuse an abortion to a woman who wants one. He proposes permissive legislation to this effect.

But he isn't happy. He still hopes for a better method of birth control "which does not require that we make a choice between the life of a conceptus and those other human values we count important." Because what is legal may not necessarily be what is moral. Legality is a shifting process of accommodations between individual rights and social needs. If legal abortions do not threaten this society, and he demonstrates that they do not, then the individual right of a woman to control her own body and plan her own family takes precedence over such abstractions as "the sanctity of life." The abstractions, however, are important—a form of "counsel." *Policy* is arrived at by weighing the arguments, balancing the interests, consulting one's scruples, deciding, and still not feeling happy. "The sanctity of life" is one of the few useful moral weapons we possess to oppose what might be called an economizing of human behavior, the kind of reductionism represented by, say, Ti-Grace Atkinson when she argues that a woman's "reproductive function and the fetus constitute her property" and she can destroy the fetus as she might destroy a painting.

Richard Titmuss in *The Gift Relationship* also opposes the econ-omizing of human behavior. His "problem" is blood donations. His worry is the commercialization of "the gift relationship," the gift to a stranger of life. His investigation, like Callahan's, is exhaustive —the blood-collecting systems of every country in the world with available statistics are examined. His conclusions are shocking: The paid "donor" system results in an appalling waste of 15–30 per cent of blood collected. It creates a "blood proletariat" consisting mostly of "the poor, the unskilled, the unemployed." It encourages a do-nor's lying about his health to get his money. It "represses the expression of altruism, erodes the sense of community, lowers scien-tific standards . . . [and] places immense social costs on those least able to bear them—the poor, the sick and the inept."

Titmuss establishes the economic insanity of commercial blood-collecting systems, but his primary concern is moral—or "ideolog-ical" if you prefer, an adjective that goes down easier in the secular state. His target, as Alvin Gouldner noted in his review of *The Gift Relationship*, is "the bent commitment of our type of industrial so-ciety to treat human labor as akin to other market commodities. If we can and do buy and sell a man's lifetime and energies, if we have consented to treat much of *existence* as a commodity, we must not be surprised if men do not boggle at trafficking in blood. The com-mercialization of blood tokens the extent to which the most sacred presuppositions of our culture have been penetrated and distorted by the norms of venality."

The most sacred presuppositions . . . the sanctity of life . . . what have these formless abstractions to do with the poor pedagogue and his anxiety to be relevant? Well, both Callahan and Titmuss have examined a problem in terms of the policies we have developed, or might have developed, to deal with it; and the consequences of those policies. Both have listened to the testimonies of science, medicine, law, sociology, philosophy, statistical analysis, religion and ideology. Both make us painfully aware of scruples and ramifica-tions, deceit and muddleheadedness, problems of *forming* a policy which are anterior to the problem that wants solving. I can't think why a college course couldn't be constructed around either book or either problem. Or another, similar, problem. Invite delegates from the various academic disciplines to state their case, defend their methodology, prove their ethical or practical pertinence, leak a little of their wisdom. Demonstrate how complicated policy making really is. *That* would be an education. The teacher would pay his dues as a citizen; the student would learn that truth is not some instantaneous relevation, immutably obvious in the fires of an existential moment, but only the grubby approximation of a shared ideal.

(September 1971)

Predestination Without Grace

Things being what they are, which is not what most of us would wish them to be, one can't walk down the streets of the mind these days without getting mugged by a Single Cause. The Single Cause usually has an accomplice, the Single Cure. Original Sin, sexism, anality, atavistic aggressive impulses, the school and/or economic system, the death of God, Vietnam, Dostoyevsky, Chairman Mao and Mayor Lindsay are among the Single Causes. Marijuana, Sesame Street, R. D. Laing, waterbeds, tactical nuclear weapons, Aesthetic Realism, the Living Theater, the polymorphous perverse, Esalen and Jane Fonda are among the Single Cures.

But—and the superstition is especially virulent among those of a literary or humanist sensibility—science increasingly plays the part of the heavy, the single *casus belli*. Science, which brought you technology, which brought you pollution, data banks, napalm, wire taps, antiballistics missiles, genetic engineering, college board exams and toothpaste with sex appeal; science, which has steadily reduced the number of things for which God can be held accountable and thereby pinned the rap on man . . . *that* science. And those scientists. There was no room for those scientists in Jacques Barzun's House of Intellect; and so they moved into Lewis Mumford's Pentagon of Power, where, according to Norman O. Brown, they are engaged in manipulations of symbolic excrement.

We have come a long way from Prometheus to Faust to Frankenstein, a typically Western way of flip-flop, attraction-repulsion, revel and remorse. The bringer of fire has become the Hun at the gate—a high Vincent Price to pay for all those old movies about mad scientists. The black magician, the wicked witch and the ship of death have always inflamed the literary imagination; why not Dr. Strangelove? The alchemist who used to be an artist has now metamorphosed into a systems analyst; for the book of secrets we have substituted the flow chart. No matter that, when Dr. Strangelove actually appears, it is in the form of thirteen college professors—professors not of physics, biology or chemistry, but professors of history, urban studies, government, economics—professing *machismo*, getting us into Southeast Asia the way Pericles got the Athenians into the Peloponnesian War. Never mind—Off the scientist! He knows something the rest of us don't, a secret and anti-democratic expertise; and we have come to believe that the end of all knowledge is manipulation and we revenge ourselves on this last elite by writing novels and making movies in which scientists perform poorly in bed, just like psychoanalysts. Norman Mailer knows.

"We" in this case are Mailers *manqués*, tenants in the rent-controlled brownstone of the humanist sensibility: If we can't be Faust, we might as well be Parsifal. We subscribe to individuality, to subjective experience; what else is Art about? We want to be Platonists, operating on an ideal scale of values—and along come these wonks with slide rules sewn into their sports jackets, these *utilitarians* with their impersonal instruments, their college board exams, weighing us as though each of us weren't *unique*. "They" are telling us that they can measure our merriment and our desperation and that we don't deviate very much from the norm. On the whole, one prefers Jane Fonda.

Now, if you were to ask your favorite scientist, as I did mine, what accounts for this hate affair, this pathological anti-scientism among the humanists, he or she might explain it this way: Scientists are telling us that we aren't central, but peripheral, to the business of the universe; that we aren't created in the image of God but are rather a lucky concert of atoms; that we aren't masters of our fate or captains of our soul but puppets of our past, jerking on strings attached to prior causes—"Predestination without grace," someone called it, a gloomy truth, and one that propels humanists into unseemly trysts with the gratuitous, the cruel, the random and the Absurd . . .

At three o'clock in the morning
You pause before my door;

At three o'clock in the morning
It's always Either/Or.

I remove my silk foulard,
You let down your Kierke-guard—

EX–IS–TENZ!

When the going gets tough the humanist gets subjective: Don't
tell *me* there aren't any shadows on the wall of the cave. Science has
created a world in which men do things not because they want to,
but simply because they know how. Everything that can be done
will be done. What kind of a world is that? Besides, how come scientists have it easier finding jobs in and out of the universities? How
come they get so much money to support their research and the rest
of us get so little?

To which the scientist replies: The only definition of free will that
makes any modern sense is man's ability to postpone action while
he scans the possibilities. And science is cumulative; it learns from
its mistakes; it learns *because* of its mistakes. What do art and literature learn from a fourth-rate painting or novel? Art and literature
always have to start all over again each time. Obviously, society is
going to invest in cumulative wisdom. Go on with your tortured
soul—pawn it for a laboratory smock!

Art is *I*, said Claude Bernard; science is *we*.

And yet, and yet, and yet . . . the humanists (subjective to the
last) enjoy their long-playing records, their inexpensive paperback
books, their air conditioning, motor-boating, mechanical pacemak-
ers in the heart, transportation to Martha's Vineyard or East Hampton, polio vaccines, no more malaria or yellow fever, "public"
television, waiting for Godard, the prosthetic extensions of man into
wonders we could not imagine and vistas beyond the power of the
naked eye to perceive. Health, food, communication, convenience,
survival. So much for the contributions of scientists to the societies
in which we, all of us I's, accidentally happen upon each other. And
the scientists (utilitarian to the core)—against what do they measure? What standard of decency, mercy, justice? Which are the laws
of men and how do they differ from the laws of matter, of falling

bodies and sucking vacuums? Quantity implies quality as a measure of its meaning, its human suitability; quality is a *value*. Utilitarianism ultimately proposes a laissez-faire economy of the psychological as well as the material goods: conflicting interests will somehow chance upon an equilibrium, in the moral as well as mercantile state. But it doesn't work. The notion of justice has to be worked up by humanists who never let go of their intuition into the suffering of an individual: how much is supportable? What is *fair?* Which are the proper uses of power? Institutions are necessary to distribute the material goods and protect the spiritual goods. Science provides the power to distribute; humanism must define what is spiritually necessary; both have to work out the whys, hows, whens of codifying, enforcing and insuring that what we agree to be good for each of us individually and all of us collectively will be institutionalized.

If science is too much identified by the humanists as the Single Cause of all our ills, then a Single Cure is bound to be in the wings —a single cure that looks suspiciously like anti-intellectualism. None of us can afford the sort of mindless whine that says it's so difficult to make sense out of things that the fault must reside in the very idea of trying to make sense out of things—not so long as the *I* is not alone. And the *I* isn't alone: we are the only animals with an accessible history; community is our condition; ours is a social disease—a permanent dependency on others that requires a contract, usually among strangers. Thinking, analyzing, extrapolating, as Jorge Luis Borges has reminded us, "are not anomalous acts; they are the normal respiration of intelligence." Let us respire.

(July 1971)

The Tube

Television

There is a concept which corrupts and upsets all others. I refer not to
Evil, whose limited realm is that of ethics. I refer to the infinite. I
once longed to compile its mobile history. The numerous Hydra (the
swamp monster which amounts to a prefiguration or emblem of geo-
metric progressions) would lend convenient horror to its portico; it
would be crowned by the sordid nightmares of Kafka . . . Five or
seven years of metaphysical, theological and mathematical apprenticeship would allow me (perhaps) to plan decorously such a book. It is
useless to add that life forbids me that hope and even that adverb.

JORGE LUIS BORGES, *Avatars of the Tortoise*

Poor Borges. The infinite was to him what television is to those of
us who review it—a "minimum labyrinth," a library of Babel, where
the light is ever "insufficient, incessant." He had to settle for fragments, gnomic riddles, as we settle for notices, a column or two of
type on what the swamp monster did last week. At least Borges,
along with his "apparent desperations," has the "secret consolation"
of blindness; there is no way he can be made to watch the network
reruns which begin in early March. Reruns in March . . . convenient
horror. The series programs don't last as long as the football season:
the football season *is* infinite.

Which are the secret consolations of the TV reviewer? His apparent desperations are obvious. (1) Nobody takes you seriously—learn
a trade, says your mother; weave baskets, find God, sell Mortimer
Adler door to door, eat your Marcusian Rice Crispies. You are un-
serious because (2) you are powerless to alter events or cloud men's
minds. By the time your comment appears in print, the object of it
has vanished. You are powerless even to inspire a panicked blip on
the encephalograms of the Sixth Avenue cretins who packaged the
objectionable. You are powerless because (3) millions of people saw
exactly what you saw, have already made up—or short-sheeted—their
minds about it, and told Mr. Nielsen.

And so (4) you waste an enormous amount of time and energy
writing about community programming on UHF, the FCC fairness

doctrine, media conglomerates, managed news, Marshall McLuhan, the cassette revolution, self-censorship on public television, who will control the new cable channels, how much video violence contributes to anti-social behavior—all to prove that you are just as serious as Borges. After all, 96 per cent of American homes have at least one TV set; the average set is on at least six hours a day; the average sixteen-year-old has spent as much time watching TV as he has spent in school; and TV Guide outsells every other magazine in the nation. TV is more serious than venereal disease.

But no one is convinced. If your reviews are read, it is by those who seek a confirmation, either of their own gut reaction to a new sit-com or of their suspicion that you are a jerk. You can no more review TV according to agreed-upon criteria than you can review politics or sports or old girl friends—or compile a mobile history of the infinite. The lout on the next barstool also considers himself an expert; "Seen in this manner," says Borges, "all our acts are just, but they are also indifferent. There are no moral or intellectual merits." Less attention was paid in March of 1972 to Senator John Pastore's hearings on the impact of televised violence than was paid to spring-training baseball.

However, the consolations make up for the desperations. (A) You are being *paid* to watch television, which means that you don't have to apologize for doing what all your friends do secretly and feel guilty about. (B) It is something you can actually do with your children, instead of reading *Babar* aloud for the 157th time or running a staple through your thumb. And (C) being powerless is liberating. You can say what you want about the play and the actors; it won't close, and they won't be fired, on your account. Since television is about everything, you can review everything. Attention may not be paid, but hostilities will be projected, and you'll be the healthier for the projecting of them, even if your society is not. As Borges put it, "We took out our heavy revolvers (all of a sudden there were revolvers in the dream) and joyfully killed the Gods."

I became a TV reviewer by accident. I'd been writing book reviews for Dave Scherman at *Life* magazine. When in May 1969 I became a daily book reviewer for the *Times*, I could not, obviously, review any books for *Life*. Dave was looking around for a television columnist, remembered an article I'd written for the *Times Magazine* on the

Children's Television Workshop and asked me to try it. It was a clear case of sponsoring a bad habit. When, in January 1971, I became the editor of the *Times Book Review*, it was considered inappropriate to be a TV reviewer for *Life* at the same time. So I disappeared and "Cyclops" was born. *Life* still occasionally receives letters thanking the magazine for getting rid of me in favor of Cyclops, or demanding my return and the firing of Cyclops. So much for a distinctive prose style.

1971

What sort of a year was it? The mind is a vacuum tube. The memory is artificial turf, videotape, consisting of images of George Plimpton, Archie Bunker, Zorba the Mayor; beneath it lie the bodies of four thousand lobotomized network vice-presidents, sewn together at their pineal glands and Achilles' heels. On the playing field itself, Congressmen and FCC commissioners and the bureaucrats of public television scrimmage with cleated prose and padded brains. Above it all broods the moon of Mr. Nixon, out of phase, making one thing perfectly clear . . .

Why is it that one thinks of La Fontaine—"the age without pity"? And of Rousseau—"the sleep of reason"? La Fontaine and Rousseau were talking about childhood. One thinks of childhood because one has just finished reading a news bulletin: Sandy Duncan is recuperating from eye surgery and her show is off the air; a CBS substitute is something called "Me and the Chimp." And suddenly one thing actually is perfectly clear. This was the year that children's programming came of age on television. It is *all* children's programming.

I'm not talking about "Sesame Street," "The Electric Company," "Story Theatre" or George Heinemann's "Take a Giant Step," estimable programs all. They have identified and gone after the appropriate age groups. But what about all the other hours? Are eight-year-olds the only age group in the country? So it seems.

How else explain the violence, which after all is a cartoon for people pretending to be adults. Bugs Bunny with napalm. Two seasons ago the networks flirted briefly with our social concerns; the relation-

ship was never consummated. This past year there wasn't a night of
the week without two cops and robbers shows, not counting the
made-for-TV movies that seemed stitched together out of film
footage left over after *The Untouchables* wasted themselves. Detectives with various infirmities variously inflicted other infirmities
on a variety of mindless evildoers: guns, knives, bombs, car wrecks,
hypodermic needles, electric shock. The occult made a comeback:
let's hear it for vampirism and necrophilia. We've arrived at a fair
operational definition of pornography, from its Greek source (having to do with harlots) to its aesthetic implications ("little or no
artistic merit"). All pornography is ultimately intended for children,
of whatever age. And the violence high is addictive.

How else explain our drowning in the vicariousness of sports? Football on Saturdays, Sundays and Mondays. The World Series at
night. Hockey, basketball, roller derby, moose hunting and the FBI.
It is beside the point that television is in the process of ruining
many of these sports for the participants—time-outs for commercials
interrupting the flow of an ice hockey or basketball game; the artificial turf that looks so green on your color screen sending half the
National Football League to the hospital. So much televised fun-
and-games amounts almost to a prophylaxis against the disease of
reality. Our only sweat is electronic; Howard Cosell becomes the
president of our awareness.

And take our President. Please. *There's* children's programming.
So what if his words and gestures seem slightly out of synch; if his
vertical hold seems spastic; if his eyes sometimes seem like broken
TV sets, behind which, inside the locked projection booth of the
skull, a little six-inch Mr. Nixon goes on endlessly re-running the late
shows of the 1950's in black-and-white. He is the Ed Sullivan of policy making, a new act every week. Decisions—freeze the wages,
go to China—are made on prime-time TV. Surprise! Just what you
least expected. Caught you with your preconceptions down around
your knees. Government by jack-in-the-box. No time for questions,
no newspaper reporters, damn few press conferences, screw the Senate, and Mr. Nielsen can't do anything about it because it's on all
the channels. Look what daddy brought home from the office: an
invasion of Cambodia! A Henry Kissinger doll: wind him up and he
disappears—to Paris, to Peking. Politics is the art of the commercial.
One imagines Mr. Nixon, his arms aloft in the famous "V," as a

slingshot, flinging our heads through the TV screen into stunned disbelief.

Infantilism. Meanwhile, Shirley MacLaine and Anthony Quinn have been knifed, and Henry Fonda is being shuffled around for professional football. "The Good Life," "Sarge," "The Partners" and "The Funny Side" have soured, been busted, divorced and run out of laughs. Make way for "Me and the Chimp" or "Sanford and Son" (a black "All in the Family," proving that the networks are willing to insult the intelligence of everyone, regardless of race, color or creed). There's a Japanese science-fiction movie on tonight . . . *Gammera the Invincible*. A giant prehistoric turtle threatens to destroy first Brian Donlevy and finally the world. Why bother? Turtles don't watch enough television. I have seen the world, and it is "Romper Room."

(December 31, 1971)

The Next Ten Years

Once upon a time, one of the nice things about being an American was that we believed there were technological solutions to social and moral problems. It's been a tough decade for that sort of naïvete; there are bloody thumbprints of the irrational all over our computer print-outs. But the notion of man's perfectibility via his machines dies hard. We still believe in antiballistic missile systems and TV, to win wars and educate the public.

About silos and multiple warheads I am not paid to think, and thus refuse to do so. About television . . . well, the shining scenarios are already upon us. An article in these pages a few weeks ago described some of them. A cable can already carry thirty TV channels into every home. UHF is a potential source of community and minority programming. Home taping of network shows is a couple of years away. Cassettes are being developed that will permit us to build up a library of cartridges; at our convenience, we will be able to plug in and turn on whatever program appeals to us, just like LP records. Experiments with computers suggest the possibility of "entertainment" as well as "data" banks; properly equipped, we will need only to dial a number and the information or the suspense we desire will appear on our home screens, plucked from a world of infinite variety.

Of these scenarios, the dial-a-program-from-the-computer-bank is the most attractive, because it would encourage the production—at minimal expense—of almost anything, almost any old cultural scratch for whatever itch comes over us, stored and waiting for the phone to ring. TV would finish off the print media, either by being more various than the competition or by absorbing it—delivering our daily newspaper and any magazine or book we selected. TV would challenge the educational system, by teaching in the home. TV would bring us Broadway, off-Broadway and even Brooklyn, without baby-sitting, car-parking or ticket-buying problems. A star fleet of communications satellites would weave a seamless web of information over the earth. Con III, effort zero.

A pretty picture. Men and women might even stay home while working, the ultimate extension of the telephone. We live, after all, in a "service environment," with police cars, laundry wagons, taxis, fried-chicken trucks and garage-door openers competing for frequencies along the electromagnetic spectrum, for their fair slice of the land mobile radio pie. Why leave your living room to get mugged? Order your clothes and Christmas presents from video catalogues; earn a college diploma instead of regressing with the "Tonight" show; watch old wars instead of fighting new ones. And if it amuses you, tune in any time you want to *How the West Was Lost*, a musical adaptation of the jeremiad by Lee Harvey Oswald Spengler, with Max Lerner playing the part of the White Liberal, Sonny Liston as the Goth, and Elizabeth Taylor as Democracy.

Democracy. Who has plunged into the cassette business? CBS, RCA, Sony, Ampex, Avco, that's who. Where's the money in CATV? In better images of the same old tripe, and telecasts of home-town sporting events—as General Electric is well aware. What do we see on UHF? Bad Hollywood movies dubbed into Spanish, and re-runs of *Sesame Street*. How about communications satellites? "Should we," asks Nicholas Johnson, "permit the entire universe to be divided up, with Comsat taking the heavens and AT&T taking the earth?" A cry of despair, because Mr. Johnson is a lame-duck Federal Communications Commissioner, and knows that the politically appointed FCC isn't up to controlling the new exploitation any more than it was up to managing the old. Richard Nixon will try to do the same thing to the FCC that he is trying to do to the Supreme Court—and he will get away with it because, unlike the Supreme Court, the FCC is a matter of indifference to most Americans.

There aren't any technological solutions to social and moral problems, unless you count George Blanda in the last few seconds of any Oakland Raiders football game. There *are* political solutions, but they depend on the President of the United States appointing to the FCC men who will cast a cold eye on media conglomerates, the apportionment of phone lines to educational networks, the amount of time devoted to public service broadcasting and the number of commercials permitted each half hour, the role of advertisers in determining the "acceptability" of program content, the access of minorities to the awareness of the majority. Otherwise, the new technology just adds up to a more effective packaging of the old damaged goods. No "global village," but millions of separate electronic bubbles wherein millions of disaffiliated individual prisoners passively consume shadows—a gray Muzak of the eye, a visual hum of machines whose only purpose is to hum us unto our entropic obliteration.

(January 8, 1971)

EMMYS

A Short Rap with the Moonmen

Wallace Stevens called it "blank uneasiness." William Kuhns calls it "new fantasy-reality ratios." I call it mental dropsy—the excessive accumulation of bile in the brain cavity. It happened to me during the Emmy Awards.

There was Barbara Bain copping her third straight best-leading-actress-in-a-dramatic-farce trophy: she who isn't fit to wear a pair of Diana Rigg's discarded leotards. And Carl Betz acclaimed as best leading actor, etc., in a series canceled by ABC. And the also-canceled Smothers Brothers honored for "outstanding writing achievement in comedy, variety or music." And, winning drama-writing honors, J. P. Miller's soap opera in Odets-throes, "The People Next Door." Plus more accolades for Cosby and Capote, to prove how much we appreciate America's two great minority groups. Not to mention that retarded little boy who wasn't allowed on stage to accept his plaque, presumably because it would too perfectly symbolize the state of the industry.

Which dropsy drove me Monday morning to Lou's Fruit Juice Bar, where the Fraternal Order of Tube-Grooving Moonmen meet to drink ether and dig the gaps in each other's perception. The Moonmen grew up with General Sarnoff, logging (like all under-thirties) 15,000 hours of TV time to 10,800 hours of school time before they graduated from high school. As Norman Mailer says, "They had had their minds jabbed and poked and twitched and probed and finally galvanized into surrealistic modes of response by commercials . . . forced willy-nilly to build their idea of the space-time continuum (and therefore their nervous system) on the jumps and cracks and leaps and breaks . . ."

Because the Moonmen cherish a dedicated agnosticism about reality itself, I hoped for consolation. But because I monger words, and words are guilty of association with rational comment and abstract idea, they suspected me. "What rough beast slouches toward us in non-prime time?" they asked.

"My sensorium needs a tune-up," I replied. "Don Adams and Hope Lange and Werner Klemperer all got Emmys. 'College Bowl' has gone on summer vacation, and Glenn Campbell seems a tab-top can of non-caloric charm, a sort of plasticized hillbilly, and I can't relate to reruns of 'The Flying Nun.' Between Johnny Cash and 'The Prisoner' is a vast waste of time."

"Time," said the Moonmen, "is crystallized guilt."

"The King Family is a bummer. I ran out of cigarettes watching 'Captain Kangaroo.' "

"How did Antonioni put it? Dispense with 'the superannuated casuistry of positives and negatives.' You presuppose a value system. There are no values anymore, only strategies for survival. Have you ever tried 'Maryknoll Story Time'? It zaps you right in the synaptic cleft."

"Ed Sullivan, I am becoming bored!"

"The new media, via electrical dilation of our senses, creates a simultaneity of stimulus and response, a cosmic membrane, a de-Chardinian noosphere which, by abolishing sequence, abolishes *becoming*. We *be*."

"But isn't being an even bigger trap than becoming?"

"Being is a lapse of haste."

"But if you are outside a context of becoming, haven't you already gone by? It seems to me that the only real faces on TV belong to Richard Daley and Joe Namath. If the nature of a culture's sensibility is best revealed in its concept of pleasure, then we are lost."

"Don't jump to confusions. Bell Telephone is experimenting with an eight-thousand-line TV image. Think what that will do to the synaptic cleft. ABC has a voodoo program coming up. And next season Doris Day moves to the city. Just as pop painters turned our physical garbage—our soup cans and comic strips—into art, so TV programmers turn our intellectual garbage into entertainment."

"The only entertainment on TV right now is the commercials."

"And why not? How did Gore Vidal put it? 'The relationship between consumer and advertiser is the last demonstration of *necessary* love in the West, and its principal form of expression is the television commercial.' "

"Then we hate ourselves that much?"

"Why not?" said the Tube-Grooving Moonmen. "It's cheaper than miniature golf."

(June 1970)

The Irony of a 'Succès d'Emmy'

"The fourth; the dimension of stillness," wrote Ezra Pound; "And the power over wild beasts." You don't ordinarily associate Ezra Pound with television, unless it's to observe that one or the other has more to feel guilty about than proud of. But there are moments, usually at night, when TV seems genuinely to be "the dimension of stillness" instead of the dimension of silliness, and you wonder whether Marshall McLuhan might have been on to something after all: cruising a Möbius loop in the lunar module of your mind, looking out at an endless instant replay of frozen images suspended in emptiness.

The murder of Lee Harvey Oswald in a Dallas police station; heavyweight George Foreman with an American flag in his hand at the Olympic Games in Mexico City; a man named Armstrong walking on the moon; Mary Travers in concert; the expression on Dick Cavett's face when Captain Robert Marasco revealed that—since "eliminating with extreme prejudice" a double agent in Southeast Asia—he had gone into the life insurance business, and Cavett's audience laughed. Moments.

One such moment occurred the other night at the Emmy Awards. Hal Holbrook was accepting his trophy for best leading actor, male, in a continuing dramatic series, *The Senator*. *The Senator*, one of the segments on NBC's "The Bold Ones," had already picked up awards in a bewildering variety of categories. It had also already been canceled. A moment, then, for ironic dilations? For the critic's little goose step of petulance, word-waltz of outrage? One need only observe that Emmys are often inflicted on victims of the industry, a black kiss, a form of conscience money, heartily applauded—we know we're contemptible and that knowledge somehow makes us less so—and then one goes on with one's thumb-sucking. Why Flip Wilson, and not Carol Burnett? How come the people who create the public affairs specials were made second-class citizens on a fourth-rate entertainment program? What sort of perceptual sponginess and soul-rot accounts for prizing "All in the Family" above "The Mary Tyler Moore Show"? Although TV has much to feel guilty about, aren't the displacements and projections of that guilt sometimes uglier than its origins?

But such thumb-sucking, or nit-picking, or scab-scratching, is reflexive. It has nothing to do with the moment. The moment consisted of Mr. Holbrook, earnest and perplexed, pawing at the podium with his right hand in staccato stabs of emphasis; the head of hair (nobody tugs *my* forelock); those Sorensenian epiphanies of political speech. Where have we seen it all before, besides of course on *The Senator* segments of "The Bold Ones"? We have seen it on a decade of newsreels.

And so the Kennedys have apparently been canceled. Hal Holbrook did his best. There wasn't a program that didn't invite us to admire his amalgam of John, Bobby and Ted: the senator in shirt sleeves, with the jacket slung over his shoulder; the beautiful wife, bored as only beauty can be in the cellars of hugger-mugger; the education bill or the guerrilla war against poverty or the outmaneuvering of troglodytic state party chairmen; money, glamour, ambition, wit and moral zeal, five violent boarders in the rooming house of the same skull. Mr. Holbrook tried, but a manipulation of our fantasy images of Camelot just couldn't win at the ratings game. The Texas School Book Depository, the kitchen of the Ambassador Hotel in Los Angeles and the bridge at Chappaquiddick pre-empted this program.

The Senator was probably no more cynical in its conception than this column is being in its dissection of it. It's only that we've all become so accustomed to the programming of emotional environments that the distinction between art and merchandising has escaped us. There is no stillness in our dimension; only static and reruns. A hand stabbing a podium for a moment is required to quiet our howls, our repetition-compulsions. What does it mean when a nation turns tragedy into comic books?

And finally, even in the stillness, is there any "power over wild beasts"? Is there, to borrow from another poem by Ezra Pound, "in the green deep of an eye . . . Crystal waves weaving toward the great healing," a clarity to disclose "the splendour and wreckage"? I think not. I think there is only Archie Bunker.

(June 18, 1971)

The Pick of the Litter

Television reviewers are supposed to stomp on the corpse of the annual Emmy Awards presentation. We are, after all, frustrated people. Nobody takes us seriously. And stomping on the Emmys is a more socially acceptable means of relieving our frustrations than, say, mugging a Girl Scout. And it's perfectly true that last month, after two hours and fifteen minutes of the usual Emmy nonsense, I felt like John Cameron Swayze strapped to a rubber duck and held under scotch and water for three months: is the brain still ticking?

Johnny Carson was the host. According to Michael Novak, "The innocence of Johnny Carson's face insults the night." Carson started out as though he intended to insult not only the night, but the last forty years of human history—with a couple of snappy one-liners about Eva Braun, Adolf Hitler and planned parenthood. He was followed by Norman Lear, who won the first of a six-pack of Emmys for "All in the Family." Mr. Lear told us that he had been telling himself that, "It won't happen again and maybe it oughtn't to happen again." Unfortunately, it did.

Norman Lear was followed by a multiple presentation of twenty-nine Emmys to the people who had done distinguished work in the news and documentary fields. It is the continuing disgrace of the Emmy business that the only men and women in television with a shred of social conscience are treated like retarded children or Stone Age tribesmen. Their achievements are remarked almost in secret a week or two before the show; they are whisked to Hollywood, where they appear en masse on stage to bask for an instant in the lights before getting the hook—as though they were shameful (like Mylai) but somehow cute (like our autistic children). Even the spoken citations and the visual effects were out of synch. The industry knows what secret lurks in the heart of the industry: five minutes out of 135 minutes to honor news and documentaries is more than enough to remind us of bad debts and bad faith.

By this time, I was enjoying the Dr. Pepper commercials more than the program. The Academy would once more ignore Mary Tyler Moore while citing her supporting cast. (Edward Asner was, however, amusing—this was his second Emmy; he promised to mate the two and give the Academy "the pick of the litter.") The Academy would, astonishingly, subscribe to Leonard Bernstein's own exalted opinion of himself: Mr. Bernstein, on the occasion of Beethoven's birthday, used Ludwig as a sort of hectograph tray of gelatin on which he pressed heroic images of Leonard Bernstein; it was Emmied. Paul Lynde appeared with the chimp from "Me and the Chimp" and said something about a feminine hygiene spray that convulsed the audience. (These people's brains need to be sprayed.) Johnny Mann appeared with his singing chimps to desecrate the flag in the most embarrassing performance of this or any other TV season. (After which, Carson brought down the house by announcing: "War bonds are on sale in the lobby." For the first time, I liked Carson.) The bead chains hanging behind the podium swayed randomly from the motions of departed ushers, like disappointed whips.

But—and here one must stop stomping—the technical incompetence of the show obscured the fact that most of the awards this year were well deserved. Who can complain about Peter Falk (for "Columbo"), Roone Arledge (for sports), Glenda Jackson (for *Elizabeth R*), Carol Burnett (for being her admirable self), Carol Burnett again (for her writers, one of whom remarked quite properly that "It's about time"), public TV (for covering the Pentagon Papers less gutlessly than commercial TV managed to do), *The Trial of Mary Lincoln* (NET Opera) and the Trial of Frank Stanton (for reminding Congress that the First Amendment is not a piece of Kleenex you use to blow your political horn)? If it was somewhat embarrassing to American TV that British TV received so many awards, it was a tribute to the Academy that they bit the bullet. And finally, there was the Emmy for Dick Cavett, at a time when ABC is trying to lock him up in a plastic coffin and make him hum Muzak. The Emmy in the past has been sometimes a kiss after death, conscience money to canceled excellence; but this one to Cavett, just maybe, might save him from the whores of Mr. Nielsen and the eunuchs at his own network. I'll trade six Archie Bunkers for one Dick Cavett any day.

(June 16, 1972)

P.S. Two days after these Emmy Awards, the Academy revised the rules to make sure British TV wouldn't embarrass them so much. It's like the Olympic Committee declaring that only clubfoots can compete in the long jump, only dwarves in the pole vault. I apologize for praising the bastards.

The Barbara Walters Problem

Of course, nobody should be watching television on a weekday morning anyway. Father should be in the kitchen making an omelet, mother should be in the bathroom shaving, and the children should be in the cellar shoveling coal. And if—out of guilt, ennui, lack of imagination or masochism—you happen to be watching television on a weekday morning, it certainly shouldn't be the news. The news with dew on it is unbearable. Mornings are squeaky. Whatever happened during the night that might be newsworthy is definitely not going to be squeaky; it is going to be a fanged, slavering blob. Besides which, the color on a TV set at seven o'clock in the morning never seems to be quite true; it is as if events during the night had been laundered, and ran together.

Nevertheless, I was watching television the other morning, probably to get the latest primary results or check out the scores of the West Coast ball games. Naturally, I watched the "Today" show. Obviously, I am now going to have to try to come to grips with the Barbara Walters problem.

"Today" has been around for twenty years. Remember Dave Garroway and that chimpanzee? Between six and seven million people watch it every morning. It makes more money than any other NBC-TV program except the "Tonight" show. Barbara Walters and Johnny Carson are like bookends propping up the folio, the novel, of our waking day; or clamps applied to either side of our frontal lobes. On the whole, I prefer Barbara Walters: unlike Carson, she is not preserved in the aspic of her own self-esteem. But she *is* afraid of silence; she plunges and gropes; she flails about in conversations as though they were trap doors and the bottom is likely to fall out of whatever is being discussed. She makes me nervous.

She has a new partner since Hugh Downs, tired of getting up at five o'clock in the morning, disappeared into the mists to count his money. (Hugh Downs I always thought of as the Harold Macmillan of television: unflappable SuperHugh, hunting for conclusions as though they were grouse, instead of jumping to them like Barbara Walters.) Frank McGee has taken over, and there is much talk among regular watchers of "Today" about the Walters-McGee "rapport," or the evolving of it, or the lack of it. (Frank McGee will always be associated in my mind with the assassination of John Kennedy: he reported it, he palpably suffered through it, and he often seemed during those heartsick days the only decent thing the rest of us could cling to, a man trying to do his job and keep from crying at the same time. I like Frank McGee very much.)

It has been said, for instance, that Barbara Walters became an aggressive interviewer because Hugh Downs was too polite to ask embarrassing questions, and sufficiently grave to permit Miss Walters to run around him without reducing the show to a shambles. Now Frank McGee is said to be asking the penetrating questions, which permits Miss Walters to be more "womanly," whatever that means. I don't see it. McGee looked more comfortable the other morning reporting from Moscow than he has seemed in the studio. Walters appears to have rushed into the vacuum created by Downs's absence, without quite knowing how to occupy it. She opens her mouth in desperation.

There are the little seminars on what's happened to our assassins during the last nine years; on equal opportunity for women; on what form improved Soviet-American trade relations might assume; on whether heroin should be made legally available to addicts. There is Joe Garagiola, his head gleaming like a hubcap, in search of chuckles. There is Frank Blair, proclaiming the news bulletins as though they had been chiseled on stone tablets. There are authors moving warily into a discussion of their books, as though the studio were Haiphong harbor. There is not, thank God, any music. But there is always Barbara Walters, energy looking for a lightning rod down which to dissipate itself. "Today" has become her show, at least since President Nixon allowed her to interview him and then took her to China as a reward. She makes the morning squeak, like a toothbrush. I wonder if the Chinese found her scrutable?

(May 24, 1972)

Morning Is Less Than Electric

Last week Mao's Revenge came to our house, perhaps in exchange for Henry Kissinger. Mao's Revenge is a virus that inflames the self-pity membrane and the suicide gland, rendering the victim incapable of walking, talking, reading, breathing or anything else except washing down his tiny time capsules with Thunderbird and watching, through the Phlegm Curtain, daytime television.

Daytime television is the excreta of the network elephants on their way toward prime time and beyond, to the boneyard of the late movies. After "Captain Kangaroo" (which appeals to the paranoid in all of us), after "The Galloping Gourmet" (which appeals to the Anglophobe in me), after "Not for Women Only," "Woman!," "What Every Woman Wants to Know" and "Dinah Shore" (has Gloria Steinem lived in vain?), daytime television consists of:

(1) Reruns of "Lucille Ball," "My Three Sons," "Family Affair," "Bewitched," and "Gomer Pyle, USMC";

(2) Game shows like "Concentration," "Hollywood Squares," "Who, What or Where," "Stump the Stars," "Password," "It's Your Bet," "Let's Make a Deal," "Three on a Match," "Newlywed Game," "Dating Game";

(3) Detergents like "Love of Life," "Where the Heart Is," "Search for Tomorrow," "Paul Bernard—Psychiatrist," "As the World Turns," "Love Is a Many Splendored Thing," "Days of Our Lives," "Guiding Light," "Secret Storm," "Another World," "General Hospital," "Edge of Night," "Bright Promise";

(4) Rotten movies;

(5) Mike Douglas.

It's like being locked inside the *Reader's Digest* for the rest of your life. On the detergents, men mess up the world and women clean up the mess—another form of housework, this time in the Heartbreak House of the soul. On the game shows, unemployed actors embarrass themselves and the amateurs are worked like slot machines, their eyes full of bananas and lemons, their arms making bandit motions, while the studio audience goes through menopausal seizures. On the reruns, we are reminded of what CBS did to the mental life of the postwar generation, making life into dog chow, the canned laugh, the rubber bone, the rural worm that's always turning. Mike Douglas is Dinah Shore in drag.

One longs for *Sesame Street*, for surely, as Sartre put it, "Man is not the sum of what he has," at least at two in the afternoon, "but the totality of what he does not yet have, of what he might have. And if we steep ourselves thus in the future, is not the formless brutality of the present thereby attenuated?"

Not really. Daytime television is a conspiracy against the future, the present and the past, reality itself. Contrary to Sartre, "the single event" *does* "spring on us like a thief." As the stomach turns, we search all the days of our lives for a bright promise in another world, following the guiding light through the secret storm to the edge of night where the heart is, and end up in a general hospital. We have been mugged. It's a plot against housewives, shut-ins, the temporarily invalid, preschoolers, the human spirit.

And yet it is a plot worth $300 million a year for the networks. Until recently, CBS owned 50 per cent of that daytime $300 million. Now we hear that CBS is in trouble—it couldn't happen to a nicer network—because "Splendor," "Storm," "Heart" and "Love of Life" are slipping. NBC's games are bleeding Mr. Nielsen. ABC, which specializes in sports and movies, has decided to pit movies against the games and the detergents. B. Donald Grant, who built up the NBC challenge to CBS, has now been hired away from NBC by CBS. Mr. Grant's last official act before switching networks was to commission a "Peyton Place" serial. There is nothing any of us can do but not get sick.

To quote Sartre again, "Everything we see and experience impels us to say, 'This can't last.' And yet change is not even conceivable, except in the form of a cataclysm."

(February 3, 1972)

Nausea in the Afternoon

It has drizzled on you for a month; charity shrinks. You're trapped in New York City over a long summer weekend; hope doesn't spring, it autumns. You wander into a midtown Chinese bar for a pisco sour and the Mets game: faith moves bowels. And, naturally, it is raining even in Montreal; a washout with a French accent. But the bartender has taken so much trouble to achieve a pisco sour, and the color TV set is already warmed up, and although you've already done a column about daytime TV you were sick at the time and maybe you missed some nuances—so you watch:

(a) *Three on a Match*, and/or *Let's Make a Deal*
(b) *The Newlywed Game*, and/or suicide.

You don't remember which host afflicted which game show, for the same reason that you don't remember which urea derivative was responsible for which custom-compounded plastic. They all make the pisco sour.

Does anybody know what's going on on NBC and ABC while decent people are supposed to be eating lunch? Conscripts, refugees, miscreants, the flotsam of an affluent society are press-ganged into embarrassing themselves for half an hour in front of *millions* of analgesiacs. Bastards-of-ceremony whip them into giggledom. Dashboards and control panels elaborated unto gimcrackery swallow, spit, hiccough and vomit. Klaxons admonish. Categories—"Famous Bald Heads" is my personal favorite—flap like lapwings around the studio. Simpletons sigh, simper, seethe and savage one another. Never before have greed and speed conspired at such a stupefying tryst. Who wrote *Aunt Jemima's Cookbook?* I'm sorry, your thyme is upchuck.

Three on a Match is so complicated—their tic-tac-toe had to go into systems analysis to find out why it hates itself—that even the advertising agencies can't figure it out. Therefore there isn't any advertising, unless you count commercials for how NBC intended to cover the political conventions and why drunks shouldn't drive. It's like watching an Apollo lift-off, only with rubber bands. But it's a great mistake to switch channels. On ABC, they're making a deal. Some weirdo prowls up and down the aisles, waving hundred-dollar bills, asking members of the studio audience whether they've got a whale tooth or Linda Kasabian's autograph or Spanish fly. If they do have it, they can either keep the cash or opt for the unseen. The unseen—a Polaris submarine, Dean Martin's bladder, thirty-four years on the jungleboat at Disneyland, capital punishment—sits behind a curtain. Zowie.

Neither program is in a class with *The Newlywed Game*, ABC's midday answer to the Salem witch trials. To qualify as contestants you must be a recently married couple within pogo-sticking distance of Los Angeles; otherwise, skyjack a lapwing. A bunch of men troop onto the stage and guess how their wives would respond to such questions as, "Last night, your hugging and kissing were (1) heavy-weight, (2) middleweight, (3) lightweight." I'm *serious*. I'm *always* serious. This was a *real* question. Then of course the wives appear and prove their husbands dunderheads. The sexes are reversed for the next round of hugger-muggering. Cute enough to make your teeth ache.

I wish Karl Marx were alive to watch *The Newlywed Game*. I wish Sigmund Freud were alive to do the same thing. I wish the two of them were newlywed, living at Malibu on a rented surfboard, so they qualified for the program. I'd like to see the Hegelian dialectic interpreted as a sex act, Hamlet pedaling his Oedipal cycle all the way to the United Fruit Company, workers risible, *Das Kapital mit Traumdeutung*. Hell, I'd like to see Simone de Beauvoir and Jean-Paul Sartre glaring at each other because they blew their big chance at free dining-room furniture. Id Kant happen, *Herren*, you will say. But it does, every weekday at 2 P.M., and the days get weaker by the minute.

(August 1972)

A Late-Night Talker Who Knows How to Listen

Now (as our President puts it), I want to make one thing perfectly clear: people shouldn't watch television at all after 11:30 P.M. They should play Monopoly, or read the Koran, or busy themselves spawning the next generation of surly ingrates. There may be an excuse for old movie freaks, if Dennis Morgan and Virginia Mayo happen to turn you on. But talk shows? All those capped teeth, those mindless sniggers, those silicone starlets who will open next week as Ophelia at the Little Theatre in Arrears, East Parking Lot, Why Not?, Nebraska . . . no. Talk show MC's ought to appear each night with warnings stenciled on their foreheads—"Caution: This Program May Be Hazardous to Your Mental Health."

Dick Cavett of course is different. He is neither an aging imp in support hosiery, nor a sincere oaf. He comes on like a Holden Caul-

field who spent some time in graduate school. He seems, un-
ashamedly, to have read books. He doesn't mug at the camera while
his guests are talking; he doesn't interrupt them with puerilities; and
he hasn't yet perfected the sort of late evening laugh that cracks
plastic.

By the time this thank-you note appears, Mr. Cavett will have been
ABC's answer to insomnia for some seven weeks. It's worth noting
what distinguishes him from the competition, aside from the fact
that he isn't a jerk.

First, there are the people he invites. In a one-week period Mr.
Cavett talked to, among others, Townsend Hoopes, the author of
The Limits of Intervention, an inside account of Vietnam policy
making during the Johnson years; Kevin Phillips, the author of *The
Emerging Republican Majority,* which outlined the so-called "Southern strategy" whereby Richard Nixon hopes to perpetuate his White
House occupancy without the permission of the Eastern seaboard and
the major urban areas of the nation; Dr. George Wald, the Harvard
biologist who suddenly last March became an important spokesman
for the anti-war movement; I. F. Stone, to my mind one of the few
honest journalists in the country and certainly one of the best; and
Jimmy (the Greek) Snyder, the Las Vegas oddsmaker who establishes the betting line on football and who for the second year in a
row believed all those press releases from the National Football
League.

Second, there is the format into which these guests are inserted.
They aren't saved until the last ten minutes of the program, when
no one will be watching. They don't exist as mere electronic phan-
tasms, here after one commercial, gone before the next. Mr. Cavett
averages about four talking guests a program; the singers sing and
then leave; the talkers get a chance to explain themselves at some
length to a host who has done his homework. Mr. Cavett, moreover,
is not afraid of controversy (unlike Mr. Carson), nor is he flabbergasted by it (unlike Mr. Griffin, who has made his incredulity a life
style—the whole world is always putting him on).

Third, there is the studio audience. Mr. Cavett's audience seems
different in kind from the other shows, not to consist largely of rejects from the long holiday lines in front of Radio City Music Hall or
Times Square pedestrians shanghaied by studio buses to keep up the
body count. There are even beards in Mr. Cavett's audience—

although his attempts to replace his opening monologue with their questions have been mostly unfortunate.

But finally the program depends on the stamina and ingenuity of Mr. Cavett himself. His short editorial on Oakland Raider quarterback Daryle Lamonica—Lamonica's two ultimate ambitions were to win the Super Bowl and kill the "Big Five" African animals; Cavett expressed satisfaction that the Kansas City Chiefs took care of Lamonica properly—was alone more interesting than most talk shows in their entirety.

The question is: Will enough people who watch TV late at night, instead of doing something useful, watch Mr. Cavett and keep him on the air beyond his one-year contract? I doubt it. He lacks a certain something . . . he lacks the requisite fatuity.

(November 1970)

Late-Night Hope for the Republic

First, the good news. Dick Cavett will be back in 1972. As we watch Merv Griffin sink slowly, too slowly, into a sea of sniggers and sighs, it is possible to reflect that there is hope for the Republic. One network, at least, is programming for adults after the late news and will persist in doing so despite the bad news.

The bad news is the rumor that ABC is having trouble selling the Cavett show to audiences outside the big cities. The real majority, or Middle America, or whatever our rural heartland is being called this week by the people whose racket it is to convert human complexities into headline phrases, would apparently prefer to watch movies at night. This need only be bad news if ABC worries too much about it and starts strong-arming Cavett's producers: mix it up, kids; put in a little mindlessness; stump the band; bring on the party hats and the squirt guns.

After all, there's no reason why one network can't continue to program for the big cities while waiting for the heartland to recuperate from its fatigue. And fatigue it is, a weariness after all the noise, the demonstrations, the fancy footwork at the United Nations, Mr. Kissinger's jet-setting, Mr. Lindsay's philanthropic gift of himself to the Democratic Party and the grateful voters. In the past year, a series of extraordinary books—Richard Hammer's *The Court-Martial of Lt. Calley*, Don Oberdorfer's *Tet!*, Anthony Austin's *The President's War*, John Franklin Campbell's *The Foreign Affairs Fudge Factory*, Victor Navasky's *Kennedy Justice*, Ronald J. Glasser's *365 Days*—has been published, examining our foreign and domestic policies and platitudes. Hardly anybody is reading these books. But they will be invaluably around when the nation has the strength to look at itself again in the bloody mirror. So, I hope, will Dick Cavett.

For Cavett is writing his own sort of book, a continuing moral inquiry almost unique on commercial television and certainly unique among TV talk shows. (David Susskind tries, but simply cannot resist the impulse to inflict himself on a subject and smother it.) Cavett regularly looks at our institutions and listens to our ethical wheezes. That looking and listening can take the form of a program devoted entirely to ten-year-olds astonishing in their intelligence and the articulating of it; or a program on the Knapp Commission's investigation of police corruption in New York City; or the extraordinary ninety minutes with Captain Robert Marasco, ex-Green Beret; or the confrontation between John Kerry and his accusers; or, most notably, the appearance and the non-appearance of Lieutenant Colonel Anthony Herbert, the war hero whom the army would prefer to have practicing his salute instead of talking to the American public.

Cavett asks the questions that are slowly forming, or should have formed, in the mind of his audience. He always allows the guest to respond. He follows and develops a conversation instead of driving it, like a dune buggy on an ego trip, into pit stops for a cheap laugh or a snide aside. His face itself reflects the intensity of the discussion, and he is not above looking honestly pained when a studio audience laughs at something morally outrageous. (In other words, he doesn't sniff the spoor of an audience's bias and then join them in that bias against the guest.) His own disquietude never assumes the shape of a posture or a self-promotion. He doesn't weep or toady. He is there to let us see the faces and hear the voices of the men and women who have been out in reality, and whose scars of conscience glow in the dark.

As a result, the Cavett show has become almost a form of diplomacy, an open negotiation among acts, ideals and attitudes, a nightly

witness. Not every night, of course. There will be evenings of balderdash, of book chat, of show-busyness and anecdotage. But it is never
a circus; there are no trained animals and there is no manure. Cavett's
dignity enhances our own. I hope he survives many seasons of our
discontent, because then he will be helping us to survive them as
well.

(December 10, 1971)

Charlie Brown in a Rep Tie

I wonder if Merv Griffin is a majority stockholder in Metromedia
Television. Somebody up there loves him. When CBS traded him in
—for late-night movies and two bottles of low-calorie cranberry juice
to be named later—there was Metromedia. You want to keep on
making a fool of yourself in public, Merv? Fine, said Metromedia,
we'll let you do it every weekday night from eight-thirty to ten
o'clock.

Of course, Metromedia already had someone doing a talk show in
that time slot. Captain Jet-Lag: David Frost. But David Frost apparently didn't own any stock. They sentenced David Frost to eleven-
thirty and the impossible dream of competing with Johnny Carson.
Merv must be served.

And so there he was the other night, the week the reruns took
over, "premiering" with the new, new, new *Merv Griffin Sclerosis.*
The studio audience in the balcony complained early on that they
couldn't hear him. They must have been masochists. The Griffin
routine never varies. Merv always comes on like Charlie Brown in a
rep tie. The rep tie seems to be trying to climb around his neck to his
ears and open up a barber pole for business. There are the usual
waltz steps—he is asking us not to hurt him. There is the usual
monologue—which hangs there, like an eel hooked onto a tree branch
overnight to die from twitching. There are the usual guests—Carson
leftovers; you keep hoping for a camera pan to show the keys sticking
out of their backs. There are the usual, the incessant, interruptions—
Merv is reminding us that he exists, that he has feelings, too. "Too"
includes opossums.

The whole thing is embarrassingly personal, the dirty underwear of our emotions, a hybrid of Nelson Rockefeller, Kahlil Gibran, Little Beaver, Gunga Din and *The Little White Cloud That Cried*. Throw this man a security blanket! It's the most astonishing use of television as a therapeutic tool I've ever seen—giving a man a program in order to give him confidence in himself. And still he doesn't quite believe it. Merv never quite believes; there is an air about him of the perfect victim, waiting to be kidnapped by events.

But the night was young. Florence Henderson was substituting for Dick Cavett. Richard Harris was substituting for Carson. Why not check out David Frost in *his* new time slot, just to see if Metromedia knows something that CBS doesn't? David was interviewing Elizabeth Taylor.

Elizabeth Taylor hasn't been interesting since *Ivanhoe*, unless you count Eddie Fisher, the Merv Griffin of an earlier era. And on this particular evening she seemed to have had a little too much of the cranberry juice before they started taping. So it was easy to concentrate on David Frost. Frost suffers from overbite. When his guests are famous, the bite is ingratiating, a kind of hickey. When they are not famous, the bite can be savage. But it always makes the teeth ache. He is ever burrowing in, as though people were grain bins. His research staff works too hard, supplying him with too many questions, all of which he asks, after consulting his Bill Buckley clipboard. It's like being attacked by a penguin.

Frost, however, can't be judged wholly on the basis of his baby talk with Elizabeth Taylor. The atmosphere is not usually so oxygen-deprived. His guests tend to be more interesting than Griffin's or Carson's. Half of his questions are intelligent. If he is going to hurt anybody in his new time slot, it will probably be Dick Cavett, who asks intelligent questions of interesting guests without yipping at their breasts. Carson's audience will follow *him* even to Hollywood.

The CBS movies are stealing the audiences of the independent stations, which run senescent movies every night. What's left—about 13 per cent of the insomniac vote—will likely split between Cavett and Frost, killing off both of them in the ratings. And Merv . . . there will always be a Merv, a Nixonburger, whose purpose it is to satisfy the American need for someone we can safely love because he seems to be worse off than we are.

(May 1972)

Whose Justice Do You Trust?

Who cares whether the networks produce their own prime-time entertainment programs, or the advertising agencies produce them, or the backlot Hollywood joyboys do it, or (Acting) Attorney General Richard Kleindienst in between ITT settlements and Senate committee hearings, or my grandmother?

As everybody knows by now, the anti-trust division of the Justice Department is suing the networks. The networks are accused of compelling "outside program suppliers" to sell them an "ownership interest" in every program bought for broadcast, or otherwise the program won't get bought. "Ownership interest" means a share of the take on rebroadcast, syndication and foreign sales of a program. Eighty per cent of prime-time entertainment programs are produced right now by outside suppliers; the networks, of course, are the principal buyers; and if the networks are using their economic clout to club the suppliers into giving them a slice of the money pie, well, maybe they should be sued. The Justice Department wants the networks out of the program-production business altogether, and it wants the courts to forbid the networks from making any profit on a program beyond the first-run exhibition of it.

Quite properly, everything the Nixon administration does is perceived through binoculars of profound suspicion. Is the Administration trying to scare the networks during an election year? Is it trying, against the grain of all that ITT publicity, to make Mr. Kleindienst look like an intrepid trust-buster? The president of CBS-TV has already muttered darkly that the purpose of the suit is to take away the networks' control of what they broadcast and when they broadcast it—although nothing in the suit has anything to do with that control. One of Nader's Raiders has, surprisingly, expressed approval of the suit because it attacks the basic "structure" of an industry instead of worrying about "a little price-fixing here and there." And most of the TV critics are reminded of the bad old days when the advertising agencies gave us payola, plugola and rigged quiz shows.

All of which may be of consuming interest to economists, network executives, filmmakers and Nixon-watchers, but what difference does it make to the TV viewer? The TV viewer, if he is a masochist, may try on the one hand to understand the technology of television (cable systems, cassettes) and, on the other hand, the economics of the industry (ownership interests). But what really matters to him, to *us*—if we're not among the 12,000 people wired into Mr. Nielsen's pineal gland—is what appears and what doesn't appear on the TV screen.

Millions of us like to watch Dick Cavett. Not, apparently, enough millions of us, because ABC has told him flatly that unless his Nielsen ratings improve he's off the air. Does that mean that ABC isn't making money off Dick Cavett? It does not. It means that ABC isn't making as much money off Dick Cavett as NBC is making off Johnny Carson or as CBS is making off a batch of rotten movies. Millions of us are going to be disenfranchised because we're a minority, and there isn't room after the late news for a minority program even if the minority is several millions. To his credit, Mr. Cavett told his audience exactly what he thought of ABC. But would admen from Mad Ave or "independent" hacks from Burbank be any less cowardly and rapacious than the network apparatchiks?

So long as all of us are wired into the notion that good programming means lowest-common-denominator programming on every channel, television of, by and for the cretin—that the intensity and devotion of a "special" audience of several millions for a favorite program is of no use to advertisers and therefore to the bursaries of rip-off time-salesmen—that serving the public means serving the product—we deserve the reruns that start in March, the two-hour "pilots" that will be next season's series flops, the computerized laugh-track by night and the jerks with tears in the daylight. Not just the quiz shows, but the whole industry is rigged. On the whole, I'd prefer my grandmother.

(May 4, 1972)

SITUATIONS VARIOUSLY COMEDIC

Bigotry as a Dirty Joke

All in the Family is a wretched program. Why review a wretched program? Well, why fix the septic tank or scrub the sink with a magic scouring pad? Every once in a while a reviewer must assume the role of a Roto-Rooter, stick himself down the clogged drain of the culture he happens to live in, and try to clean away the obstruction.

Carroll O'Connor plays the part of your friendly neighborhood bigot, the American workingman as Norman Lear and CBS conceive of him, William Bendix with a bad mouth, going on for half an hour every Tuesday night about the spooks and spics and wops and fags. He mugs a lot. Jean Stapleton plays his wife, slightly out of sync, one of those women—like Ruby Keeler—who never seems to belong in the situation in which they find themselves but who tries hard, thereby earning from the audience an admiration heavily laced with contempt. Sally Struthers plays their daughter; she's married to Rob Reiner (Carl Reiner's son), who plays a slightly long-haired Polack college pinko. Sally and Rob live with Carroll and Jean. They are always having Sunday dinner, the occasion for Mr. O'Connor to spit out his snappy one-liners on the inferiority of alien races, colors and creeds.

Just as most TV commercials are not really insulting to women (they are insulting to *people*), *All in the Family* is not merely insulting to minorities; it is insulting to Mr. O'Connor, Miss Stapleton, Miss Struthers, Mr. Reiner, the American workingman, CBS and everybody who watches the program. Bigotry becomes a form of dirty joke. We are invited to snigger. Invited, hell—we are *instructed* to snigger, like morons in a nursery school, before each episode. And we are piously assured that laughter cures, cauterizes, exorcises, even when it's canned. Fearless programming! About as fearless as the underground press's decision to use men's-room graffiti as a model for newspaper illustration, which in turn is about as fearless as pinching your little sister.

Take a recent, typical example. Mr. Reiner brings home a long-haired friend whom Mr. O'Connor suspects of being a homosexual. Mr. O'Connor complains about it at his local beer parlor. Mr. O'Connor is made to intuit that one of his drinking buddies, a heavily muscled ex-college football star, just may be, well, *that* way too. Mr. O'Connor refuses to believe it. End of program, after much mincing around. Mr. O'Connor always winds up refusing to believe; how else could the sit-com drag its asininity on to next week?

And what are *we* supposed to believe? That limp-wristed longhairs may look like homosexuals but aren't necessarily so disposed, while the short-haired athlete on the next stool lapping up draught beer and bellowing at the TV set is suspect? Don't say nasty things about homosexuals, your best friend may be one? Very funny. Cauterizing. Implicit in the sit-com is stasis; it's a condition, not a movement toward or away from revelation, and therefore it's naturally immune to theories of drama, abstractions about catharsis. OK. But what *is* the condition of *All in the Family?* Why is what Archie Bunker says considered to be laughable?

I don't object to this vulgarity because of my ideological delinquencies, my toilet training, my SAT scores, my Higher Seriousness or my chromosomatic complexion. I object because the program is a double-edged lie. Cutting one way, the lie tells us that workingmen are mindless buffoons; their opinions, unlike ours, are unrelated to social, psychological or political conditions; their knee-jerk responses to stimuli are so farcical as to be amusing. (See Studs Terkel on "The Great American Dream Machine" for evidence overwhelmingly to the contrary.) Cutting the other way, the lie tells us that Mr. O'Connor's Archie is, anyway, charming. Forgivable. Purely a premise, a *given*, in no way dangerous, certainly incapable of roughing up anti-war demonstrators. A bad mouth, maybe; a sloppy mind, yes; but somewhere anterior to his style of speaking and thinking is an essential decency, or harmlessness, that makes him a figure of fun. Bigotry out loud, like scatology out loud, robs the words of their subterranean power to shock or destroy—or so we are told. (Meet George Wallace; he's a *fun* person.)

But the words to begin with were only approximations of feelings which are in no way defused or defanged by making a sly joke out of them. Even as the complexities of individuals are reduced to a cartoon, so the cartoon is legitimized. A double-edged lie and a two-way pandering (we—CBS and the audience—are better than he is; he is ridiculous; but then, people actually say these things) . . . just who is the joke on?

(March 19, 1971)

P.S. This review appeared in the same issue of *Life* that featured on its cover Norman Mailer's account of the Ali-Frazier fight. Mailer's article drew 125 letters; this review drew almost 500 letters, over 90 per cent of them hating it (the review, needless to say, not the program). So much for the Zeitgeist. The program, and everybody in it except Mr. Reiner, have since won Emmys and transcendental ratings. Alas. I watch *All in the Family* about once a month now, at the urging of friends who insist that I overreacted. I still object as strongly, not that it matters to anyone but me. The one part of the review I would change today would have to do with the performances; Jean Stapleton is especially good. But talk about your rip-offs . . . stealing laughs from bigotry, and in the process legitimizing the expression of it, and moving it to Saturday night for the edification of our children, and enduring Norman Lear's explanations of how noble he is, and . . . Phtui! The drain is still clogged, and once a week most Americans wash their faces in the dirty water left in the sink, unless, like the voters for Wallace, they drink it instead.

Twist and Tact

"A *light and diplomatic bird/ Is lenient in my window tree*," wrote black poet Gwendolyn Brooks some years ago; "A *quick dilemma of the leaves/ Discloses twist and tact to me.*" Let's say, for the purposes of this column, that the "window tree" is the TV screen; that the "light and diplomatic" birds are the producers and writers of network shows; and that the "quick dilemma of the leaves" consists of the black faces the white birds are putting on prime time in this post-"Amos 'n' Andy," post-"Julia" era. After the collapse of the Sammy Davis, Jr., and Lesley Uggams variety hours, after the greening of Bill

Cosby, after the obligatory black token on every toothpaste and detergent commercial, what exactly is being disclosed?

Much twist, some tact. I don't count "Black Journal," "Black Studies" and "Soul!," which are on public television and which aren't really intended for white watching, anyway. Nor do I count "Black Arts" (CBS, Sunday mornings) and "Positively Black" (NBC, Sunday afternoons), which are tucked away where the ratings won't find them. But there is "The Jackson Five," a Saturday-morning animated cartoon based on the singing group, smack dab in the middle of the kiddie ghetto. There is "Room 222," a Mr. Novak in blackface. There is "Flip Wilson," an Andy Williams in blackface. There is, or was, *Cutter*, a *Shaft* spin-off that appeared as a segment on NBC's "Mystery Theater." And there is "Sanford and Son," a black situation comedy that recently climbed into Mr. Nielsen's sainted circle of the top ten.

Like "All in the Family," "Sanford and Son" is an idea Norman Lear stole from British television. On British television, the old man and his son were poor white cockneys. Mr. Lear has put on the blackface—with comedian Redd Foxx as the father and Demond Wilson as the son—and, at least for the first two months of the program, relied on plot lines already developed on the other side of the Atlantic. Like "Flip Wilson," most of "Sanford and Son's" writers are white, despite all the jokes about Afros and chitlins.

It's an agreeable show, as sit-coms go, a cut above "Dick Van Dyke," a cut below "Mary Tyler Moore." (I leave "All in the Family" out of it: the people you talk to about "All in the Family" react as though you were criticizing their taste in sex.) Redd Foxx is splendid as the junkman with dignity; Demond Wilson is a perfect specimen of youthful ambivalence, full of pride, anger, affection and the usual awkwardnesses; Slappy White, as the old friend Melvin, seems on the verge of becoming a regular, which might help bring back black vaudeville. If it isn't any sort of triumphant breakthrough into a new honesty and realism about race in this country, at least it escapes the middle-class claustrophobia of "Julia." Why, after all, should we expect everything that happens to be black to be automatically redeeming, or terrifying, or pregnant with symbolic meanings— unless our symbolic manipulations of the idea of blackness are so pathological that we *want* to be burned?

There is another kind of claustrophobia, however, attached to

"Sanford and Son." So far, it hasn't really gone out into the streets, where there is material rich enough to float a thousand sit-coms, and of course ten times as many tragedies. It hasn't exploited its chosen milieu as effectively as Flip Wilson—not just the storefront church, the welfare system, the numbers game, the militant sect; but the energy, music and art as well—and, like "Julia," it seems locked into a benign Moynihanism. (Widow and widower are substituted for the absent wife or husband.) Why not try young black writers like Ishmael Reed and Cecil Brown? Or, if you have to have an older one, Chester Himes? They could provide the wild humor and the dark meanings missing from "Sanford and Son," some sense of those (as Gwendolyn Brooks put it), "*Whose hours at best are wheats or beiges/ Lashed with riot-red and black./ Tabasco at the lapping wave./ Search-light in the secret crack.*" Really, and I suppose I'm being pathological about it, *Porgy sans Bess* with canned laughter is not enough.

(March 20, 1972)

Ode to a Very Active Verb

According to the second edition of Webster's New International Dictionary, to "predicate: is to proclaim, declare, affirm, commend, cry or preach up." A verb is defined as "a word which affirms or predicates something; a word which, expressing an act, occurrence or mode of being, carries the distinctive force of a predicate," assuming "variations of form and phrasing for voice, mood, tense, person and number." R. Buckminster Fuller, our leading geodesic dome, has said of himself: "I know that I am not a category. I am not a thing— a noun. I seem to be a verb."

Carol Burnett, no doubt about it, is a verb—transitive, active, reciprocal, irregular. To *burnett* is to affirm, to make funny, to dance, sing, cry, mug and gambol about in extravagant motion. *Burnetting,* every Monday night on CBS, tidies up all the conceptual confusion between subject and object that TV has dumped on the American mind for twenty years. Only for a moment, of course. While we're burnettized, who cares whether we are children of the electronic village, nodes on an information grid or lumpish eaters of shadows?

Then comes the Late News, converting everybody back into pronouns, "with little or no fixed meaning except one of relation or limitation." Burnett connects.

It is possible to play the grammar game to death. Is Richard Nixon a solecism? Is Spiro Agnew a malaprop? Is Edward Kennedy a dangling participle? Is George McGovern a qualifying clause? Enough. The verbivorous Miss Burnett devours acts, moods, modes of being. She's her own category. I come to proclaim, declare, affirm, preach up and commend her as our best comedienne, and to predicate her program as the most consistently entertaining series of the last several TV "seasons." (By the time you disagree with this, reruns of most network programs will have already begun. In March! It happens every Ides, the assassination of programs.) Burnett is a distinctive force.

Harvey Korman helps; Harvey Korman could make Dante giggle in the ninth circle of hell. Vicki Lawrence helps, although she hasn't been on as much this year as last year, and she seems—perhaps from disuse—to be thickening. Lyle Waggoner also helps, the perfect parody of the floorwalker as matinee idol, with plastic hair on his chest. The writers, who must munch morning glory seeds while watching old movies through the bottoms of empty bottles of Thunderbird, help a great deal: once a week they come up with an idea for a Vonnegut novel and press it, like Cantonese duck, into a bizarre ten minutes.

But Burnett brings everything off. To watch her swimming around the living room in an Esther Williams spoof is to learn the difference between art and, say, Marlo Thomas. More moves than Pete Maravich, a face as mobile as wet mercury; one wing of grace, the other of vulgarity, the two together whipping up a soufflé out of diamonds and sand.

To be sure, the soufflé sometimes collapses, especially in routines like the working-class family with all the dreary mother-in-law jokes. Burnett pretends to be ugly more often than such an attractive woman should be allowed to. (Remember what happened to Martha Raye? She appears these days only in Vietnam and every Saturday morning as the witch in "The Bugaloos.") Except for Emmett Kelly's unannounced visit last month, Burnett's charwoman miming at the end of every program has started showing signs of a creative sclerosis.

But . . . this review is also intended to be a verb, one that means *to love.*

(April 2, 1971)

Dean Martin: A Las Vegas of the Heart

When was it that Dean Martin ceased to be in any way amusing? I seem to have been out of town for a couple of years, or at least out of Las Vegas. The other Thursday night I came back for a visit, because "Owen Marshall, Counselor at Law" was a rerun. There was Deano, slumped inside his neon suntan, a cigarette hanging out of his mouth like a fuse . . . the drinking jokes, the cue-card jokes, the mammary gland jokes . . . The men all wore black ties and heavy leers; the women consisted of legs and navels; the choreography had been conceived by a Prussian general; the humor had been distilled from the sweat socks of junior high school hoodlets. The whole thing reminded me of acne.

I used to like Dean Martin, perhaps because once upon a time we had to make a choice between him and Jerry Lewis, and the French film critics decided that Jerry Lewis was a genius, and French film critics are always wrong. But also because Dean Martin didn't take himself seriously. He played with his TV program as though it were a Yo-Yo. He performed competently in movie Westerns out of the time-honored tradition of *machismo* rubbish—look, we said, he can *act*; it was like your pet hamster playing the xylophone. He ruined the character of Matt Helm in several spy spoofs, but better novels than Donald Hamilton's have been turned into Celluloid toilet paper. He cruised with Sinatra and such heavyweights as Peter Lawford and Joey Bishop. He didn't seem to be hurting anybody.

Now: well, now, a Thursday night with Dean Martin is the equivalent of solitary confinement with nothing to read but the *Playboy* Advisor. The only jokes that aren't off color are those that are blue. Women become "girls," and "girls" become anatomical toys—there's a group on the show called the Ding-a-Lings—wind them up and you smack your lips. A kind of plastic smut, a Las Vegas of the heart, is loosed upon the screen. And across it troop battalions of middle-aged men with muscle cramps in their raunchiness: which way to the skin flick? They don't even wear raincoats.

It isn't necessary to be solemn about sex, as though it were one of Beethoven's last quartets or an Apollo lift-off. The Elizabethans had a ribald wit. So did Hollywood in the 1930's. So does Carol Burnett. And Sonny and Cher. But what keeps that wit from being dehumanized—from being, in fact, a mask to cover up aggression—is that everyone partakes of it, regardless of gender. The women are just as witty as the men; *people* are involved; they relate to each other as personalities, as individuals with individual styles and individual dignity. They aren't *things*, tinkertoys or erector sets, to be bought with credit cards and stored in the libidinal attic for a rainy afternoon of autoeroticism.

"The Dean Martin Show" is witless. If the "girls" are objects, so, too, the men eventually become objects: there isn't wit about sex, but giggles about push-ups, sophomoric fetishism, a calculated degradation. It's not even a good night-club act, because a good night-club act becomes interesting inasmuch as it reveals the full hostility, the fear and the fantasies of power that motivate the sex joke. The Dean Martin or Las Vegas or night-club sex joke is pathological—anti-woman and anti-man, too: if I don't love, it won't hurt—and pathology *is* interesting. But it would only be *entertaining* to monsters or to people wholly incapable of love (which is probably the same thing). I can't get terribly exercised about TV commercials asking us to fly a stewardess to Miami—commerce, after all, has always been naked, and such commercials are no more insulting to women than the commercials that make a man a man because of the little cigars he smokes are insulting to men—but Deano's systematic sniggering diminishes all of us, and if the radical feminists want to picket next Thursday night, I'll join them if they'll have me.

(May 1972)

Stand Up and Cher

There is hope for Sunday evenings, after the children have been perfused: there is Cher. Cher is more beautiful and sings better than Ed Sullivan. She is more beautiful and sings better than almost anybody else on television. She has, unfortunately, a husband, about whom it is necessary to make jokes each week on CBS to keep the show moving right along between production numbers. Although Sonny is rumored to be the brains behind the act, clearly he doesn't deserve Cher. Only TV reviewers are good enough for Cher, because we have spent so many cold electric hours watching little girls (I must be sexy, I try so hard) and old girls (Pretend I still know how) that we immediately recognize a woman (*being*, as opposed to becoming and gone-by). TV reviewers have earned Cher, whereas Sonny merely married her.

Now, Sonny and Cher have been getting dyspeptic notices from the commissars of our sub- or adversary- or counter-culture, those poor little pebble-brains who hang out in the vicinity of rock music and grub a buck by writing about it. By writing, in fact, yards and yards of hyperthyroid prose which, with its emphasis on "the wisdom of the blood" and its contempt for anything other than the Id-iotic *me*, seems to have been translated from the mid-1930's German. The commissars don't like Sonny and Cher, you see, because Sonny and Cher aren't into drugs and Satanism. Cher has even been known to sing what used to be called a "standard." The rock critic—who rips off the entire past, who uses everyone else's agony (Bach, the blacks, the Orient) as so much Kleenex to blow his small mind on—accuses Sonny and Cher of ripping off Youth Culture.

Spinach. The kind of greedy, acquisitive, dog-in-the-manger spinach that, if we were talking about property instead of "cultures," would look reactionary and manipulative. Which it is. A friend of mine complains that popular music, then and now, has usually amounted to nothing more than a Taj Mahal of noise built around an unsatisfactory sex life. He's wrong, but at least he is aware that today's pubescents have no more of a monopoly on innocence and idealism than yesterday's did. One of the nice things about spending an hour with Sonny and Cher on Sunday nights is that people like Jimmy Durante, than whom there is no greater innocent, are likely to drop in. You may even hear some Cole Porter, and be reminded that Bob Dylan wasn't the first poet to work the popular side of the street. A sort of Spock of recognition results: among our mothers and fathers and grandmothers and grandfathers, there just may have been a few decent human beings after all.

Moreover, there is about the Sonny and Cher show that inspired comic touch to production numbers of which only CBS seems capable, whenever CBS decides reluctantly to program for people over the mental age of eight. The Smothers Brothers had it. Carol Burnett still has it. "Laugh-In" (NBC) has degenerated into thinking that wit consists of pistol shots, the squirt gun; no sustaining power past thirteen seconds. Tom Jones and Johnny Cash (ABC) sought the meringue and found the mud pie. Along come Sonny and Cher, grafting Gilbert and Sullivan onto the New York *Times*'s publication of excerpts from the Pentagon Papers (with Ken Berry singing, "I am the publisher of the New York *Times*," etc.) and you realize that CBS has done it again. Even the medley of commercial jingles, an old trick and a lousy one, worked with Sonny and Cher because of some extraordinarily clever continuity.

Above all, there is Cher, bringing a little Elizabethan bawdy into Plasticland, with a vocal range that ascends from the diesel truck to the clarinet, pit stops on every curve. One can only feel sorry for the commissars incapable of enjoying her. Nietzsche once compared critics to insects, which sting us not because they want our pain but because they need our blood to live. Rock critics are insects who want to be vampires. Let us renew our option on Cher, and fumigate the room.

                                                              (September 1971)

ADVENTOURISMS

Dr. Welby's Tonic Won't Harm You

Robert Young is probably the best thing to happen to doctors since Medicare. (What? You thought doctors were opposed to Medicare? They were, until in practice it proved to be quite profitable, with the government paying the bills of people who might not otherwise be patients. It's like the oil depletion allowance, with the poor playing the part of the oil and the doctors getting the allowance.) "Marcus Welby, M.D." is a commercial for an idea of medicine—the father figure who makes house calls—that seems more attractive the less it bears any relation to reality.

"Dr. Kildare," "Ben Casey," "The Doctors and the Nurses" and even the E. G. Marshall segments of "The Bold Ones" have all been built around the modern hospital as a microcosm of urban society. They have all asked us to believe in a marriage of science and moral zeal. They have gone on about crime, drugs, racial tensions, miracle cures, money problems, *coitus interruptus*. Their cameras have lingered lovingly on the instruments of deliverance, the machines of medicine—as though hardware itself, so gleaming, so full of profound blips, so relentlessly *fair*, were a sign of grace.

Such a celebration of science could only go so far before the perceptions of people who couldn't understand how the machines worked, and who didn't feel good anyway, caught up with it. Science hasn't saved our souls, and therefore we have decided that it is a mere manipulation of knowledge for the purpose of achieving power; not benign magic, but the black art of gaining control of us. The gleaming instruments were never intended to deliver us, the machines do not cure; they deflower and lobotomize the innocent. Even as hospitals are increasingly computerized—from a credit check of the suffering petitioner to his cell assignment to a preliminary diagnosis of his hemorrhoids—they become less hospitable to any fantasies of Buddha with a stethoscope. The snake strangles the sword.

And along comes Marcus Welby. He operates out of his home in Santa Monica, California, a white world of school buses and good intentions. Not that there isn't a vagrant drug problem; TV programs these days can no more get by without a drug problem than they can get by without a sponsor, and sometimes the two are consubstantial. Not that there wasn't an hour-long fling at venereal disease, estimable, award-worthy, and more than NBC would let "Mr. Novak" get away with several years ago. And not that the youth market doesn't exact its 200 pounds of flesh, the scowling Dr. Steven Kiley (James Brolin, out of Vince Edwards via Marlon Brando), who mounts a dedicated motorcycle to roar off on *his* appointed house calls.

But the general run of "Marcus Welby, M.D." goes like this: a lawyer with a terminal disease refuses to cut down on his work load; a mother gets an ulcer bringing up a retarded daughter without any outside help; a girl about to be married learns that she has leprosy; mononucleosis, emphysema, kidney machines, tuberculosis, alcoholism, malpractice, plastic surgery, rabies all descend on Santa Monica as domestic chores for Dr. Welby to take on—everything, so far, except sickle-cell anemia and rat bites. He understands and he consoles. Whether it's your plumbing or your psyche that's clogged, he dissolves the obstruction. He is Uncle Fix-It, relying sometimes on the latest medical journal, sometimes on instinct, too often dispensing a vulgarized Freudian Pablum that makes one Fromm at the mouth, always spreading the marmalade of his infinite kindliness on the crust of our discontent.

There is no harm, and much potential good, in "Marcus Welby, M.D." The scripts are remarkably uneven, varying week to week from tautness to flaccidity, from the safe to the inane. But the homily grits are edible, and maybe even nourishing. The Emmy, by which television congratulates itself for doing something the public mysteriously approves of, visits Robert Young as often as groupies are said to visit rock musicians; "Welby" rates sky-high in all the homes Mr. Nielsen chooses to wiretap. Among the millions who watch weekly there must be thousands of doctors—nighttime golf not yet having been perfected—and if those doctors take Welby's example to heart, the nation will be a better place to live in. Of course, doctors are only human, as they and we tend to forget, and like most humans they are probably inclined to use television as a substitute for reality instead of an enhancement of it or a quarrel about its terms. Who among us takes the Late News to heart and resolves forthwith to make house calls on the politically, economically, spiritually sick, even if in some cases we wouldn't have to leave the living room?

Uncle Fix-It is what we would all like all doctors—and Presidents —to be. Having congratulated ourselves for our high-minded desire, we can then turn it off, just like a TV set.

(May 14, 1971)

One of Our Myths Is Missing

It was your usual Thursday night, too hot for bowling. We were sitting around in lobster pots at Captain Nemo's Gin 'n' Bare It Tonic-Watering Spa, watching Polaris submarines go down and worrying about cable television. The cable TV people kept telling us that if only they were allowed to make enough money stealing signals from other stations, they'd be able to get into program production themselves. Think of it: another thirty channels. But—another thirty channels of what? We weren't convinced that cable TV people knew how to be any more creative than network people. So far, it was all old movies and home hockey games. Besides, paranoia was at high tide. How long before Pete Rozelle sold them the Super Bowl? And wasn't there something suspiciously *two-way* about those cables? Mightn't *they* be watching *us* while we thought *we* were watching *them?*

Then Fosfate came in. The inevitable Fosfate, our fertilizer, sprinkling his compounded self over the exhausted minds. "You ninny-hammers," he said, "are always bitching about technology, when myths are where the moxie is. Technology kills; the myth it gives us lies. I have been hither and yawn in the vast yeastland, looking for a comely myth. What do I find? Sit-coms. The westerns, with John Wayne fat and Randolph Scott dead, have decamped for Italy. Science fiction is Japanese. And the private eye has been co-opted."

At this, we muttered disapprovingly. The bloodshot private eye was, in fact, *our* "I," peering at the world through segments of red web. Fosfate polluted.

"Sellouts, every one of them!" he shouted. "Do you remember the myth? The myth was Raymond Chandler saying we're a nation of cop-haters. The cops were owned by the well-born, the Syndicate, the pols. The Southern sheriffs had all the Dodges. The private eye was the only one to *see*. The loner, the disaffiliated Quixote, the Thin Man, the Fugitive, the Saint, T.H.E. Cat, Mr. Lucky, Sam Spade, Philip Marlowe—what became of them? Richard Diamond has turned to paste. All the strings on Lew Archer's bow are broken. The cops on TV today are the good guys."

We pondered. "There was always 'Dragnet,'" we reminded him, "and 'The Naked City.' And, briefly, '87th Precinct.'"

"Objections that fooled the rule," said Fosfate. "Once we were Surfside Sixed and 77 Sunset Stripped. Now we are Hawaii Five-Ohed and Adam Twelved. Ironsided. FBIed. NYPDed. Smith Familied. Dan Augusted. Mod Squat. Even Mannix has a friend on the force. When you find a private eye today, he's on loan to authority. Like the Rand Corporation or the Hudson Institute, he's got a contract from the government. Authority is objective, myth is subjective. The difference between myth and authority is subjectivity, individuality, art, dream. If the eye is no longer private, we all become objects, incapable of dreaming."

When Fosfate gets going, he can fill up thirty channels all by himself. But he did have a point. "Perhaps," we suggested, "it started with 'Burke's Law,' combining the class privileges of the rich with the bureaucratic privileges of official authority."

"No," said Fosfate. "I blame it on the cold war and Vietnam. Reality and dream, ego and id, thesis and antithesis, authority and myth must co-exist. It was fine to have the myth of the private eye on one network while you had the authority of spies and war on the other two. Two ideas of order versus one idea of escape maintains the psychic equilibrium. But the cold war was too full of internal contradictions. One by one, the stylish spy serials—'Secret Agent,' 'I Spy,' 'The Avengers'—descended into spoof, like the Western. The mission was clearly becoming impossible. Trivialization was the consequence, which isn't good for authority. And Vietnam wasn't exactly the sort of war that inspires authoritarian drama. Without a satisfactory war to celebrate, the American public was in danger of becoming anti-social. Authority petitioned the TV cop for redress of dialectical grievances. It can't work for long, because not even a cop can be a one-man synthesis. What we desperately need now, I'm afraid, is another war, a *good* war, a war to dream on."

Momentarily heartened, we said. "Maybe Pete Rozelle can fix one up for cable TV."

Fosfate dropped acid.

(August 1971)

Private Eyes and Heavy Lids

I'd like to think that last Christmas someone gave Xeroxed copies of Edmund Wilson's essay "The Wound and the Bow" to all the TV producers on Sixth Avenue. You remember the myth of Philoctetes? Philoctetes had a suppurating wound that smelled so bad his friends wouldn't come near him. But he could shoot straight, and when his friends got into trouble they held their noses and went to him. Edmund Wilson suggests that maybe Philoctetes could shoot straight *because* of the wound. Compensation: portrait of the artist as a neurotic.

Now look at all the Philoctetes-type detectives smelling up and shooting down the home screen this season. There's "Ironside" (Raymond Burr) in a wheelchair. "Longstreet" (James Franciscus) is blind. "Cannon" (William Conrad) is fat. "McCloud" (Dennis Weaver) is a hick. "Columbo" (Peter Falk) pretends to be mentally retarded. Cade, of "Cade's County," is played by Glenn Ford, which is enough of a handicap. "Sarge" (George Kennedy) is an ex-cop turned Roman Catholic priest, which must mean something. "The Partners" (Don Adams and Rupert Crosse) are incompetent. As for "The Persuaders" (Tony Curtis and Roger Moore), "McMillan and Wife" (Rock Hudson and Susan Saint James), "Bearcats!" (Rod Taylor and Dennis Cole) and "O'Hara, United States Treasury" (David Janssen)—they don't look much like Philoctetes, but that's probably because some producers can't read and Wilson was therefore wasted on them.

What's next? "Senior Citizen Detective," a shamus in a retirement village finding out who stole the estrogen? "Junkie," paid in methadone to spy on junior high school radicals? It's all so, well, suppurating. As my wife said after watching "Cade's County," "It's not quite good enough to hold your attention; but still it's not quite bad enough to make you want to vomit." On Sixth Avenue, that might pass for an aesthetic principle.

Poor James Franciscus. Once upon a time he was known as a Richard Chamberlain who could act, and act he did in "Mr. Novak." It was canceled. Mr. Franciscus then starred in one of the worst Hollywood movies ever made, *Youngblood Hawke*, and hasn't been the same man since. As "Longstreet," a blind New Orleans insurance investigator with a guide dog named Pax (Pax!), he is ridiculous. Because the premise is ridiculous. And because the writers, who got their brains by sending in ten coupons from the backs of cereal boxes, can't think of anything better to do with him than teach him karate for the showdown fight. He does, however, cock his head almost as well as Pax.

Peter Falk can act. But "Columbo"—every third week of NBC's Mystery Movie series, along with "McCloud" and "McMillan and Wife"—is going to wear thin as a routine. The detective who seems stupid but who is actually smart is funny only the first time around. And when the writers for "McCloud" try using Columbo's tricks for *their* boy, you begin to feel your awareness has been stuffed inside a thimble. A word should be said, however, for "McMillan and Wife": Susan Saint James is an excellent reason for watching TV; Rock Hudson as her police commissioner husband proves a surprisingly adept comic actor; and the writers work overtime to find lines someone would actually be pleased to say aloud.

"Cannon" and "Sarge" are about as interesting as Metrecal wafers.

Finally, there's "Mannix" (Mike Connors), moved from Saturday nights to Wednesday nights just to aggravate the viewer, but still the best detective program on the air. Maybe it's because Connors's only handicap is being, in real life, an Armenian, or because the producers do all the little things right—the throwaway touches that tell you something about people, warming up the brandy in the snifter, air-conditioning the limousine; or because the writers always come up with more than enough plot to make an hour confusing. Whatever the reasons, it works, and will go on working after Longstreet has tripped over Columbo, thereby knocking Ironside down a flight of stairs, which would have hurt except that he landed on top of Cannon, who happened to be there because Efrem Zimbalist, Jr., who never misses, shot him while tracking a couple of Maoist kidnappers across Cade County and into ennui.

(October 22, 1971)

SUBSPECIES (1): CHILDREN

On the Street Where Kids Live

Several years ago, deploring recent movies for children, Pauline Kael said: "I see no reason why we should not respect our children at least as much as we respect ourselves." A wistful remark, and one that should be pinned above the shaving mirrors of the cyborgs who package children's programs for commercial television—although I suppose those cyborgs, looking into the mirror, see only the other side of the room.

In February 1968, probably feeling much the same way Miss Kael did, the Carnegie Corporation, Ford Foundation and U. S. Office of Education gave Joan Ganz Cooney and her Children's Television Workshop $8 million. The workshop was to produce twenty-six weeks of daily hour-long programs, in color, for distribution to educational TV stations across the country. Directed specifically at preschool children, the programs were intended not only to entertain, but to instruct: not an electronic baby-sitter but an electronic nursery school.

"Sesame Street" is the marvelous result of that effort, a brisk, witty, absorbing series which proves that professional standards of TV production aren't necessarily incompatible with intellectual rewards. An engaging host and hostess (both of them black) preside over a realistic street set (complete with garbage cans). There are puppets, cartoons, jingles and sight gags. Those commercial techniques usually employed to hustle war toys are on "Sesame Street" deployed instead to teach the alphabet, number recognition and vocabulary lessons: "Today's program is brought to you by the letter A."

The only reviews of "Sesame Street" that really count are of course those by the children who watch it. In my house there is a three-year-old bored by almost everything that isn't a pretzel and a seven-year-old who disdains all artifacts of man but books and bicycles. Both are devoted to the program, lusting even after reruns, enduring even the deliberate repetition of skits and comic strips that take the Chinese water torture approach to education.

But . . . these children, like most reviewers, are irreparably middle-class, which means that you can experiment on their modes of awareness in almost any way you want to and they will enjoy it and profit by it; the world is their hors d'oeuvre. One of the announced purposes of the Children's Television Workshop is to plug the class gap between "disadvantaged" and "middle-class" preschoolers. On the presumption that not much educational TV gets watched in the ghetto, the workshop sought to connect "Sesame Street" with day-care centers and Head Start projects, to publicize the program with ads in neighborhood newspapers, posters in barbershops and churches, promotional leaflets "stuffed into phone bills, light bills and welfare checks."

Is it working? We shall have to await the dispensations of Mr. Nielsen. It is not now, nor has it ever been, very clear how much Mr. Nielsen knows or cares about ghetto TV-watching habits. One hopes the saturation-bombing of "Sesame Street" on the public conscious-ness—190 stations now carry it; it's available six times a day in New York City alone—will sell something we desperately need. We shall also have to await the reading scores in the public schools of the chil-dren who have enjoyed the program.

Mrs. Cooney is perfectly aware that twenty-six weeks of educa-tional TV, even educational TV as superb as "Sesame Street," isn't an adequate substitute for nursery schools, any more than Head Start is an adequate substitute for a public school system that would, on all grade levels, treat all children as precious national re-sources and individuals with minds and souls deserving of respect. What happens after the first $8 million are gone? What happens if commercial networks use "Sesame Street" as an excuse for not at-tempting something similarly ambitious for their Saturday morning creative slum? What if the world isn't utterly changed for the bet-ter tomorrow morning before breakfast?

It is a beginning, of the sort no one else has been willing to under-take; action instead of rhetoric. And meanwhile—a huge meanwhile, this—we have a program of intelligence, sophistication, good humor and noble intention, to be enjoyed by preschoolers, schoolchildren and parents alike, a tribute to Mrs. Cooney and her producer David Connell and the many men and women who helped prepare the series. If it proves only that by spending as much money on every minute of children's programming as the advertising agencies spend on every minute of commercials we can reduce airwaves pollution, it proves something very important: that we should have been doing it all along, and that the trolls and mercenaries who feed garbage to our children do so because they have respect neither for themselves nor for children.

(February 1971)

Wrong Way Down Sesame Street

What are we to make of the BBC's refusal to show "Sesame Street" to English children? According to the New York Times on September 8, "Sesame Street" was "banned" by the BBC because Monica Sims, head of children's programming, worries about its "authoritarian aims," its "middle-class attitudes," its U.S. slang, its hard-sell ad technique for teaching numbers, letters and words, its "passive" educational approach. "Right answers," said Miss Sims, "are demanded and praised, and a research report refers to the program maker's aim to change children's behavior. This sounds like indoctrination and a dangerous use of television."

Three days later David Webster, a BBC representative in the United States, wrote a letter to the Times to clarify BBC's position. A tenth of BBC's programming is devoted to children, he explained; to add "Sesame Street" would mean "destroying some of our existing programs." (Why? Why not 10.5 per cent of programming devoted to children, or more programming period for everybody?) On September 12, Fred Hechinger in the Times summed up criticisms of "Sesame Street" heard here and abroad which might have accounted for the BBC attitude. One was that the program "tries by way of funny sketches to promote such virtues as honesty and cleanliness, in the view of some critics an imposition of middle-class—the majority as differentiated from the ghetto culture—standards." Personally, I was unaware that lying and dirt are considered virtues in the "ghetto culture." How come, then, there's so much complaint in the ghetto about being boycotted by the sanitation trucks, the rat and roach exterminators, the building inspectors? Just maybe the people who live in a ghetto know something that people who write about "ghetto culture" have forgotten—that there's a relationship between dirt and disease, and between honesty and trust.

Well, the BBC is having its troubles. Proposals abound in Britain for some sort of broadcasting advisory council to keep an eye on the corporation, especially after the perverse editing of programs like "Yesterday's Men," a documentary on former members of the Labour government that made Harold Wilson appear only slightly more foolish than he really is. And "Sesame Street" can take care of itself. It *will* be seen by some English children, every Saturday for thirty weeks in London—on ITV, the BBC's commercial alternative. If it succeeds, ITV may take on daily, nationwide telecasting of the program, which might bring it into direct competition with two American imports the BBC approves of—"Huckleberry Hound" and "Yogi Bear"—as well as the BBC's own "Play School," a children's series so dreary it's no wonder Miss Sims worries about "Sesame Street."

But the drivel about the "authoritarian aims" of "Sesame Street" continues on both sides of the Atlantic. Maybe it's in the nature of educationists to poor-mouth any idea they didn't dream up themselves, and in the nature of critics of education to get apoplectic about lack of perfection—*their* kind of perfection, serving their particular aims, which are never of course authoritarian. McLuhanoids object to anything that might help children learn to read, print culture being such a reactionary drag. Esaleniks are so busy climbing into each other's bathtubs to scrub off their inhibitions that any endeavor presupposing "right answers" looks like an intolerable psychic repression to them. Hustlers of "ghetto culture," black and white, have elevated a miserable condition into a whole new principle of apprehension, a way of thinking that doesn't need to count or to communicate with the other 80 per cent of the country.

"Sesame Street" isn't perfect. It isn't a substitute for day-care programs, Head Start, open schools, enriched environments, social justice. Obviously, parents and teachers should be using it as a supplement or a launching pad for a more personal educational experience in the home and classroom. But "indoctrinating" preschool children with the alphabet and numbers isn't immoral; at the very least it will prepare them to count their change and read the want ads—survival skills. What it will not do is employ those children as pawns in an ideological chess game, or as props in the psycho-dramas of self-hating members of the middle class (I am hypocritical; ergo, "middle-class values" are hypocritical). It is a modest and amusing step in the "right" direction: television for children that neither bores them to distraction nor clubs them into insensibility. If we hate ourselves so much that we end up blaming the lack of decency in the world on the hideousness of our decent instincts, then we are obliged to hate "Sesame Street," too. Otherwise, we should cherish it, and look around for other ways to put those decent impulses to work.

(April 1972)

"Mice" Deserve a Better Trap

On Sixth Avenue in Manhattan, where all the giant networks live, children are called "the mice." Charming. And now Norman Morris, who works for one of the giants, has written a book about television and "the mice" (*Television's Child*). His argument, after much repetitious huffing and some schizophrenic puffing, seems to end up roughly like this:

Granted—most TV for children is garbage. But—one group of experts is willing to testify that there is no direct relationship between televised garbage and anti-social behavior. Nevertheless—"Sesame Street" proved that children's TV needn't be garbage. Therefore—the networks might conceivably try to make their garbage a little more nourishing because they want "Sesame Street"'s Nielsens and Emmys. Meanwhile—it's up to the parent to supervise his child's garbage consumption and discuss with his child why some garbage is better than other garbage.

Mr. Morris is a full-time employee of CBS news. Although he throws some stones at Black Rock (where CBS lives), he feels that CBS has been more forthright than the other giants in meeting its obligations to the mice. (After all, there's "Captain Kangaroo.") His real targets are the "experimental psychologists," the "academicians" and "educationists," "the anti-violence crowd" and those Congressmen and parents who waste their time "counting" the number of aggressions on TV and worrying about the psychic total.

To calm the qualms of this "hysterical" bunch, Mr. Morris has consulted *clinical* psychologists and TV executives; polled parents and teachers; searched his soul. He concludes that while children might "learn" aggression from TV, they safely discharge it in their "play," not their "behavior." What's more, a little of it is good for them. The lab in which those *experimental* psychologists work is not a "real-life" situation. TV isn't responsible for crime in the streets and presidential assassinations. Nor is it a "passive" experience: look at our energetic young. And if the parents Mr. Morris polls protest that televised violence disturbs their children, well, they are probably projecting their own anxieties on their offspring. Anyway, "the suggestion that the economic and moral conflicts of commercial television can be resolved by strict federal regulations or government watchdog committees is completely impracticable. No room for such machinery can or should exist within our free enterprise system."

What, then? Mr. Morris proposes a vice-president of children's programs at each network, reporting directly to top management . . . an end to performers doing commercials personally . . . a ban on ads for vitamins and other medical products on children's TV. Agreed. But what else? Mr. Morris's only other else is parents—parents writing cards and letters, forming pressure groups, turning off TV sets, having long, meaningful conversations with their children. The notion of "accountability" does not seem to have arrived on Sixth Avenue.

Mr. Morris hasn't made any useful distinction between the *play* of children and their *behavior*. (The two are significantly related.) His contempt for experimental psychologists is vulgar. (Like clinicians, they vary in their opinions and in their contributions.) TV certainly isn't the *only* cause of psychic disturbance in the world today, but the toy manufacturers don't spend $15 million a year on TV advertising without some reasonable expectation of manipulating attitudes. (I am always astonished how often we are told that the content of a TV program doesn't do anything to our minds, but that the commercials make us want to buy things.) Our free enterprise system somehow manages to accommodate machinery for helping to resolve "the economic and moral conflicts" of food and drug manufacturers. (Aren't there other, mental, forms of botulism and overdose?)

What is missing in *Television's Child* is any sense that the nervous system, like the stomach and the lungs, deserves some social as well as individual protection. Of course, parents must be on guard against the depredations of the electronic baby-sitter. Parents must also warn their children about entering parks at night and accepting candy from strangers. That doesn't mean, after all the warnings, that other people—TV executives, government officials, federal Communications Commissioners—shouldn't be held accountable for not trying to create a world in which the parks are safe and strangers don't molest children. The networks apparently feel they have a contract with the rest of us, under whose terms they are left free to be enterprising and we, as parents, are not to be left free to trust our children in front of a TV set. It is not a contract I have signed, nor do I intend to. Either TV is part of the solution or it is part of the problem.

(August 20, 1971)

"Subsequent Aggressive Behavior"

On Monday, March 21, Senator John Pastore and his Senate communications subcommittee begin hearings on the Surgeon General's report, *Television and Growing Up: The Impact of Televised Violence*. It has been said that Senator Pastore only started disliking TV after the 1968 Democratic Convention in Chicago—those pretty pictures of police beating up kids—which cost his party the presidency. But I'm all for him this time. Somebody's got to make some sense out of a farce that's been going on for two months now.

The Surgeon General's report took two and a half years to prepare, and cost the National Institute of Mental Health a million dollars. A 279-page summary was released to the public in January, to be followed by five volumes of supporting research. When the summary appeared, most newspapers, including the New York *Times*, based their stories on the first nineteen pages and ran headlines like this: "TV Violence Held Unharmful to Youth." The crucial quotations were these: (1) ". . . there is a modest relationship between exposure to television violence and aggressive behavior or tendencies," but (2) "It must be emphasized that the causal sequence is very likely applicable only to some children who are predisposed in this direction."

Very likely . . . only . . . some. The sigh of relief on Sixth Avenue was gaseous. But almost immediately a smog of complaints rolled in. There were complaints that the newspaper stories did not adequately reflect the summary. There were complaints that the summary did not adequately reflect the results of the research. And there were, especially, complaints about the people who wrote the summary.

The people who wrote the summary—the Surgeon General's Scientific Advisory Committee on Television and Social Behavior, hereinafter referred to as the Violence 12—were described in *Science* magazine as "the network five, the naive four and the scientific three." How did it happen that the Violence 12 included an NBC vice-president, a CBS research director, two CBS consultants and a former CBS research executive? It happened because the three major networks had the option of vetoing anybody nominated to the committee whom they didn't like or were afraid of. And so they blackballed such distinguished scientists as Percy Tannenbaum of Berkeley (who contributed to the study but wasn't allowed to be on the Violence 12 that summarized it), Leon Eisenberg of Johns Hopkins Medical School, Leonard Berkowitz of the University of Wisconsin and Albert Bandura of Stanford.

Now: an earlier Surgeon General's report—the 1964 study that warned us about cigarettes—was not written or summarized by a committee weighted with tobacco industry representatives; nor was the tobacco industry permitted to blackball nominees to that committee. The last time, in fact, that the tobacco industry commanded that sort of clout was in the 1930's, when the first studies of cigarettes and health were whitewashes.

Which perhaps helps to explain why, of the sixty papers and twenty-three independent studies prepared by the Surgeon General's research staff, the one described by the senior research coordinator as the "most useful" was all but ignored in the summary. "Most useful" was a longitudinal study of nineteen-year-old boys whose viewing habits had been identified ten years ago. A "cross-lag" analysis indicated "significant correlation between viewing violence on television and subsequent aggressive behavior."

"Significant" means something more than "modest," at least in the popular imagination. I hope the Pastore hearings will make that clear. And I would suggest that the Senators and those who testify before them keep a couple of facts in mind: toy manufacturers spend $15 million a year on TV commercials, and advertisers as a whole spend $2.5 *billion* a year on TV commercials—to do what? To influence our behavior. I don't believe *that* many admen can be *that* wrong about television's capacity to encourage us to do things we might otherwise not do.

(February 1972)

The Littlest Neurotics

Sometime shortly before the Christmas holidays, during that period when we were thumped nightly on the head with one ordinary "special" after another, I sat with my children watching *The Littlest Angel*. It was the story of the shepherd boy who dies, goes to heaven, returns to earth to collect his box of "favorite things," and finally gives that box to God (E. G. Marshall) as a birthday present for the Christ child. It seemed a reasonably harmless pastiche, typical of the season, although I remember objecting silently to the idea of heaven as *work*—all those angels polishing the stars and vacuuming the cosmos; will the drudgery never end? The Protestant ethic even unto afterlife.

Then two things happened. First, during the program, when the shepherd boy, suddenly ashamed of his gift, tries to hide it from God and of course fails, my five-year-old daughter remarked: "God is sneaky. God can see around corners. God would *never* lose at hide-and-go-seek." (I made a note to call Art Linkletter.) Next, after the program, she burst into tears and couldn't sleep. It took me fifteen minutes to find out why she was so upset. She had registered the fact that, when the boy returns to earth to pick up his box, his parents can't see or hear him. That's death, when your parents can't see or hear you. Death is a scary idea. (I made another note: to think less about the Protestant ethic and more about the way my children perceived the world.)

Without leaning too heavily on such a slender reed of anecdote, I did wonder how much the adults who make programs for children know about a child's perceptions of the world. The idea of God as invincible at hide-and-go-seek and the idea of death as a situation in which your parents can't see or hear you both belong to an imagination rather more vagrant than adults have time for, wholly unafflicted with irony, making tentative connections for the first time, extrapolating promiscuously, deeply engaged. TV is, after all, a window for our children, not—as for us—a mental wastepaper basket in which we discard the day's frustrations. What might happen if children themselves were to construct the world on the other side of the window?

"Zoom" intends to find out. "Zoom" is a new weekly half-hour series on public television written by and for children ages seven to twelve. The plays, skits, riddles, rhyming games, Merrymac hand-clapping contests, recipes and jokes are suggested and performed by children. There are "Zoom" "raps," movies and guests (what it feels like to go to the hospital, impressions of racing cars, how to make a raft). There is a more-or-less Pig Latinized private language, "Ubbi-Dubbi." There are segments on how a Boston child experiences Appalachia, and how an Appalachian child perceives Boston. (It isn't an accident that the program originates from Boston's WGBH, the center of agitations by the Action for Children's Television people who want to get rid of hard-sell commercials and violence on children's programs.) Material from other children is solicited on the air and by mail, and credit in the form of a photograph and production title is given for ideas accepted.

"Zoom" does not presume to instruct, at least overtly. There is no manipulation according to a learning theory, simply a kind of "access" to the media for children, like other minority groups. It is still very middle-class. I don't object to this as much as other middle-class adults, riding their rhetorical hobbyhorses in empty circles, seem to. "Zoom"'s future will depend entirely on a national feedback system of free and fresh material. It enjoys itself too much—at a time when children are supposed to be force-fed on anguish. And maybe the cast of seven incredibly lively kids will become professionalized, and therefore boring, in the months to come. I hope not. But right now, it is enchanting.

All right. We have known since Freud that childhood isn't an age of innocence, that children are every day secretly cultivating castration anxieties and sibling rivalries, denying and repressing, the littlest neurotics. But we also know that they teach themselves to speak, not as a result of adult theory applied with adult earnestness, but because they want to and enjoy it. So they might, within a flexible framework, teach themselves about God and death, about when to play and how to create and what's been left undone and what's too silly or evil to be done at all. "Zoom" is graduate school after "Misterrogers Neighborhood," the "Great American Dream Machine" for people who are still capable of dreaming, the ultimate experiment in cinéma vérité, and enormous fun.

(January 1972)

The Family That Sings Together . . .

It happened a couple of Friday nights ago. I came home from a hard day of practicing my disdain. The children as usual were absorbed like sand in the great moon-eye of the television set. All I wanted was a pint of Bombay gin, an hour to memorize the box scores of the baseball games, and perhaps a praline to gnaw on. "Father Wisdom," said one of the children—I can never remember her name—"after you've finished memorizing the box scores of the baseball games, can we watch 'The Partridge Family'?"

"Of course not," I explained. "What's 'The Partridge Family'?"

"They sing," it was retorted.

I looked them up in the listings. Shirley Jones was in "The Partridge Family." Shirley Jones! I had never quite believed in Shirley Jones, like the Third Law of Thermodynamics; she seemed to exist, by some secret of mitosis or cloning known only to Hollywood, as a by-product or offshoot of old Pat Boone movies, associated forever in my mind with white buck shoes and old Coke bottles. No deposit, no return.

"Unfortunately," I compromised, " 'The Partridge Family' conflicts with the first half hour of 'The Name of the Game'."

" 'The Name of the Game' is a Gene Barry rerun," ululated my children. They were, of course, correct. Nor had I been practicing my disdain for nothing; all his life Gene Barry has wanted to be Gene Barry, and now at last he is. The motel of his self-esteem is booked full of little Gene Barrys; no room or need for me.

But you can't give children what they want without exacting some quid pro quo; otherwise, they will think that you love them. "Have you done your homework?" I menaced. They had. "Have you cleaned your rooms?" Assuredly. And they had taken their baths and brushed their teeth and withdrawn our troops from Vietnam and reconciled Kant's categorical imperative with Kierkegaard's Either/Or. "Well, if you are an absolutely silent majority while I gnaw on my praline, we will watch 'The Partridge Family'."

In "The Partridge Family," Shirley Jones plays the part of a mother and, presumably, a widow whose children—teen-agers, moppets—constitute a rock-music group. Some evenings and weekends, they trundle over the countryside in a psychedelic bus toward assignations of amplification. David Cassidy, the eldest son (and Miss Jones's stepson in real life), usually leads them in song. He and Miss Jones use their own voices; the others are dubbed. The music is domesticated, homogenized rock, sort of Lester Lanin on medium speed, as far from the Rolling Stones as Mick Jagger is from Nat King Cole or the human soul, with just a hint of Community Sing. Yet it pleases and an album has climbed the charts and already people want David Cassidy to speak out against Vietnam and mushrooms.

Most episodes of "The Partridge Family" are really excuses for the one new song each week. The dramatic bread around the musical Spam sandwich is guaranteed stale: the girl who runs away to find her father; the little boy who suspects he's adopted; the horrors of high school social life (why can't our children face up to the fact that they are expected to be as unhappy while young as we were?), etc. But the Partridges—a plastic version of Salinger's Glass family, quiz kids into music instead of mysticism and Fat Ladies—seem to enjoy themselves and each other. Some adhesive is applied to the generation gap, sticking us together for another thirty minutes. And the result, unlike the real world of rock, is surprisingly wholesome.

Well, I like Shirley Jones more than I like Pat Boone. And David Madden, as the grumpy agent, gives the children something to hiss at, a bear with bad breath and bad knees. And young Mr. Cassidy, while I wouldn't want my daughter to marry one, is worth somewhat more than a barrel of Monkees. And on Friday nights this fraughtful spring we all sit around the moon-eye tripping out on a psychedelic bus, even if the children haven't settled that Alaskan pipeline question and the SALT talks before I get home. It's as American as memorizing box scores; one family, on TV, does things together; another family, at home, watches and pretends it's doing something together. Ah, but even television reviewers get tired of flexing their disdain.

(April 30, 1971)

Why Lassie Can't Come Home

Depending on whom you choose to believe, Lassie is either thirty-three, thirty-one or thirty years old this month. Eric Knight's original short story about a Yorkshire collie was published in *The Saturday Evening Post* in 1938; his novel *Lassie Come-Home* appeared in 1940; and Lassie's thirtieth birthday will be officially celebrated this week with a new edition of the book from Holt, the original publishers, while MGM rereleases the original 1943 Roddy McDowell-Liz Taylor movie. For over half of those years—seventeen, to be exact—Lassie has been televised.

And will continue to be. For her eighteenth year on TV, Lassie no longer needs CBS, NBC or ABC. She has her own syndicate, called the Lassie Television Network, which has sold her new series in 206 markets representing 96 per cent of the nation's TV homes. According to a press release, "The 1971–72 season promises to be a very special one as the all-new episodes bring Lassie to a unique home and loving family." Film locations include "the Sonora area of California's mother-lode gold country," "the lush and beautiful Santa Ynez Valley," and, God help us, "the Strategic Air Command headquarters in Nebraska." (Who writes these press releases, anyway? Hermann Hesse? Cassius Clay?)

Does anyone remember what the original Lassie was all about? Here's your sophisticated TV reviewer, on a jet plane leaving La-Guardia, pulling from his attaché case not a confidential memorandum on the dollar crisis, nor a copy of *Commentary*, nor a bilingual paperback selection of the poems of Rainer Maria Rilke, but the Holt Library Edition of Eric Knight's *Lassie Come-Home*. The TV reviewer pretends that the book is an amusing joke played on him by his secretary. What, after all, will the stewardesses think? He tries on and discards various expressions of affable inappetence as he riffles the pages. In fifteen minutes, his eyes are wet and his nose is running. Not all your love stories are written by Yale professors . . .

The pre-TV Lassie didn't grow up in the mother-lode country of California, nor anywhere near the Nebraska headquarters of the Strategic Air Command. She grew up in the English mining town of Greenall Bridge, during the Depression. She was sold for fifteen pounds to the bad-tempered Duke of Rudding when the coal mine was shut down and Lassie's owner, Sam Carraclough, couldn't afford to feed his family. She escaped so many times from the duke that he finally had her shipped off to his estate in Scotland. Most of *Lassie Come-Home* deals with her final escape and her 1,000-mile odyssey from the highlands of Scotland home to the flatlands of Yorkshire. It sits squarely in the picaresque tradition, only this time Tom Jones is a collie. The heel heels.

Major Eric Knight, who died in an airplane crash in the jungle of Dutch Guiana during World War II, could write up a storm (remember *The Flying Yorkshireman?*). There is wit and hilarity in *Lassie Come-Home*, an excellent ear for dialect—some of which has been plasticized in the new Holt edition so as not to tax the kiddies—a savage eye for spotting differences in social and economic class, a wealth of knowledge about dogs and men. There is also irony in the ending, when the duke discovers that to get the dog he has wanted for five years he must buy the man who owns her, which he does. Karl Marx, welcome to the kennel.

What has happened to Lassie in three decades should not, of course, have happened to a dog, even the President of the United States. The sentimentalizing and the inflating, the scouring away of Lassie's social context, the Disneyization of her in books and on television have left us with Super-Collie—the brain of Herman Kahn grafted onto the body of the Hound of Heaven. The TV Lassie, like Dr. Doolittle, talks to the animals; she psychoanalyzes human beings; and she patrols the American West as though she were a four-legged FBI. J. Edgar Woof. Super-Collie bears no more resemblance to Eric Knight's Lassie than *Shaft* bears to big-city private detection, black, white or mauve. And she's bound to make you look at your own mutt and wonder if somebody's put stupidity pills in the Gaines-burger.

Major Knight's widow, incidentally, doesn't share in Lassie's TV money trough, since there were no such things as "TV rights" at the time the book was sold to MGM. Maybe she wouldn't want to share in what's happened since. "Honest is honest," Sam Carraclough used to say, "and there's no two ways about it." He was wrong; there's eighteen years about, and without, it.

(October 29, 1971)

Prisoners of Corn

It happens every week: I miss the first half of "The FBI." I miss it because the rest of the family wants to watch "The Wonderful World of Disney." The rest of the family hasn't read Richard Schickel's excellent biography of Walt Disney; the rest of the family hasn't even read anthropologist Edmund Carpenter's review of Schickel's book, in which he talks about "controlled environments." I am the only one on Sunday nights who knows that we are being manipulated—prisoners in a sort of space capsule of the imagination, being force-fed on recycled sentimentalities, wired by our lacrimal glands to a Mission Control in Anaheim, California. But I have used up all my credibility, after six hours of basketball, baseball, hockey, golf and bowling. And so we watch "The Wonderful World of Disney."

There are horses and foxes and lynxes and spider monkeys and sheep and even a coatimundi. There are boys who want to climb mountains and girls who want to become policemen and a family band that doesn't know what it wants to do and people like Dean Jones and John Davidson and James MacArthur (before he became a Hawaiian cop) and Hayley Mills (before she grew up) and Don Murray (who never grew up)—you know, *good* people, American faces, Middle American spider monkeys, your lovable coatimundis of a denatured nature, a tame wilderness, an innocent heart, a moral lollipop. There are the self-cannibalizations—shows that were originally released as films, shows that become films, shows that consist of snippets from several old films, shows that consist of new dramatizations of old songs. Not to mention the animated cartoons, which are unmentionable.

I wonder if B. F. Skinner watches "The Wonderful World of Disney." Mr. Skinner is the behavioral psychologist who believes that a little bit of free will goes a long way toward killing us. Mr. Skinner would like to remake the modern world in the image of nineteenth-century small-town America, with nineteenth-century small-town American values like hard work and sexual abstinence. (Never mind what small towns were really like.) Mr. Skinner would do his remaking by "positive reinforcements." A controlled environment. Wire everybody into an economy of scarcity, and zap them with good feelings (material rewards) whenever they behave themselves. Mr. Skinner taught pigeons to quadrille by positively reinforcing them with food pellets. Talk about your clockwork orange.

And that *is* Disneyland, the nineteenth-century orange, the time capsule, whose sections of rind are closing over us from California and Florida. Under the dome there will be Muzak, a nature without pity or terror; the only evildoers will be busybodies; all the dwarves will be cute; all the sex will be sublimated; none of the animals will bite; every reinforcement will be positive; the quietly good (all wisdom is inarticulate), the plucky (all courage is the moral stamina of innocence), the steadfast (one thinks of Walter Brennan), the clean of heart and the clean of hands (animated *people*, nineteenth-century cartoons) will inherit the parking lot with the Richfield mini-cars and the band of merry burghers flexing their perceptions like accordions. No greed, no death, no cities. Beauty is cute and cute is beauty; that is all you're going to be allowed to know.

On Sunday nights in my house this sort of animadverting is considered to be a consequence of heartburn. And so it is. I will never forgive Disney for what he did to *Alice in Wonderland*, any more than I will forgive the psychoanalytic critics and the Jefferson Airplane for what *they* did to Alice. And someday the prince *doesn't* come. And the South sang some songs that weren't so prettily Remusized, especially in the nineteenth-century. And so the heart does burn—because it isn't clockwork.

(April 1972)

Frozen Instants: TV at Its Best (Football and Television)

Four months, five cartons of cigarettes and twenty-two six-packs of beer ago, I disappeared into my living room to watch televised football. Now it is over. I have returned to my wife and children with a migraine and a tragic intuition.

The intuition has to do with the nature of time and the American beast and the medium which feeds us images of ourselves. The U. S. Bureau of Narcotics and Dangerous Drugs is currently worried about tetrahydrocannabinol, a colorless, odorless artificial marijuana being synthesized abroad. The bureau is afraid it will be smuggled into this country as after-shave lotion. The bureau needs my intuition.

For marijuana's principal effect on the mind is time distortion. It elongates each instant, creating an infinitely plastic *now*. Anybody who has watched all the exhibition, college, pro, divisional play-off, league championship, Super Bowl and all-star football games on television—from camera angles in the end zone, from a blimp, between the center's legs; in Slo-Mo, split-screen, stop-action, instant replay—knows that Americans don't want their instants elongated. They want them frozen and decisive, brutal and absolute. Television is more dangerous than tetrahydrocannabinol because it panders to our longing for each instant to be definitive, for someone to win and someone to lose, *against* the clock. We are haters of time.

Football absorbed my Saturdays and Sundays for four months in a way that baseball, congressional hearings, space flights, comedy and dramatic hours never could, because football is a love-hate relationship with the clock. The stately grace of baseball, the pastoral dream, the ritualized exchange of innings (theoretically, and often practically, interminable) has nothing to do with the clock. The difference between baseball and football is the difference between art and war. Sudden death! Since television is a remorseless mirror of our psychic state, football was destined to become our most popular sport. This fall it will invade prime-time TV on Monday nights. Next year—who knows?—the season may last as long as the war in Vietnam.

Of course, it took TV a long time to understand what, in fact, it was doing. In the old days, CBS planted its cameras like trees along the sidelines and followed the NFL quarterback and the offensive ends and the ball: the trigger, the bullet and the victim. It took Roone Arledge, president of ABC Sports, to exploit the many possibilities of the brutal instant. When Arledge, the most imaginative man in the industry, started handling AFL games, he introduced the odd camera angles and the replays that trebled the number of action-packed instants in any given game. After the AFL shifted to NBC, Arledge went on experimenting with the college games. His inventiveness has infected the other two networks, and he will have to keep it up, for that inventiveness is desperately required to protect us from the floorwalkers and morticians (I except only Paul Christman and Al DeRogatis) who report and "analyze" the game.

The ultimate triumph of instants on TV last year was, naturally, Arledge's coverage of the Summer Olympics, at a cost of $4.5 million for the rights, with a crew of 450 and almost fifty different cameras. We saw, enthralled, not only the results of a hundred human competitions, but two instants, live and brutal, that only TV could bring us: Tommie Smith and John Carlos raising black-gloved fists and lowering their heads during our national anthem at the awards ceremony; and Vera Caslavska, the Czech gymnast, turning away her head during the Soviet anthem. Political instants, definitive, undeniable. TV is beginning to realize that it is at its most effective as an eye on the living, bleeding instant. Joe Namath's white shoes, the lift-off of a rocket from a launching pad, black faces, street riots, assassinations, even the manufactured and manipulated "instants" on Rowan and Martin's "Laugh-In" (the metaphysical pratfall) bring an explosive immediacy into the living room and bring, as well, a pretense of life. For the brutal instant always belongs to someone else, doesn't it? We are passive recipients of it, voyeurs on other people's moments of self-definition. We have, in our living rooms, abandoned the making of history for the consumption of it.

Still, football is best. I shall miss it during the long months to come, when there is nothing to do on Sunday afternoons but sit around smoking my after-shave lotion.

(February 1970)

ABC's Wide World of Sports

ABC's "Wide World of Sports" was ten years old this spring, which, of course, is the mental age of those of us who watch it. A whole decade of auto-crash championships, figure-skating exhibitions, world land-speed records, computerized prizefights, Japanese all-star games, twenty-four-hour Le Mans endurances, Duke Kahanamoku surf classics, Mickey Mantle retirements, female jockeys, demolition derbys, pocket billiards, target diving, motorcycling, barrel jumping, roller-skating, iceboating, kick boxing, dune-buggying, parachuting, dogsledding, snowmobiling, wrist wrestling, lumberjacking, skateboarding and rattlesnake hunting!

One imagines Roone Arledge to be a huge electronic fly buzzing over the globe, his banks of eyes alert to every bit of shadow, change of light, sign of movement. Sport is perceived. A voice goes out over the monitor: Send for Jim McKay. Jim McKay, the host of "Wide World of Sports," has gone more than two million miles to thirty-five countries on six continents for more than 100 different sorts of games. He finally arrived—as an entry in the latest edition of Who's Who in America. He could properly be described as an anthropologist.

"Wide World of Sports" goes on every week all year long. In a decade it has been pre-empted only by college football, one baseball game, an occasional golf tournament and the assassinations of John and Robert Kennedy. The week before John Kennedy's assassination, there was a 200-car demolition derby at Langhorne, Pennsylvania, and a United States vs. Argentina water polo match at Long Beach, California; the week after, there was the Grey Cup game for the Canadian professional football championship. The week before Robert Kennedy's assassination, there was a "Tournament of

Thrills" auto-crash championship at Las Vegas, Nevada; the week after, there was the Indianapolis "500."

If Mr. Arledge is an electronic fly and Mr. McKay is an anthropologist—and Howard Cosell is, well, Howard Cosell, only more so —what are we, those of us who on Sunday afternoons can think of nothing else to do but peer into a magic box at weak images of other men's flirtations with death? According to Proverbs (26:14): "As the door turneth upon its hinges, so doth the slothful upon his bed." According to Lord Chesterton, that old bore who was always clubbing his son with platitudes: "There are some pleasures that degrade a gentleman as much as some trades do. Sottish drinking, indiscriminate gluttony, driving coaches, rustic sports such as fox chases, horse races, etc., are, in my opinion, infinitely below the honest and industrious profession of a tailor and a shoemaker, which are said to *déroger*."

Then there was Alexander Smith, in *Dreamthorp* (1863): "I am not an actor, I am a spectator only. My sole occupation is sightseeing. In a certain imperial idleness, I amuse myself with the world." Surely Freud had much to say about it, what with repetition compulsions and neurotic ceremonials and all, but I've loaned his *Collected Papers* to Jim McKay. Not to mention Wilfrid Sheed in *Max Jamison* (on the dangers of reviewing your life as though you were reviewing a play about to close out of town) and Frederick Exley in *A Fan's Notes* (on the dangers of believing that Frank Gifford may be the only success you will ever have) and Robert Coover in *The Universal Baseball Association* (on the dangers of your "imperial idleness" turning into existential guilt).

But "Wide World of Sports" is at the very least more innocent than other so-called sports programs I can think of, programs on which movie stars and athletes kill their betters, their betters being animals who are not to blame for the profound ennui of movie stars and athletes. Why not let all the two-inch heroes do our living and dying for us? Television has definitely improved. When organic farmer J. I. Rodale died recently during a taping of the "Dick Cavett Show," Mr. Cavett substituted another show; Jack Paar would have run the whole exciting episode and sermonized about it. There goes Roone Arledge now, overhead. He's discovered sex. Send for Jim McKay! Bolt the bedroom door.

(July 9, 1971)

The Basketball Is Black

By the time you read this, they will have vanished from your screen: all those tall men in their underwear. Milwaukee will have won the National Basketball Association play-offs after only two years of Lew Alcindor. The gunners and the dribble freaks will have split to assignations of varying danger—some in court to argue the terms of contracts; some on the road to check up on fried-chicken franchises; some to the surgeon for knife work on the knees. The city game, as Pete Axthelm called it because so much of it begins on urban playgrounds, will have gone back to the playgrounds for another summer of one-on-one.

Professional basketball came late to TV, as it came late to dignity. Part of the problem was its own fault. In the early years, defense was a dirty word. Emotional and incompetent officiating made a farce of many games. Unspoken racial quotas seldom allowed the best five men to take the floor as a team. A brutal and often insane schedule— over 100 games a season, counting the play-offs; sometimes four games in five nights—almost guaranteed unevenness of play.

And part of the problem was New York's fault. Reality is defined as that part of the world which New York chooses to acknowledge as existing. New York, the Rome from which all media flow, needed a winner, and only when New York started building a winner was professional basketball deemed a reality worthy of fat television contracts. A shaky one, at that. When Baltimore beat the Knicks last month in the final game of the Eastern divisional playoffs, Chris Schenkel on ABC had some difficulty—Chris Schenkel *always* has some difficulty—hiding his disappointments. Baltimore? Against Milwaukee? Where were the major TV advertising markets? What happened to New York, Los Angeles, Chicago?

But animadverting upon Chris Schenkel is a mug's game, like badmouthing a clubfoot who tries the *entrechat six*. The Nijinsky of electronic sports reporting Chris Schenkel is not. Televised basketball does, however, have something to tell us in spite of its commentators. For openers, those tall men in their shorts can't make a mistake without our seeing it, and yet team play wins all the championships. (Hockey's too quick and football too muddled for instant blame. Baseball is a tapestry of tedium interrupted by splashes of individual excellence; the best baseball team is the best collection of talented individuals. And golf, well . . . great big man hitting little bitty ball: golf on TV is not a sport, it's a cure for insomnia.)

For seconds, when one basketball player is better than another, you know it in your living room. No sophistry is possible. The best basketball players today are, of course, black. Which perhaps accounts for the death of the quota. I have seen Atlanta, New York and Milwaukee this season send all-black teams onto the floor, and not a cracker crumbled. Which may also account for the fact that, unlike baseball and football, basketball has had three blacks as head coaches of professional teams—Bill Russell (Boston), Al Attles (San Francisco) and Lenny Wilkens (Seattle). One-on-one, and Whitey loses.

There's no point in turning this into a liberal soap opera—*Equal Opportunity Is Beating the Twenty-Four-second Clock*—because professional basketball *is* a meat market. Already the competition between the NBA and the rival American Basketball Association has resulted in a raiding of the colleges for undergraduate tenderloin, causing college coaches—whose careers depend on the buying of bodies—to whine all the way to their high school fleshpots. (Television will decide this one, just the way NBC and Joe Namath forced a merger of the National and American football leagues.) Ken Durrett, Artis Gilmore, Jim McDaniels, Sidney Wicks, Johnny Neumann, Elmore Smith, Howard Porter, Austin Carr and Julius Irving are all millionaires before they've even played a professional game. (All but Neumann are black.)

But follow the wide-angled lens. It's as revealing as Captain Robert Marasco on "The Dick Cavett Show." Get a close-up of Wes Unseld, at six feet seven and a half inches short for a pro center, blocking out and leading a fast break. See Willis Reed on one of his stoic picks, making himself a wall behind which the guards shoot. Watch Lew Alcindor, moody, contemptuous, now the chocolate stork, now a scythe . . . notice those faces, the incredible dignity. Earl Monroe sinks baskets that are impossible even on slow-motion replays: *there's* a Nijinsky for you. Those faces—a televised reality bigger than New York. If they don't trouble the American imagination, then we are stupid. What a game! Sign those guys up for commercial spots before they scare us into accepting their manhood.

(May 28, 1971)

They Hardly Ever Knock the Product

Ho (another baseball All-Star game has come and gone) hum. Faster than grass grows, more gripping than canasta, able to achieve sleep in a single inning—our midsummer classic! Of course, these opening lines were worked out subconsciously the day before they hit six home runs out of Tiger Stadium during gale winds that gusted up to thirty-one miles an hour on prime-time television. Like Vida Blue, TV reviewers aren't perfect. But we seek perfection always, and we never find it in sports announcing, either at the All-Star game or during the regular season.

Curt Gowdy and Tony Kubek "handled" the All-Star game, as they do NBC's game of the week on Saturday afternoons and some Monday evenings. This time Lindsey Nelson, the Mets announcer, was there to assist them, looking like a combination of Captain Video and Mickey Mouse, in one of his notorious sports jackets straight off the rack at the local linoleum factory. Gowdy was the old unflappable pro he always is, a kind of Walter Cronkite of sports broadcasting. Tony Kubek, the "color analyst," was eager and earnest and inoffensive. Lindsey Nelson did things like interviewing Mrs. Tom Seaver and Mrs. Bud Harrelson between innings. I don't know why.

What Gowdy, Kubek and Nelson didn't say was, however, more interesting than what they did say. They didn't tell us why the Detroit fans booed Baltimore manager Earl Weaver when he was introduced before the game. (Weaver had been reluctant to name Detroit first baseman Norm Cash to the team.) They didn't explain why the American League players were slow to come out of the dugout as they were introduced. (A joke: they wanted Weaver to stand out there for a while in front of the hostile audience.) They didn't allude to an All-Star "first"—for the first time both starting pitchers were black. (In fact, all four National League pitchers—Ellis, Marichal, Jenkins, Wilson—were black, quite a change from ten or fifteen years ago, when black pitchers were as rare in baseball as black quarterbacks are in pro football today—also unmentioned in the broadcasting booth.) Nor did they bother to comment on the peculiar strike zone created by plate umpire Frank Umont: it was as tall as Frank Howard and as wide as Sardi's.

Quibbles, yes. But they point up the tendency of TV sports announcers to pretend that the game we're watching exists wholly outside of any social, historical or commercial context; that all umpires are the products of a cloning process that began with the conscience of Albert Camus; that there is no race question except the pennant race question, no avarice, no stupidity. (Remember the Super Bowl two years ago, Kansas City and Minnesota? The announcers kept referring to the "enormous pressure" on Kansas City quarterback Len Dawson. They never explained that the "pressure" was due to accusations that Dawson associated with gamblers. On TV, people like pitcher Denny McLain have "troubles." You have to read newspapers to find out that those troubles are related to bookmaking.) There will never be any avarice or stupidity, even after the 1980 World Series between the Warsaw Braves and the Calcutta Giants.

Don't knock the product, especially since the club owners determine whether or not you've got a job. Red Barber knows; the Yankees got rid of him when they started going downhill and needed a PR man instead of a journalist. Vin Scully in Los Angeles is not a PR man. Neither was Ned Martin in Boston the last time I heard him. "If you've just tuned in," he said once, "welcome to the debacle." And, another time, "It's not much of a night for baseball, but a great night for walking along the Potomac with a bottle of May wine." Baltimore sportscasters are generally good. There was a man in Pittsburgh years ago, in the dark days, who clearly expected the Pirates to lose and was flabbergasted when they brought off a double play.

But most of the mouths apparently conceive of sports reporting as a minor league apprenticeship to prepare them for the big time of selling refrigerators and automobiles. They advertise instead of reporting. Oddly enough, the TV watcher gets more honesty from the technological gimmicks—instant replay, slow motion, etc.—than from the men who man them. Which may explain why the Mets tried recently to cut down on the number of instant replays televised during each game. Who wants Ralph Nader doing a General Motors commercial? These games are serious.

(August 1971)

TV AND THE PUBLIC

Some Public Credit Where It's Due

On a recent summer Sunday, the New York *Times* devoted its television page entirely to articles on public TV. There was nothing sinister about it. Unless you count the Apollo 15 lift-off next week, or the terrible suspense of extra-inning baseball games, or Lloyd Bridges pretending to be Thomas Jefferson on *Continental Congress*, there is really very little to look forward to on commercial television until August, when Sonny and Cher take over Ed Sullivan's variety slot. What's an editor or a reviewer to do? He can meditate on the fate of poor Susan Saint James, who has been sentenced after the cancellation of "The Name of the Game" to be Rock Hudson's wife in a new fall series. He can make snide remarks about reruns: "The Men from Shiloh" recently repeated a 1969 "Virginian" episode; "Gunsmoke" went all the way back to 1967 for some healthy violence. Or he can, in desperation, take a long look at the only TV network whose season doesn't end in March.

TV Guide was moved to write an editorial about the *Times* television page. Now, *TV Guide* is about as critical of the industry as the backs of cereal boxes are critical of their contents. It consists of program listings inside a sandwich of press releases, a seemingly endless stream of sneak-peeks at the psychology of television stars (Troy Donahue wants to play *Hamlet* because he was frightened by a bottle of Man-Tan when he was six months old), and a sort of institutionalized defensiveness: why is everybody picking on us? (Nick Johnson emerges from the bound volumes of *TV Guide* as a publicity-seeking meanie. It's like those producers who grumble about "highbrow" critics. Apparently, a "highbrow" critic is a critic who doesn't like what he sees.)

As late as spring 1968, *TV Guide* was publishing such articles as the one that told us plain, ordinary commercial TV provides "automatic, first-step reading lessons," that televised baseball games and quiz shows teach children arithmetic, that Dean Martin teaches all of us Italian, and that "Dr. Kildare" and "Ben Casey" teach "some useful things about psychoanalysis." How much? "Our study of TV's ghost teachers has turned up a remarkable statistic: No less than one tenth of the entertainment programming on television was found to be educative in one way or another . . ." Remarkable, indeed! What's happened is that *TV Guide*, after years of serving the industry, has developed the mind of a producer. Oh, yes, there is violence on television, but there's violence in the world, etc. It's a game of table tennis played between the ears on either side of an empty head.

The editorial on the *Times* was a classic example. *TV Guide* began by complaining mildly about all the attention to "public-TV activities." It went on to admit that "public television is doing many worthwhile things for minority audiences." It then lamented the fact that, "With certain noteworthy exceptions, commercial television must be bland in order to reach huge audiences. Certainly no one envies public TV its freedom more than the men who run commercial TV." Followed by second thoughts: Congress worries about public TV because "it is not easy to enforce surveillance over the accuracy and fairness of public-service broadcasting on *one* public station—much less 200 of them. . . . Perhaps we should study the British experience and restructure our public system so that, like theirs, it can be a bit more independent *of* but still responsible *to* government. Public television is much more than just another channel on the dial. It can become a tremendously important factor in our society."

What are they saying? Examine the assumptions. Commercial TV *must* be bland. (Because huge audiences mean huge revenues, and the purpose of television is to make money.) Public TV *must* be placed under surveillance. (But not commercial TV, which, after all, is "just another channel on the dial." We envy the "freedom" of public TV; that's why we want to take it away.) The public system *needs* "restructuring." (How can you be "more independent *of* but still responsible *to* government"? Certainly not the way the BBC does it. If television has to be responsible to something, it should be to its artists and to the community it purports to serve.)

Everything is being said and nothing is being said. When commercial TV produces a children's program of the caliber of "Sesame Street," a magazine program of the caliber of "The Great American Dream Machine," a public-affairs program as uncompromising as

Banks and the Poor, a dramatic series half as good as the average BBC import, an "Advocates" approach to controversial issues, a Nader-like *caveat emptor* effort that doesn't grovel before the brand-name money gods who pay the salaries of the network vice-presidents, it too will be "important"—and maybe even of interest to the editors of summer television pages. Until then, we'll have to settle for network news programs reporting on what government thinks being "responsible to government" means. It means keeping your mouth shut.

(August 1971)

Sorry, No Soap for Fyodor

"I am simply . . . nothing but annoyances." Or: "It sounded like delirium. Who could make head or tail of it?" Or: "This was distinctly a blunder." All quotations are from Fyodor Dostoyevsky's *The Possessed* (Constance Garnett translation) and all apply to NET's new "Masterpiece Theatre" import, a six-part trivialization of the novel. Watching an episode the other night, I was struck, like Stepan Trofimovitch, by "an attack of hysterical remorse."

How did this happen? What is to be done? A couple of years ago Jorge Luis Borges at his most wrongheaded said that "one never feels anything in a Russian novel to be true because the characters are always explaining themselves to each other." Borges makes the mistake of knowing more about novels than he does about Russians. But it almost seems as though the British Broadcasting Corporation, which originally dramatized Dostoyevsky, and the Mobil Oil Corporation, which put up a grant, and the Public Broadcasting Service, which syndicates the episodes across the country, have conspired to prove Borges correct. Or maybe they thought, perversely, to justify an old Dostoyevskian complaint: that everything characteristically Russian, "everything that is ours, preeminently national—and therefore, everything genuinely artistic—is unintelligible to Europe."

The Possessed is Dostoyevsky at his most ambivalent, the pan-Slavic ideologue deciding at age fifty to ridicule young radicals, insofar as he perceived their godlessness and nihilism. Irving Howe in his superb essay on *The Possessed* has pointed out that Dostoyevsky knew "next to nothing about the populist-terrorists of the *Narodnaya Volya* or about the incipient Marxists just beginning to appear in Russia at the time he wrote his book." But he knew the type, precisely because half of him belonged to it; and thus his characters passed through ridicule into tragedy, the artist being (thankfully) greater than the ideologue. "In the world of Dostoyevsky," says Mr. Howe, "no one is spared, but there is a supreme consolation: no one is excluded."

Now, what the BBC has done to this passionate ambivalence is to turn it into a bloody vaudeville; and I mean "bloody" in the literal, not the British slanguistical, sense: the rape, the several suicides, the many murders of the novel are here, in gloating detail. The ambivalence got left at the Finland Station. Each character seems a marker on some vast grid of abstractions, moved about to groan and moan about his soul or the peasantry or liberal values or filial pieties —a series of monologues, a comic-stripping of the original mountain—and then to meet his arbitrary fate, with a point score totaled up before and after each episode by the inevitable Alistair Cooke, playing the part of Walter Cronkite on the Sunday Evening Historical and Literary News. See the crowd kill Lisa . . . see Nikolay hang himself . . . see Verhovensky play solitaire. So much for radicalism! Victor Serge meets Arthur Miller meets Miller Barber and they golf around Stalingrad using wood on their internal contradictions.

Considering the unfortunate circumstances, the acting is fairly good. Rosalie Crutchley as Mme. Varvara is splendid. But what has happened is that the style of the BBC's *Forsyte Saga* has been foisted on the BBC's *The Possessed*. It doesn't work. An old bore like Galsworthy needed television to pump him back to life; Galsworthying Dostoyevsky is like Kerouacking Shakespeare—artificial respiration becomes the artifice of desperation. Without spending much of this magazine's valuable space on another rerun of the old "Which Medium Is Most Appropriate for Which Message?" parlor game—how few first-rate novels have made for first-rate movies or TV programs, how many second-rate novels have made for first-rate movies or TV programs—it seems to me that Dostoyevsky, for both his faults and virtues, belongs between covers, not on a twenty-

four-inch screen; the novels themselves are electricity enough. One
doesn't ask Brooks Robinson to write cantatas.

But of course we will go on watching the episodes each week, as
we go on watching "All in the Family," under the illusion that the
one will give us the word on radicals, Russia, revolution, ideology,
as the other gives us the world of workingmen and bigotry. The
word lies, like the rug under which we sweep everything that we
don't want to know.

(June 4, 1971)

A Marvelous Nightingale

"I like to compose music more than the music itself," said Igor
Stravinsky in an interview shortly before his death last spring. For
Stravinsky, a blank sheet of paper on which to scribble was like "waking up in the morning"; he looked forward to it. Because it is impossible to televise the workings of a man's mind, we must be
content next Monday night, November 22, with only "the music
itself."

To be sure, the NET Opera Theater's ninety-minute tribute to
Stravinsky makes a stab at getting inside the man's head. Vera Stravinsky, his widow, and Robert Craft, his amanuensis and alter ego,
remember him fondly. There is much puttering among relics—his
piano, his notebooks, the drawings of him on a wall. There are film
clips and stills and snippets of opinion plucked out of old interviews—Stravinsky characterizing Beethoven's Ninth as "boring";
Stravinsky asking Cocteau to write a "banal" libretto and getting
instead something "Wagnerian" and asking Cocteau for two more
drafts in search of banality; Stravinsky admitting that he was really
opposed to the idea of opera, all those people trying to sing as they
moved around on the stage, etc.

But none of this adds up to more than a page or two out of *Retro-
spectives and Conclusions* (1969) or any other volume of the seemingly endless series of books Stravinsky and Craft conspired at over
the years. Like Robert Frost, Stravinsky in his declining years con-
cocted—or had Craft concoct for him—a public personality a little
too good to be true to the private man behind it. This, a privilege

perhaps of genius, is the personality of the film clips. We are stuck with it, at least until Craft decides to give us an unauthorized biography. That is, until Craft recognizes that he is an extraordinary writer in his own right and needn't store his talent in the armored car of Stravinsky's reputation in order to ride around safely.

The music, itself, however. *Stravinsky Remembered* consists mostly of a new production of *Le Rossignol*, the opera Stravinsky interrupted in 1909 to work on *L'Oiseau de Feu* and *Le Sacre du Printemps* ballets. It is based on Hans Christian Andersen's fairy tale, *The Emperor and the Nightingale*. A nightingale that sings every night to the fishermen is invited to perform at the court of the emperor of China and does so beautifully. Ambassadors arrive from Japan with a mechanical nightingale. The real one flies away; the emperor falls ill; he is saved from death by the nightingale's reappearance and song.

It is superb. Since its debut in 1914, *Le Rossignol* has depended on voices. Peter Herman Adler has found those voices, in Reri Grist as the Nightingale, Sidney Johnson as the Fisherman and Lili Chookasian as Death. With such voices, the rest of the stage-busyness wouldn't matter very much. But the direction (Kirk Browning), the choreography (John Butler) and the color effects are as good as the voices. Mr. Adler has obliged Stravinsky by keeping Miss Grist, Mr. Johnson and Miss Chookasian off the stage; substitutes do all their on-camera moving around. Mr. Adler videotaped the dancers, the substitutes and the lesser on-camera singers in a New York studio; he then taped the orchestral version with the Boston Symphony and the three principal singers, mixed the components, and here we are.

At a very nice place indeed. Opera on television has come of age, with better sound quality than I can remember and better color control, too. The old debate on *Le Rossignol*—Ravel liked it, Debussy didn't—is over, at least in my ears. Ravel was right.

(November 19, 1971)

Shuffling the Archetypes

It had to happen. The BBC just got overconfident. After all, they had been turning out serializations of absorbing historical hugger-mugger—*English* historical hugger-mugger—ever since *The Forsyte Saga*, and the only reply from this side of the Atlantic was cops and robbers shows. And so they decided to intervene directly in the American fantasy life. The result is a dramatization in eight episodes of James Fenimore Cooper's *The Last of the Mohicans*. While it is not nearly so offensive as the BBC's other experiment in transcultural vamping—the travesty of Dostoyevsky's *The Possessed*—it is profoundly silly.

Mohicans is silly because, in this day and age, you simply can't play it straight. In the 146 years since Cooper's novel was published, a compost of interpretations and stylizations has grown over it. There have been two movie versions, which owed more to the conventions of the Hollywood Western than they did to the book itself, complicating the perceptual problem. And *Mohicans* has been hit with heavier literary criticism than even *Moby Dick* could stand. You can't see the artifact for the exegesis.

First, there was Mark Twain, who complained in a delightful essay that Cooper's Indians knew so little about the wilderness they were supposed to inhabit, they wouldn't have lasted a week in the woods. Then D. H. Lawrence came along, finding in Cooper the nineteenth-century gentleman, "a correct, a clockwork man," with "the great national Grouch" grinding inside him, which he called "COSMIC URGE." He loved his myth more than he did his wife, because he had a wife and, fortunately, could never have the myth. Lawrence formulated the problem this way:

Wish Fulfillment	Actuality
THE WIGWAM *vs.*	MY HOTEL
CHINGACHGOOK *vs.*	MY WIFE
NATTY BUMPPO *vs.*	MY HUMBLE SELF

Thus, Natty Bumppo—Deerslayer, Pathfinder, Leatherstocking— "a saint with a gun"; and Chingachgook, "The Noble Red Brother"; and what they formed in the woods, "a stark, stripped human relationship of two men, deeper than the deeps of sex . . . the stark, loveless, wordless unison of two men who have come to the bottom of themselves"; and the myth of "the essential white America . . . The essential American soul is hard, isolate, stoic, and a killer. It has never yet melted."

Finally, Leslie A. Fiedler, in *An End to Innocence*, said out loud what Lawrence only hinted at. What really worried Cooper was miscegenation. "Natty Bumppo, the man who always boasts of having 'no cross' in *his* blood, flees by nature from the defilement of all women, but never with so absolute a revulsion as he displays toward the *squaw* . . . and the threat of the dark-skinned rapist sends pale woman after pale woman skittering through Cooper's imagined wilderness. Even poor Cora, who already has a fatal drop of alien blood that cuts her off from any marriage with a white man, in so far as she is white cannot be mated with Uncas, the noblest of the redmen. Only in death can they be joined in an embrace as chaste as that of males. There's no good woman but a dead woman! Yet Chingachgook and the Deerslayer are permitted to sit night after night over their campfire in the purest domestic bliss."

Well. How was the BBC to cope with such material? Ernest Hemingway lost his life and Lyndon Johnson lost his presidency because they both wanted to be Natty Bumppo. What do the British know about it? The British don't even know what was said to Mrs. Moore in the Marabar caves, and *that* novel was written by an Englishman. The BBC does not cope. Nor does it camp. It just shuffles the archetypes around on the small screen solemnly, until the mind gets so small, watching, that it can't contain the point. And so it dozes. I'm sorry, Alistair Cooke, but your Urges aren't Cosmic enough for James Fenimore Cooper.

(March 30, 1972)

Soft Vonnegut

As if there weren't already more than enough to worry about—why was NBC's coverage of the Winter Olympics so unsatisfying; why don't more people watch "Sonny and Cher" on Monday nights; could I have been wrong about "Cannon" and "Monty Nash," both of

286

THIS PEN FOR HIRE

which seem to have improved mightily during the last several months?—now one must worry about Kurt Vonnegut, Jr.

NET Playhouse persuaded Mr. Vonnegut to whip up an hour and a half of television last week called *Between Time and Timbuktu—A Space Fantasy*. The idea is a simple and amusing one. Stony Stevenson (played by Bill Hickey) wins a jingle contest sponsored by "Blast-off," the space food of the astronauts. First prize in the contest is being blasted off from Mission Control into the "chrono-synclastic infundibulum," or time-space warp. Thus our first poet-astronaut experiences human history, past and future, simultaneously, and comments on it.

Human history turns out to consist mainly of dramatized snippets from Mr. Vonnegut's novels and short stories. The chrono-synclastic infundibulum is borrowed from *The Sirens of Titan*. The wholly technologized society, in which only engineers work, is borrowed from *Player Piano*. Bokonism (with Kevin McCarthy playing the part of the prophet of "harmless lies") is borrowed from *Cat's Cradle*. The "suicide parlor" in an age of overpopulation and the handicapping of human beings to keep anybody from being in any way better than anyone else are both borrowed from stories in *Welcome to the Monkey House*. There is a sprinkling of Rosewater, and a segment from Vonnegut's play *Happy Birthday, Wanda June*. And the notion that we have to be careful about what we pretend to be, because we tend to end up being what we have pretended, was first proposed in *Mother Night*.

It is a very funny hour and a half, because (1) Mr. Vonnegut is a very funny writer; (2) Mr. Hickey as the tender-minded poet-astronaut is marvelous—the schlemiel is no longer Jewish-specific, he is the awkward sensitive adolescent in all of us; and (3) Bob and Ray, who play Walter Gesundheit and ex-astronaut Bud Williams, Jr., at Mission Control, are hilarious—even if their routine was largely perfected a couple of years ago in Norman Lear's movie *Cold Turkey*. Mr. Vonnegut's night-terrors—conformity, the military mind, technological despotism, being stranded in Schenectady, New York—are the bad dreams of most reasonable men and women these days, and even the partial realities. Soul-devouring Molochs patrol the mindscape in helicopters, strafing all the niceness.

And yet . . . I worry about Mr. Vonnegut. He once said in a speech that the trouble with Americans is that we don't know how

to end things, we are good at starting, big on middles, lousy in finishing up. And he cheerfully admitted that the charge was true of
his novels, as well. He would equally cheerfully admit, I'm sure, that
implicit in everything he writes is a simple anti-rationalism, a fear
that all science is manipulative and therefore evil, a sense that problems can't be solved and the best we can do is compose poems or
concoct paradoxes about them. Niceness is elevated to an aesthetic,
even a moral, principle. How, then, do those who are nice avoid
becoming victims? Well, Mr. Vonnegut is bad on endings, and he
doesn't really know. Sometimes he just gives us the victimization—
Ice 9, or the "So it goes" of *Slaughterhouse Five*—and sometimes he
softly sentimentalizes.

The habit of sentimentalizing, the element of softness, is nowhere more apparent than in this NET space fantasy. Confronted at
the end with Hitler (evil: "I am death, and I am final"), what do
the poet-astronaut and Mr. Vonnegut propose? How do they defend themselves, and niceness? With "inner space," "the moon,
the sun, the stars," creativity. Stony Stevenson tells Hitler what the
game is all about: "Death against . . . imagination." A platitude, not
of much utility in a death camp or in Southeast Asia or Harlem, for
that matter. No planning, no hard work, no laws, no agonizing moral
choices. Just imagination, a kind of piety of niceness, a jingle. It is
not enough, but it helps explain why Mr. Vonnegut's agreeable
fictions are so popular among the young.

(February 1972)

TV VS. THE PUBLIC

There's Bad News Tonight

Well, these are recessed times. Money is tight and Glenn Campbell is cutting down on his hair spray and the news is bad. So bad that the headlines tramp like a defeated army over one's throbbing optic nerve and into one's shallow brain pan. So bad that in Washington, New York, Los Angeles, Louisville, Kansas City, Omaha and Cincinnati, the local TV news teams have developed a whole new style of presentation which seems to consist mainly in insulting one another while insulting their audience. A form of the "extended family"—which might be described, with apologies to William Faulkner, as a Snopesism—it has murdered whatever awareness we waste on the six o'clock or eleven o'clock hurricane warnings. TV newsmen and newswomen belittle their colleagues in order to belittle the news. History, always so tedious and inconvenient, becomes a metaphysical pratfall. The "happy talk" or "chitchat" format of the New Electronic Journalism giggles its way to apocalypse, as though Merv Griffin were some sort of first principle in epistemology.

We need a new word to hint at this trivialization of reportage. I'm tempted to call it *Eye-Witless News,* but I'd settle for *Malapropaganda.* Malapropaganda may be Snopesized as that process by which incompetence is converted into cuteness; we forgive a member of our family (video or nuclear) for his many sins against intelligence and decency because if we didn't who would take out the garbage? Meanwhile, reality is reduced to one-liners and temperamental quirks. A Roger Grimsby, a Willard Scott, a George Putnam or a Mort Crim transcends hijackings, blizzards, Ronald Reagan and crime-in-the-streets by virtue of his personality. Instead of Schopenhauer we get Neil Simon: the gag that chokes. Or Ed McMahonliness: promote the news by parodying yourself, your embarrassments.

So far, network newscasters have not succumbed to this sophomore smirk. On CBS, Walter Cronkite still comes on like a combination of God and Willy Loman, selling disaster on a shoeshine and a jowl. NBC has fallen into confusion since the departure of Chet Huntley; David Brinkley is sunk into an abysmal sneer; Frank McGee often isn't around, and John Chancellor appears to be apologizing for his stint at the Voice of America by bad-mouthing Richard Nixon, who needs bad-mouthing about as much as Spiro Agnew needs publicity. Harry Reasoner has defected to ABC, where he and Howard K. Smith play Ping-Pong with the news, one putting an ironic topspin on a gloomy dispatch, the other smashing probabilities out the window; they switch sides every other game to editorialize.

Of the three network news shows, Reasoner and Smith seem most appropriate to our recessed times. They look like a pair of defeated Congressmen, or unemployed advertising executives, or headwaiters marooned at Nedick's. They can't be excused, of course, for squeezing Frank Reynolds off the airwaves. Nor should Smith be allowed to talk one night about the difficulties of quizzing a President, and Reasoner the next night refrain from analyzing how well (or poorly) Smith handled those difficulties. But they are terribly sincere, and ABC has packaged that sincerity as it packages football games, with flow charts and other arty background noise, pins in the eye.

Does it matter, this merchandising of disaster, whether the form is malapropagandistic (if I mispronounce the name of the village we bombed, and everybody laughs about it, the village wasn't really bombed) or lumpishly serious (a little girl died and her death diminishes even the meteorologist)? Would it matter, on a slow day, if Smith set fire to Reasoner's sideburns? Yes. The anthropologist Edmund Carpenter, author of *They Became What They Beheld* and the brain behind Marshall McLuhan's blarney, has suggested that in the age of Sarnoff electricity subverts diplomacy. Nations negotiate not at peace tables in Paris but according to the impact of images inflicted on all us children of the Electronic Village—images of protest, of prisoners of war, of weary death-making. Statecraft submits to Neilsen ratings. Americans get out of Cambodia and Russians don't execute dissidents because a kind of poll of indignation has been televised. If, however, the news is conceived of as entertainment, we react to it like an audience instead of an electorate; we chuckle instead of screaming. When the last American ground troops are removed from Vietnam, so will go the last American cameramen. The bombing will go on, but we won't see the flowering death of non-electronic villages; we'll see, if anything, a flow chart on mega-tonnage, and now to Jim with the sports . . . thanks, Roger, you old athlete's foot, you . . .

(February 5, 1971)

Chicago's "Underground News"

One of the many deficiencies of novelists and revolutionaries these days is that they seldom make any attempt to penetrate the mind of what the newspapers like to call the Middle American. Novelists are too busy writing novels about the corruption of language, and revo-lutionaries are too busy eating absolute truth for breakfast, to do much imaginative projecting. What goes on in the Middle American mind—assuming that the Middle American mind, unlike the New York mind or the Youth mind, is monolithic, which is of course a false assumption—when it perceives the modern world? Is there a triggering fantasy?

If I were a Middle American, the first thing I'd worry about would be the ears. There seem to be fewer ears in the world, at least in the image of the world on television, and much more hair than there used to be. You never see the ears of the young, and most of the time you don't see the ears of singers and comedians, and the ears of professors and detectives and athletes and statesmen are disap-pearing, and there are all these helmets of hair on television, a mar-tial look associated with old Fuzzy Wuzzy movies. If they have no ears, how can they hear the eternal verities?

The second thing I'd worry about would be waterbeds. What *is* a waterbed? It sounds like something to drown in, and yet there is an overpowering insinuation of hanky-panky. What do people *do* on a waterbed? The unspeakable. One imagines, if one has been brought up on co-ed jokes and has always felt indignantly that col-lege girls are wasted on college boys (a reward for bad behavior), the young in earless calisthenics, a nude game of water polo, with long hair floating on the libidinal pool.

These imaginative projections, available free of charge to novelists and revolutionaries, were inspired by watching several tapes of a new Chicago TV program, "The Underground News." "The Under-

ground News" beams nightly for half an hour to the counter-culture
and anybody else in the UHF signal range of Station WSNS, Channel 44 . . . Middle America. Host Chuck Collins, a twenty-one-year-
old student at Lake Forest College, appears before the camera in what
looks like a modified fatigue jacket. Behind him is a photograph of
the late Jimi Hendrix. The sound track is likely to be crawling with
Beatles. There are very few ears, much hair, and some great advertisements for waterbeds.

Collins is the counter-culture's answer to Perry Como. Whether
he is interviewing Weathermen, Abbie and Anita Hoffman, black
militants, Mark Lane or Jane Fonda, he's so loose he seems about
to fall apart with a sigh and lie on the studio floor like a mound of
old pajamas. He never argues with his guests, even those with whom
he might reasonably be expected to disagree; he lets them talk themselves into silence, down a ladder of "uh's," "huh's" and "wow's,"
without ever gasping for breath in moments of dead air. Even his
editorial commentaries seem more perplexed by the idiocies of the
world than splenetic about the obscenities in it.

"The Underground News" is oddly relaxing. The commercials,
witty and somewhat amateurish owing to the lifeless studio sound
surrounding them, do not threaten because they do not take themselves seriously. Sometimes the guests appear not to take themselves
seriously, either. Abbie Hoffman recently complained about his difficulties in publishing and distributing his new book, entitled *Steal
This Book*, and then confided to the audience that "I was trying
to write a book that no one would publish" and it was hard work.
Anita Hoffman, the author of a harmless bit of semi-fictional rubbish
called *Trashing*, said she liked writing orgy scenes because they
made her feel "horny." Collins laughed earlessly.

Now, it would be possible to come on all heavily solemn about
the commercialization of youth culture, the rip-off of rock, the capi-
talistic subway stops of "The Underground News" on its way to
raising our consciousness of waterbeds. A flexing of the moral biceps.
And it would be equally possible to say smug things about revolution-
as-show-biz: Collins hasn't exactly unleashed a lot of dangerous in-
tellects into our living rooms. But I keep thinking about all those
Middle Americans who just might tune in—Chuck Collins is such
a *nice* name—and find out their children aren't monsters. "The
Underground News" is one of the too few creative games being

played on the UHF channels so many of us held out so much hope
for. It is also one of the few things going on in Chicago besides Mike
Royko that might make life a little more bearable. A waterbed of
the airwaves could put Procrustes to sleep, and God knows he must
be tired after all he's done to our century.

(July 2, 1971)

It's Put-Put Time in California

Put-put time is ten o'clock of a southern California night, when
the charcoal has burned low in the bowl of the barbecue rotisserie
on the patio and the air is scented with oil and oranges and strong
men remove aprons scriven with hortatory insignia and women weep
into tumblers of Thunderbird and somewhere in the desert moon-
maddened lizards lurk, omophagous or (more dangerous still)
plastic-eating.

Put-put time is George Putnam with a version of the news. George
Putnam gets $300,000 a year from Metromedia's KTTV, Channel
11, Los Angeles, for his version of the news. He is on every afternoon
from four to five, every evening from ten to eleven; but the nights
are better because southern California nights are full of dread—as
though the desert were about to yawn and in yawning swallow up
all the chili bars, shrimp canteens, used-car lots, miniature golf
courses—and George Putnam is a surfer on the dread wave. George
Putnam is the Aimee Semple McPherson of electronic journalism.

He seems to have only one eyebrow, always cocked, like a horizon-
tal parenthesis above his disbelief, never to be closed, a lapse into
innuendo so profound that mere reporting will never be resumed.
He speaks in italics; whole clauses lean to the right and fall off the
edges of awareness. He dwells in the present tense, as though divin-
ing news by a weather vane spinning in the winds of his own mind;
as though inventing the news on the spot, which in fact he sometimes does: the style becomes the event. It's not what students did
this day, or the Vietcong, or *Newsweek*; it's how George Putnam
says "students," "Communists," "news magazines"; how he bulges
his eyes, twists his head, confides to the camera, makes of the ether
itself a sort of submarine sandwich of sincerity and dismay.

Show-biz TV reporting began in Los Angeles, as have so many things that will ultimately destroy this nation. Even the best of the old-time TV newsmen in Los Angeles were performers before they were reporters. Remember Clete Roberts in his trench coat? Philip Marlowe with a microphone, he was. The logical extension of Clete Roberts, more than a decade later, was Tom Redding, the retired police chief one channel tried to inflict on its viewers in the guise of a reporter. Redding laid on the ennui with a trowel, his little brick-like thoughts ultimately locking the viewer into a cell of one-minute commentaries that seemed like a life sentence. But the precedent of putting the persona before the facts is well established in California, both on TV and in politics.

And George Putnam has been there for over twenty years, boosting the ratings of each station to which he jumps, annoying other newsmen because he so seldom does the legwork on his stories. He considers himself a crusader, and is known sometimes to carry a .38 revolver. He is a master of the empty-chair technique: Joe Heavy was invited to be on tonight's inquest but was too gutless to show; this is the chair Joe Heavy should have occupied while we explained why he is an excrescence; let us talk to the empty chair. He pioneered in editorializing; the "One Reporter's Opinion" segment of his program comes on with a gravity that pulls down the heart and makes the feet sleep. Once upon a time, George Putnam cared about discrimination and narcotics. Now he has discovered old people and prayers. (The Supreme Court decision against praying in the schools was a step "in the direction of eventually erasing from our American heritage God, patriotism and the true understanding of the sacred privilege of being an American under God.")

Now, also, he is in trouble. Not because there isn't an appetite in southern California for evangelism, and not only because George Putnam isn't comfortable in the new TV news world of "happy talk," the chitchat of studio families (insult the meteorologist and make fun of the sports reporter's drinking habits). George is basically a loner—Rona Barrett's vamping seems slightly to embarrass him; Hal Fishman is a combination of Cohn & Schine on the old Joe McCarthy Show, out of place—but George is in trouble because he is paying the price of show-biz journalism. The other night the men in aprons and the women on Thunderbird watched George editorialize on the plight of old people and wondered aloud whether George had a mother he wanted to get rid of and found Leisure World too expensive. By making himself an actor, he's made the news a fiction, and his audience criticizes his performance instead of learning anything.

(June 25, 1971)

Walter Was There, Anyway

CBS has looked into its memory bank for an old idea and found "You Are There," the video version of Madame Tussaud's wax museum. "You Are There" went out of business fourteen years ago. Maybe the idea has been gathering interest ever since. Why not let a new generation of tube-boobies eavesdrop on another round of Great Moments in Western Civilization—like Amelia Earhart getting lost (was she or wasn't she on a secret mission for the U. S. Government?) and Woodrow Wilson getting huffy (yes, Mr. Lodge, the Zimmerman Telegram is authentic, but I can't tell you how come I'm so sure, because my promise to another gentleman is more important than the need of the U. S. Senate to know anything). Walter Cronkite again plays the part of Methuselah, which was written for him by God.

Indeed, Walter Cronkite is the only plausible aspect of this second coming of "You Are There." One believes that Walter Cronkite probably *was* there, wherever and whenever there was. Walter Cronkite has always been there. He is as much a part of our modern consciousness as are parking lots and bewilderment. He will be the anchor man when Sirius the Dog Star decides to sterilize all earthlings as an antiseptic precaution on behalf of the cosmos.

But the others . . . One is embarrassed for all those veteran CBS newsmen—Morley Safer, Dan Rather, Douglas Edwards, Hughes Rudd, Dan Schorr, etc.—press-ganged into making fools of themselves by pretending that the President of the United States would tolerate a cameraman in his private chambers while he exchanges lack of confidences with a Senator. And one is dismayed that an actress of Geraldine Brooks's quality should flounder so in the role of Amelia Earhart, twitching her way through the part as though she were sometimes supposed to be an Oberlin girl at a sit-in and other times Antigone. Perhaps they are all embarrassed. Who wouldn't be, camping up the historical pluperfect, with the old hokey baritone in the old hokey echo chamber? I'm sorry, Mother, they seem to be admitting, it rained on my credibility and I shrank.

Agreed, "You Are There" is a harmless half hour, mildly educational, apparently intended this time for children. Still, even eight-year-olds have seen these people, these electronic journalists, before —at *real* assassinations and moon shots, reporting surreal body counts, meddling with their microphones in public and private griefs. The psychological hangover after employing them as actors is not to make the fiction more persuasive but to make the reality less so. The technique of television news coverage is applied so heavily on historical anecdote that all we see is the technique, and we suddenly realize that it *is* technique, a kind of show biz. Parody ultimately swallows the parodist, as laughter turns into a self-devouring yawn: witness Jorge Luis Borges, writing reviews of nonexistent books and selling them as short stories. If we can't believe Walter Cronkite, faith in anything is impossible. Next week Willie Mays will be promoting lung cancer.

More basically, the historical anecdote is 90 per cent anecdote and 10 per cent history. If there is anything that the young, to whom "You Are There" addresses itself, need especially to know, it is that history can never be capsulized into a single day. Decisions aren't sudden, but are the sly insinuations of policy. And policy isn't the product of a moment's existential revelation, but an accretion of conflicting counsels, preconceptions, altruisms, work and weariness. When the moment and the policy try to synthesize a decision, you simply aren't there. To pretend that you are is to trivialize the issues, to make bubble gum out of the muscle of all that we know and need to know.

(March 1972)

The Show Biz Conservative

A season or so ago, William F. Buckley, Jr.—columnist, editor, TV roustabout, ex-candidate for mayor of New York and sometime consultant for the U. S. Information Agency—made an appearance on

Rowan and Martin's "Laugh-In." There was an impromptu press conference. One of the questions went like this: "Mr. Buckley, I notice that on your own program you are always sitting down. Is this because you can't think on your feet?" Buckley hesitated only for a moment, and then slowly, gravely replied: "It is hard . . . to stand up . . . under the weight . . . of all that I know." A moment of pure Buckley: the conservative as show biz.

Now Bill Buckley has taken his show biz—his clipboard and his ball-point pen and his eyebrows and his promiscuous analogies—to non-commercial television. There must be a sinister explanation. He has never been infatuated with non-commercial television. ("Spend a long day with the BBC," he once said, "and they are *all* long days . . .") Has the free enterprise system failed him? Is federal funding of public affairs programs all right only with a Republican President? Does the Public Broadcasting Service conceive of "Firing Line" as so much conservative sand in the carburetor of "The Great American Dream Machine"? Did Bill Buckley, having been Gored in the élan Vidal, switch channels—like Mr. Nixon switching states after his "last press conference"—just to rehabilitate himself?

It doesn't matter. Non-commercial television has always been an adult extension course in solemnity. Remedial Seriousness. Or a kind of secular church, an electronic pulpit, from which Fathers Qualm promulgate many liberal pieties and not much joy. Buckley makes jokes in the back row or the back pew; Dread Relativism scares him no more than it scares our radical young Luddites. After all, he was attacking the evils of Big Government and the amorality of college professors before Mark Rudd munched Pablum. Buckley is a character who emerged from a Fitzgerald novel and turned the wrong way; his is the fatal desire to displease in a world where the anxiety to please is a substitute for the fear of God.

Which is to say, he has style, and he has been smart enough to stick to his style—aristocratic (there is as much of the South in him as there is Irish Catholicism), witty, a little jeering—instead of adapting himself to the democratic mediocrity of the medium. He speaks in numbered paragraphs and usually assigns letters to each dependent clause. He is a great activator of nouns: "fanaticized," "hobgoblinized," "martyrized." He is a master of the invidious juxtaposition. (For example, when a seventeen-year-old Negro in a Los Angeles high school referred to Johann Sebastian Bach as "that old, dead punk," Buckley observed: "To call the greatest genius who ever lived an 'old, dead punk,' the least of whose cantatas will do more to elevate the human spirit than all the black student unions born and unborn, is not so much contemptible as pitiable: conducive of that kind of separation one feels from animals, rather than from other human beings." Notice the juxtaposition.)

And he uses his formidable vocabulary as a weapon. Words like "nugatory," "usufruct," "enthymematic," "asymptotic," "propaedeutic" and "endogamous" cast a spell over his readers and his viewers. Each word is used precisely; the cumulative effect is one of a *routine*. Lenny Bruce used different words, not quite so precisely, but to the same effect. Jack Benny has his silences and his folded arms; Bob Hope, his leer; the Kennedys, their quotations. Buckley hits you between the eyes with a usufruct, and by the time you remember what it means, he has gone on to the next numbered paragraph and you never catch up with the transition in his logic. Muhammad Ali brought much the same approach to prizefighting, to use an invidious juxtaposition.

It's a routine that works best on guests so sincere in their liberal pieties that they huff and puff after every deft insinuation. It works worst with guests like Groucho Marx, Norman Mailer and Allen Ginsberg, who have their own highly developed shtick. Ginsberg went right on Om-ing over Buckley's paragraphs. But whether it works or not, it makes for dazzling show biz, which is what TV is all about. No matter which set of abstractions you mainline on, "Firing Line" inspires a lofty sort of voyeurism: the conservative matador, the liberal bull, and we are all ears.

(September 1971)

From the Other Side of the Desk

My days of innocent aggression are over. I am no more the merchant of psychic yard goods, hacking off as many inches of words as any old editor asks for—eight pages on masochistic cyclothymia in Shakespeare's tragedies? Consider it done. Fourteen pages on the theory of the bite in vampire movies? You bet.

For over a year now, *I* have been "any old editor," hiring other pens, discovering what other editors have always known: that writers are children, necessary and unreliable and bad spellers. Moreover, they are constantly interfering with the real business of editors, which is to put out fires. There are many fires. One "media industry newsletter" says that *The New York Times Book Review* hates books. Another "media industry newsletter" says that we review only those books that are advertised in our pages. The president of a publishing house writes a letter to literary agents accusing us of imitating The New York Review of Noam Chomsky. The editor of a black magazine charges us with honkie recidivism. A prominent West Side intellectual complains that we are trying to "re-establish" the WASP novel. A prominent radical sociologist threatens to sue us for not printing his essay. A prominent elder poet gets huffy when we won't let him review his boyfriend's book. Gay liberationists declare that they will anally assault us for not thinking E. M. Forster's *Maurice* is the greatest thing since meatloaf. Eli Siegel's Aesthetic Realists *do* assault us, at the office, for not thinking that homosexuality can be "cured" by night school Hegelianism (opposites have more fun). *Esquire* runs an article saying that we haven't really changed very much after a year, even though the new editor's politics are "decidedly leftist." *Partisan Review* runs an article referring to "the new young conservative editor" at the *Book Review.* The air quality in Manhattan is unacceptable.

This is what happens when you have been institutionalized. Before institutionalization, you can only be blamed for so much, because there is only so much you have the energy to do, even poorly, as an individual. Americans are usually ready to tolerate an unobstructed *me.* Look it up in the Social Contract—each of us has a right to be inadequate. After institutionalization, "you" becomes "one." One wears suits. One does not remove one's jacket. One is protected by one's secretaries from one's friends, who seem to special-

ize in fourteenth-century Croatian oral epics; from distempered
assistant professors of French, who feel they have a monopoly on
Proust's disingenuous riposte to Sainte-Beuve; from Mrs. James
Drought, who has confused an indifference to her husband's fiction
with a conspiracy to destroy him; from grammarians in a snit and
radical feminists with sheep shears and paranoid Canadians and
Century Clubbies hustling for their friends and the janissaries of
Xerox, RCA, CBS, CRM, etc., all of whom own publishing houses;
from, as Dean Rusk used to say, "the other side." One is minister
to a flock of twenty-four, most of whom are paid to read the books
one gives to them and to tell one what they think of them. One is
paid to meditate on those reports, sift the suggestions, select a reviewer, and determine the perfect number of words for each review.
One must then exact a Sicilian oath from the reviewer that he will
deliver his copy on time, which he never does—his son was busted
for dealing cocaine, his mother-in-law was hijacked to Zanzibar, his
wife ran off with a Mortimer Adler Great Books salesman—and one
sits around waiting for an article that will be inevitably four times
the suggested word-length. (The most astonishing excuse I have ever
heard from a reviewer who failed to turn in his copy on time was
the explanation that his wife was having her period.) One is then
obliged each week to decide which articles will be least embarrassing
to publish. One is not allowed to be inadequate, because institutionalization means accountability. One looks into the shaving mirror
and sometimes sees only the other side of the room, where a quotation from Pasternak is tacked: *To open a window is like opening a
vein.*

Pasternak? Well, delusions are part of an editor's job, not delusions of grandeur, but of persecution. "All his behavior in exile is
marked by this conflict between the necessity and the impossibility
of action. He senses the conflict, but is never clearly conscious of it.
Even when he glimpses the impossibility, he sees it as extraneous,
temporary, and resulting merely from persecution and physical isolation. This unawareness gives him the strength to struggle on
against odds perhaps more fearful than any historic figure has ever
faced." Thus, according to Isaac Deutscher, Trotsky in Mexico. And
when they come with the alpenstock—when, that is to say, they take
away my clipboard and arrange for a lateral transfer to *Family Circle*
—the autopsy probably won't show "a brain of 'extraordinary di-

mensions,' weighing two pounds and thirteen ounces," but, certainly, "the heart . . . was very large."

If not Trotsky, then Job. The comforters in one delusional system are the same as the ax-men in the other, a Nat "Eliphaz" Hentoff, in *The Village Voice*; a George "Bildad" Frazier, in the Boston *Globe*. (Zophar, like all trade-book publishers, is out to lunch on an expense account. "Your magazine," says Zophar, "is thirty per cent of the dollar market for books." He means that there are not very many other spots to place book ads, especially since the *Saturday Review* has been Bernie Cornfeldized. Zophar has a slide rule running between his ears; behind the transparent plastic eyes, I'm being measured on a logarithmic scale. I've got 7,000 words by William H. Gass on Paul Valéry. Zophar's big spring book is the first true story on what goes on in Baltimore massage parlors, by a Greek hermaphrodite named Agnewt. On the dollar market, Gass is de-Valéried. The gnomes of B. Dalton work the remainder bins like slot machines.) In other fantasies, one is Sisyphus, Cunégonde, Eddie Fisher, Captain Kangaroo, Ferdinand the Bull.

The forest is full of publicity girls. Instead of arrows in their quiver, they carry credit cards and spring lists. Their mouths are bows; each thin message inflicts a wound. It is a fine forest. I go there often. The publicity girls, who in a better world would be editors, have no natural sense of logarithm. They believe in the first novel, an orphan which I once committed myself, in the days before institutionalization, and which no one reviewed. We know that it is just as hard to write a bad book as it is to write a good one, and we respect the dignity of labor. They rhapsodize: an interior monologue about incest in the barrios of El Paso; Roland Barthes would love it. I explain that only 35 per cent of the *Book Review* is editorial; 65 per cent is advertising. (The admen tell me every Friday morning how much editorial I'll be permitted to publish.) There is cognac drizzling on the leaves of the trees in the forest. Outside is the real world, admen driving slide rules into traffic jams; the best-seller list is Times Square at high-roller noon. Why do these young women now look at me as though my name were Moscow Trial?

"The idea of a perfect and immortal commonwealth," said David Hume, "will always be found as chimerical as that of a perfect and immortal man." Hume, as usual, was right; but we persist in tink-

ering with the world and with ourselves. The hope for improvement
distinguishes people from cranberries.

Editing a magazine has none of the grosser ego-satisfactions of
writing a regular column, with your name on the marquee; but there
are subtle pleasures attached to it. One of them, in its lowest form,
is the sense of planning a campaign instead of scribbling dispatches
on bandages in the trenches on the bloody front. Another, hopefully
more elevated, is the sense of growing up from "I" to "we." "Art
is I," said Claude Bernard; "science is we." So is society "we"; and
institutions, like the *Book Review*; and culture, even if it's literary.
There is a bias among the editors of the *Book Review*: "we" are in
the business of asking each "I" for help: what should "we" do? We
are looking for books that make some sort of connection between
the individual and society; which portray the "I" (intense feelings,
singular perceptions) trying to or failing to or refusing to accommodate itself to a social context (abstract relationships, contracts
among strangers); which partake of history, observe change, fix the
objects of love/hate/ambivalence with pincers of precise style, and
alter our way of seeing. Books are our life, and we can't help expect-
ing something salutary from them—a sensitizing after long numb-
ness, an organizing perception, perhaps even salvation by example—
personal art that trafficks with cultural continuity. It's fashionable
these days in some quarters to excuse literature from the responsibilities of citizenship, to perceive it as "autonomous," a-historical,
a-moral, a-social. (In much the same way, apologists for television
think that by calling it an "entertainment medium" they can escape
criticism.) Well, it is not "our" fashion: the writer is autonomous;
what he writes is not.

A small bias, then, but our own, which we are attempting to in-
flate into a principle. Such an inflation is only so much hot air unless the space, the "cultural space," it seeks to occupy is defined.
We want the *Book Review* to be something more than a shopping
guide, a *Good Housekeeping* seal of approval or disapproval stamped
on every defenseless verbal artifact the instant it pops out of the
print factory—then on, remorselessly, to the next batch. The magazine as a whole has somehow to embody the motions it notices in
the culture. We will review books we never before considered
suitable for review. We will return regularly for second and third
looks at books that have acquired a momentum after their publica-

tion that we couldn't have guessed at at the time of our original review. We will institutionalize hindsight, which, after all, is one of the things culture is about. We will launch introspections, publish career essays, interview everybody in sight, put poetry and science on the front page, even, occasionally, declare war.

In doing so, we have to talk to one another, over grog and gruel, in a democracy so participatory that the editor will lose some arguments, which of course is bad for print culture; but a democracy so glossal that the editor will usually be forced to hear things he hadn't thought of, which is at least good for the editor. We will then deploy, in one of those places where the accident of sanction happens, under poster art, among mountains of galley proofs, to typewriters and telephones. Not at all like cranberries.

There is satisfaction in that. And even—dare I say it?—a sense of mission in an age of hobbies.